Silence, Screen, and Spectacle

Remapping Cultural History

General Editor: **Jo Labanyi** (Director, King Juan Carlos I of Spain Center and Professor in the Department of Spanish and Portuguese, New York University)

This series challenges theoretical paradigms by exploring areas of culture that have previously received little attention. Its volumes discuss parts of the world that do not easily fit within dominant northern European or North American theoretical models, or that make a significant contribution to rethinking the ways in which cultural history is theorized and narrated.

Silence, Screen, and Spectacle

Rethinking Social Memory in the Age of Information

Edited by
Lindsey A. Freeman, Benjamin Nienass,
and Rachel Daniell

berghahn
NEW YORK · OXFORD
www.berghahnbooks.com

First edition published in 2014 by

Berghahn Books

www.berghahnbooks.com

© 2014, 2017 Lindsey A. Freeman, Benjamin Nienass, and Rachel Daniell
First paperback edition published in 2017

Library of Congress Cataloging-in-Publication Data

Silence, screen, and spectacle : rethinking social memory in the age of
 information / edited by Lindsey A. Freeman, Benjamin Nienass, and Rachel
 Daniell.
      pages cm. — (Remapping cultural history ; volume 14)
 Includes bibliographical references and index.
 ISBN 978-1-78238-280-5 (hardback) — ISBN: 978-1-78533-355-2 (paperback)—ISBN 978-1-78238-281-2 (ebook)
   1. Mass media and history. 2. Collective memory. 3. Memorialization.
 4. Mass media—Technological innovations—Social aspects. 5. Information
 technology—Social aspects. I. Freeman, Lindsey A. II. Nienass, Benjamin.
 III. Daniell, Rachel.
   P96.H55.S55 2014
   302.23—dc23

                                                                2013023291

British Library Cataloguing in Publication Data

A catalogue record for this book is available from the British Library.

ISBN: 978-1-78238-280-5 hardback
ISBN: 978-1-78533-355-2 paperback
ISBN: 978-1-78238-281-2 ebook

Contents

Part III. Silence and Memory: Erasures, Storytelling, and Kitsch

Illustrations

Acknowledgments

We would like to thank series editor Jo Labanyi for her insightful input and for making our book part of the Remapping Cultural History series; Marion Berghahn, Ann DeVita, Elizabeth Berg, Adam Capitanio, Ben Parker, and the entire Berghahn Books staff for their work making the book a reality; Vera Zolberg for her keen eye on early drafts and her long-standing support; Jonathan Bach and Ross Poole for their creative insight and tireless efforts; Robert Kirkbride for always showing up, even when on sabbatical; Maury Botton for his magical way with the visual image and the written word; Rachel Garver for her textual dexterity; Jessi Lee Jackson for her editing corroboration; the New School Interdisciplinary Memory Group past and present (especially Amy Sodaro, Adam Brown, Yifat Gutman, Naomi Angel, and Laliv Melamed) for camaraderie and inspiration; and to all of those who helped and encouraged our woolgathering along the way.

Introduction

Rethinking Social Memory in the Age of Information

Lindsey A. Freeman, Benjamin Nienass, and Rachel Daniell

The clamor of the past can be almost deafening: it preoccupies us through speech, texts, screens, spaces, and commemorative spectacles; it makes demands on us to settle scores, uncover the "truth," and search for justice; it begs for enshrinement in museums and memorials; and it shapes our understanding of the present and the future. However noisy and ceaseless the demands of memory and of the past may seem, in every act of remembering there is something silenced, suppressed, or forgotten. Memory's inherent selectivity means that for every narrative, representation, image, or sound evoking the past, there are others that have become silent—deliberately forgotten, carelessly omitted, or simply neglected. In an age of information the relationships between remembering and forgetting, deleting and saving, posting and archiving have changed. It is the tension between loud and often spectacular histories and those forgotten pasts we strain to hear that this volume seeks to address.

For those who study social memory, the tension between silence and spectacle is especially productive. As the past often serves as a screen on which we project our present ambitions and future aspirations (Huyssen 2003; Rothberg 2008; Freeman, Nienass, and Melamed 2013), both what is silenced and what is loudly remembered tell us much about the present and what we expect of the future. This tension illuminates what has been selected for remembering and why; allows for alternative memories and understandings to emerge; reminds us that forgetting may sometimes seem necessary; and ultimately deepens our theoretical and empirical understanding of memory and its processes.

In this volume, we employ Guy Debord's notion of the spectacle as a conceptual apparatus through which to examine the changes of the contemporary landscape of social memory. We utilize Debord's canonical 1967 text as an inspiration, rather than an instruction manual. For Debord, the spectacle was characterized by an obsession with, or, at least an inability to look beyond, the present moment. We seek to answer how this concept might be developed now, in an age that has been criticized as an era dissatisfied with the present, nervous about the future, and obsessed with the past. We argue that this is precisely the moment to reintroduce the notion of spectacle. Perhaps now "spectacle" can be thought of not as a tool of distraction employed solely by hegemonic powers, but instead as a device used to answer Walter Benjamin's (2003 [1940]) plea to "explode the continuum of history," to bring our attention to now-time. By drawing on Foucault's concept of spectacle as a metaphor that can encompass dynamic heterochronic experiences (1968), rather than simply describe a snapshot of halted social interaction, we attempt to update Debord's theory in order to contribute to theories of social memory.

The relationship between memory and spectacle merits particular attention. According to the logic of spectacle, "[w]hen the spectacle stops talking about something for three days, it is as if it did not exist. For it has then gone on to talk about something else, and it is that which henceforth, in short, exists" (Debord 1998 [1967]: 20). For Benjamin, one of the outcomes of a modern society characterized by spectacle was the "impoverishment of memory" and the "standardization of perception" (Crary 1989: 103). One counter-strategy to this dulling and amnesia-inducing spectacle lies in memory. In evoking past images and narratives that are threatened by the radical presentism of the spectacle, memory can help build a repository for critique and political change. For both Debord and Benjamin, counter-spectacle also implies a notion of counter-memory. It is precisely because past, present, and future become indistinguishable in the spectacle that a new focus on the past can break up these impoverishing and standardizing tendencies to interrupt the flow of present moments.

Following Debord and Benjamin, the strategy for defying spectacle does not necessarily include direct access to a past or present reality or truth, but rather must, at least in part, also employ spectacular means—it is a matter of "using the tools of spectacle against itself" (Debord 1994 [1967]: 15; Martel 2006: 89). Spectacle, seen as the drawing in of careful attention, and not simply distraction, provides a chance to look at the past with new eyes, to focus our attention from different angles in order to allow for critical reflection and perhaps even social and political action. That is not to say that some of the characteristics of spectacle criticized by Debord and Benjamin do not still stupefy and attempt to thwart critical thought and political endeavor. Yet, there is something vital to be discovered through this lens of spectacle, enacted through new media, such as the Internet and social networking sites, or older media, such as photographs and museums that have been mobilized in new ways.

The chapters in this volume address the interplay of silence, screen, and spectacle while raising a number of pressing questions about absence, the politics of forgetting, and the challenges of new media, which will be increasingly important for future studies of social memory and communication. What does silencing the past mean in the age of digital media? Is silence still largely the product of hegemonic projects? Or, rather, is it now a byproduct of chaotic and cacophonous memory debates as a result of an "all access" approach to the past? Is silence perhaps a consequence of numerous parallel spectacles—of too much noise—or, is silence still best understood as either absence or the repression of one narrative by another? In other words, is the lack of a unifying narrative a silence in itself? Should the diversification of narratives be viewed as a welcome challenge to oppressive memories controlled by the few? If so, then how do we renegotiate the co-existence of different views about the past in an age of increased access and augmented storage capabilities? Does the proliferation of screens, from Times Square to Tahir Square, mean more opportunity for screening memory or for screen memories? And how do we tease out the complex relationship of spectacle to screens and silence?

Spectacular Memory: Memory and Appearance in the Age of Information

Social memory in the age of information is shaped by new relationships to attention and distraction. We have crossed "certain thresholds of acceleration within the general machinery of culture, with all its techniques for handling, recording, and storing information," which has resulted in an "acceleration of history," or, more specifically, the way we perceive and organize history (Derrida 1984: 20; Nora 1989). New technologies of mass communication and social media have shifted our engagement with the present and the past, new challenges to the ethics of memory have arisen, as well as new opportunities for once-silenced memories to appear or reappear. Along with Avishai Margalit (2002), we see social memories "not as a simple aggregate of individual memories," but instead as memories that require the aggregation of "different perspectives" through communication. In contemporary times, there are more means and opportunities to communicate than ever before, but that does not mean that the lines of communication or the ability to be heard is equal for everyone. Communication gets a voiceover, subtitles, and flashing sidebar content, and is interrupted with breaking news or by a test of the emergency broadcast system; messages and communiqués are shouted over, silenced, muffled, suppressed, and unplugged.

Spectacle can either draw attention to or complicate our ethical engagement with the past. While Debord sought a true unity with the past, as opposed to the false unity displayed by the "society of the spectacle," we argue that ethical remembering requires plurality and dexterity with respect to communication and reception. Communication must be more than just information; it must carry with it "the ability to share experiences" (Benjamin 2003 [1980]: 143), and it must emerge from a diversity of voices and mediums to reach equally diverse listeners and responders.

In "Haunted by the Spectre of Communism: Spectacle and Silence in Hungary's House of Terror," Amy Sodaro shows how one spectacular museum falls short of this goal and instead is used as a "political device" that attempts to stage support for the current government by simplifying the nation's past. The House of Terror purports to be a space of moral education by showcasing the oppressive regimes that controlled Hungary throughout much of the twentieth century, but, as Sodaro illustrates, there are limits to the success a museum of this sort—a museum of terror—can achieve. In fact, the space ultimately functions as a kind of stun technology that overloads the visitor's circuits with stories and sounds of torture and torment. The museum's theatrics, which are architectural, aural, and visual, bombard the visitor with selected memories, keeping most of the past out of the script. Sodaro rightly calls this process "the sacrifice of information" which results in "more of a communist crimes theme park than museum."

Within the museal space of the House of Terror dramatic sounds and images do most of the communicative work with only minimal text; each room has a single quote that is intended to impart the essence of the past on display there. Yet, one pithy phrase cannot be expected to carry a complicated social and political past with multiple regimes of terror and numerous historical actors. And because this is a national museum, Sodaro writes, "the museum's silences become official forgetting by the Hungarian political establishment." The problem is not in the brevity, but rather in the assumption that this is *all* there is to be said. Of course with every act of remembering there are parts of the past that are left out, obscured, deliberately or accidently forgotten, but when a mnemonic space, such as the House of Terror, attempts only to convey a feeling of heightened fear and oppression, memory is quashed anew. In spaces such as these, mock violence can result in real violence to memory.

National museums dedicated to painful pasts are productive spaces to focus on for the study of the changing social memory landscape, especially when they address wrongful acts committed by the nation-state. Increasingly, apologizing for past sins has become an imperative for nation-states across the globe and a source of internal and external legitimacy (Olick 2007; Nienass 2013). In "Making Visible: Reflexive Narratives at the Manzanar U.S. National Historic Site," Rachel Daniell focuses on the "self-reflexivity" on display at a former World War II Japanese American incarceration camp, now a U.S. National Historic Site. There is a marked tension in Daniell's case, where the recognition of the historic site is attributed to years of grassroots activism but in the end is funded by the state. Daniell questions what kinds of knowledge can be produced in state-sponsored historic sites, in spaces where what is commemorated is "the repressive actions of the same government that is its primary funder and architect." While the museum at Manzanar is undoubtedly a state spectacle, can the "activist heritage" that worked for the creation of the museum be passed on to a new generation of visitors? Can including the activist origins of what has become a state-run site of memory within the spectacle inspire more "productive remembering" (Huyssen 2003)? Daniell argues that sites such as Manzanar do have the potential to go beyond their own histories to address larger questions of state power and domination. In other words, new self-reflexive museal spaces can re-link lines of communication among past, present, and future concerns.

Memories circulate; they travel, defy spatial and temporal constraints, disappear, and reappear. They can potentially divide communities—such as national communities cut along racial and colonial lines, as seen in Naomi Angel's "The Everyday as Spectacle: Archival Imagery and the Work of Reconciliation in Canada." As memories re-emerge, as they "flash up in an instant," they drag traces of the past into the now (Benjamin 1968). At these moments, recognition can be sparked and new interpretations can occur, but we should be careful not to conceive of this process as straightforward. Multiple looks and multiple ways of looking are required. With seized memory-images come questions of "truth," evidence, and witnessing, as well as queries of the social, political, and cultural structures and processes around these memories: how they have been produced, nurtured, buried, or preserved.

Angel addresses how photographs from the Indian Residential Schools of Canada function as "spectacle," as a "social relation among people, mediated by images" (Debord 1994: 12). She shows how the photographs, the spectacular images mediating social relationships, were designed, developed, and reproduced through the colonial darkroom. Like many images on display in Manzanar, the image at the focus of Angel's chapter has an "everydayness" or "ordinariness" that becomes poignant when critically considered; an illustration of Barthes's assertion that "[p]hotography is subversive not when it frightens, repels or even stigmatizes, but when it is pensive, when it thinks" (1981: 38).

Angel shows how a photograph can endlessly signify (think) and inspire thought. The potential for the thinking spectacle is precisely the possibility we see in the contemporary social memory landscape. The possibility is productive, but can also be disorienting, so we must pay close attention to the multiple readings images from the past can reveal. This is what the anthropologist Kathleen Stewart might call "slow theory"[1]; it takes time to develop. For example, the photograph of children that Angel addresses can be read as evidence of ordinariness or as proof of colonial brutality. The trick is that it should be read as both. A photograph such as this should not be simply information, which closes in on itself with a gesture of finality, but rather a memory trigger—a vehicle for narrative (Benjamin 2003 [1940]; S. Stewart 1993).

The crimes of colonial oppression magnified by everydayness become harsher in their accepted banality. The image, if not read on multiple levels, risks functioning as a "memory stand-in," which blocks or screens out the brutal history of the Indian schools. The danger of this photograph and others like it is that the harsh reality of the past can be so easily concealed by the appearance of everydayness. Looking back from the twenty-first century, the images of the last century's aboriginal school children can and should be read as the colonial state's "self-portrait of power" (Debord, 1994: 19). Armed with this knowledge, Angel shows that these images can re-circulate in the present, undergoing constant resignification. In the hands of relatives and friends of those depicted, the portraits are not only of the state's oppression, but also of loved ones in the course of their everyday lives. These images become spectacular in their resurfacing, as survivors from a past event. While there are recoveries of lost pasts to be found in these images, in this circulation and re-circulation of knowledge, understanding, facts, truths, and even names and dates are inevitably lost and forgotten. What has been lost complicates the current process of reconciliation in present day Canada. To understand what *has* happened in order to imagine what *can* and *should* happen is a difficult task, but an absolute necessity if a deeper past is to be revealed and a richer future is to be constructed.

Screening Absence: New Technology, Affect, and Memory

Communications and memory scholar Peter C. van Wyck writes that in the twenty-first century, "we have come to understand the previous century as a time that authored the *unspeakable*" (2010: x). Catastrophic events piled up, rendering understanding and remembering difficult tasks in themselves and their communication even more challenging. What emerged from the challenge of the *unspeakable* were not only silences, but also new ways to transmit knowledge of and about the past—new methods of "screening." In the contemporary age, remembrance is shaped not only through more traditional ways of commemorating and mourning, such as festivals, monuments, and memorials, but also by video activism, social media, and digital archiving. These new forms of memory and communication technologies work "not only as 'screens' … but also as collective surfaces and media for the production of memory" (Sosa, this volume). What these technologies often screen is absence or silence, becoming fecund spaces that open up possibilities for critical thinking in the vein of John Cage's provocative 4′33″ recording—a spectacular performance where the musician "plays" silence for four and a half minutes, effectively screening silence for the listening audience in a way that allows them to hear it anew. As Cage shows, when a person actively produces silence, there is no possibility for "true" silence; there is always something being communicated.

Cecilia Sosa's chapter, "Viral Affiliations: Facebook, Queer Kinship, and the Memory of the Disappeared in Contemporary Argentina," takes up a particularly poignant example of how absence can be screened through new technologies, spreading through far-flung social networks at a rate that would have been inconceivable just decades before. Sosa compares two activist campaigns that sought to draw attention to the thousands of disappeared persons who were victims of state violence during the 1976–1983 military dictatorship in Argentina. The first concerns the *Siluetazo* (the Silhouette campaign) of the early 1980s. This venture resulted in the posting of thousands of life-sized painted silhouettes around Buenos Aires, standing in for those persons missing from that city and elsewhere—their bodies' whereabouts, and even whether they were living or dead, still unknown. In the second case, which is the focus of the chapter, Sosa analyzes a Facebook campaign launched three decades later on March 24, 2010, the anniversary of the dictatorship's seizing of power. The Facebook effort asked participants to remove their profile pictures, in effect to "disappear" their images in an act of commemoration and resistance. Facebook's default profile image—the wavy outline of a head and shoulders—echoed the *Siluetazo* outlines of the past. Other participants chose to replace their own profile pictures with those of disappeared persons. These contemporary online campaign strategies have been mobilized in similar ways for other resistance and memorial movements, including the move to transform profile pictures on Facebook to black squares in order to protest the execution of Troy

Davis by the U.S. state of Georgia in 2011 or the Facebook status updates intended for broad circulation that end with the phrase "please repost." Social networking sites provide a different kind of group forum in which participants can be in each other's "presence" and remember together.

The new visual memorial strategies addressed by Sosa are employed through social media, through spaces that are geographically fluid. These spaces become digital monuments to absence. Yet, while they draw attention to what has been lost, they also communicate memory in new ways. Vinitzky-Serrousi and Teeger have pointed to the fact that "silence can ... be used to facilitate recollection, [while] talk can be used to enhance amnesia" (2010: 1104). In the spaces Sosa addresses, absence is displayed through a proliferation of empty profile frames that make the larger absence present.

Sosa shows how virtual social spaces link and re-link communication lines where the transmission of stories from the past to the present may have been interrupted. Through her case studies, Sosa demonstrates how memories of a previous generation can be "queered," connected with, communicated, and re-interpreted beyond the bloodlines of the family or nation. Sosa's work on Argentina shows a "postmemory" that goes beyond a "DNA performance" and extends to communities of affinity (Taylor 2003; Butler 2005; Hirsch 2008). Imagining the future sometimes means smuggling the missing or disappeared parts of the past—its absences—into conceptions of what is possible. The spectacle of absence in Sosa's chapter is an interruption that allows for the severed ties to the past to be re-sewn in new ways.

The proliferating technologies of video production and circulation also offer new ways of screening memory. Laliv Melamed's chapter "Learning by Heart: Humming, Singing, Memorizing in Israeli Memorial Videos" considers the way in which the production of "domestic" Israeli memorial videos contributes to the affective impact of private storytelling and publicly shared memories. The videos, which commemorate Israeli soldiers who died in violent conflict, are aired on Israeli television on Israeli Memorial Day—they are private memories that circulate in the public sphere. Melamed shows how "domestic" videos recall the soldier as an individual first, "a singular, irreplaceable, particular lost loved one," and as a citizen of the state second. These two identities are then stitched together, as songs and images work both to trouble and to travel historical distance and political terrains.

Melamed goes on to examine the ways that folk and popular music woven into the mostly non-professionally produced videos further emotionally charge the films and work to produce affect in its viewers and listeners. The soundtrack here is of utmost importance. The songs used are widely known to the Israeli audience who view and hear the films; they are, as the author points out, popular songs that carry the ability to "sound as if [they were] directed towards and playing especially for you." Further, they provide a "haunting melody" to the memorial images—a melody which often continues in the memory of viewers once they have turned off the television. The stories accompanied by the familiar music smuggle their way into the watchers'/listeners' consciousness because the music is always already part of their memories. The melody "haunts because one actually forgot that one heard it. ... The haunting melody is the remembering of forgetting." Melamed links the "haunting melody" to involuntary memory and affect production, thereby theorizing beyond the image-based analysis that is often the focus of social memory studies.

Samuel Tobin also moves beyond the image to explore the corporeal embodiment of social memory in his study of disappearing spaces of play with the emergence of new gaming technologies. Through ethnographic and interpretative methods, Tobin shows how video arcades and the social practices they encouraged are being forgotten, while other social gaming practices are reemerging and being remembered, both aesthetically and practically, in other forms of individual and collective game play. The relationship of forgetting to fluctuating social spaces is particularly poignant in his chapter: Tobin notes the new absence of the arcade spaces that had shaped gaming culture, including the loss of Chinatown Fair on Mott Street, the last traditional video arcade in New York City, which has closed since the writing of this introduction.

When spaces of interaction disappear, previous social rituals and practices morph into new social rituals and practices—Tobin calls this process the "corporeal memory work of new game players." Tobin's research shows how we can remember these disappearing and disappeared spaces by looking for their traces in the new, while reminding us that other practices will inevitably fall off or be forgotten. And while we can lament what has been lost, we can also look for new ways to act in the future, both alone and in concert with others.

Silence and Memory: Erasures, Storytelling, and Kitsch

In contemporary times, silence appears in many guises: as a void, as avoidance, as a whisper drowned by shouting, or as cacophonous voices talking at once producing only noise. These myriad modes of silence are evidenced even in social memory practices less centered on new media—although they show up there too—such as storytelling, the construction of memorials and museums, and the organization of festivals and heritage events, as well as active ignoring and forgetting. While often ignored, this section shows how silences are active "participants" in the production of social memory.

The resurfacing of forgotten or ignored pasts, particularly as they manifest in unexpected or historically inaccurate ways, is the topic of Timothy McMillan's chapter. He takes as his case study the campus grounds and archival fields of the University of North Carolina. McMillan deftly shows how institutional memory goes through cycles of forgetting and remembering, of erasure and monumentalizing. McMillan's analysis begins to peel back layers of the complex, painful, and violent racial history of the United States. Mystifications arise when stories about this history are told too neatly, too succinctly, and when real historical persons are transmuted into merely symbolic figures on campus and elsewhere. In his examples, the namelessness of former slaves exemplified by recent UNC monuments stands in stark contrast to the individualized attention granted to other actors in UNC's memorial landscape. Ultimately we are left with a presumably self-reflective acknowledgement of "unsung" heroes, "unknown" workers, and "unnamed" activists, even in cases where more specific information is readily available on the campus itself. In McMillan's chapter we see how brokers of history play a game of hide-and-seek with the past, often guided by present concerns to such an extent that they provide "agency to those who invoke the (forgotten) black past of Chapel Hill, but in many ways den[y] agency to the actual black people being remembered." Most importantly, the campus continues to tell a story about forgetting itself, in its material traces as well as in the debates that surround each new controversy about the university's legacy and responsibility.

In "The Power of Conflicting Memories in European Transnational Social Movements," Nicole Doerr examines the relationships between storytelling and silences in the era of new transnational activist public spheres and their related forums of communication via the Internet. She takes as her case the European Social Forum, a public sphere dedicated to debating alternatives to neoliberal globalization. Through an ethnography of storytelling, Doerr shows how conflicts over silenced memories can eventually cause more tension than conflicts over power struggles that take place out in the open. The silenced memories resurface as tensions that are acted out under the pretense of other discussions. Attempts to take political action in the present become inflected with the conflicts of the past and the exclusions of differentially valued voices.

"Remembering forgetting" plays a central role in Joanna B. Michlic's account of Polish memories of Jews and the Holocaust. Michlic fleshes out the common tropes of Polish Holocaust remembrance—the Christian rescuer, the nostalgic Pole who laments the loss of a multicultural community, the neighbors who turn malicious during the fog of war—and casts them in a new light. She shows the difficulty Poles have had in integrating the darker stories of their past into the historical narrative. Her research maps a constellation of Polish responses torn between ethical demands, pragmatic short-term considerations, and the constant wish to "create" silences. Ultimately, evoking Goethe's famous dictum that "everyone hears only what he understands," Michlic provides a rather bleak outlook for a possible mediation between these different motivations.

Building on Timothy Garton Ash's (1990) concept of "refolutions," (a reform-revolution fusion), Susan C. Pearce shows how a new type of political revolution, characterized by its nonviolence and a "multi-faceted reconstruction in the realms of culture," has affected seven countries of Central and Eastern Europe that were members of the state-communist "Eastern Bloc" until 1989. Pearce looks at what happens when memories long silenced are "heard" again, when national boundaries are redrawn and leadership shifts, when the archives are cracked open and the machinations of secret police forces are laid bare. What is left, Pearce tells us, is "the unfinished business of revolution—and its partner, the unfinished business of memory."

So how does one address these two lacking processes? In her analysis of the current memorial landscapes of this region, she sees the emergence of two opposite poles of mnemonic strategy: "a nostalgic souvenirization" and a "re-traumatization." Both of these processes distance the past from the present and lack the critical and analytical tools to achieve a more complex telling of the past. The question remains then, how should nations begin to untangle the outright deceptions and tergiversated social memories of the past decades—the airbrushed photographs, the falsified or destroyed documents, the manipulated audio, and all the industries of propaganda, churning out everything from cereal to pamphlets to museums? Perhaps one answer here is to call on multidirectional memory (Rothberg 2008), to begin with a position of plurality and difference that can provide a more comprehensive analysis of the past; another option is to incorporate spectacular strategies, which utilize new forms of media and communication technologies to draw attention to the past in order to act in the present and the future.

Contributions and Connections

This volume, while firmly situated within the debates of the field of social memory studies, breaks new ground in the discussion of absence, both in terms of addressing specific "absent" or underrepresented dialogues, texts, monuments, and communities in its various case studies, as well as with regard to conceptualizing "disappearing" modes of living and relating to the past. In addition, we show the emergence of counter-memories and new communities of memory in the particular context of new technologies, as they compete with and compliment older technologies. The volume thus attempts to explicitly address new possibilities for thinking about the relationship between spectacles, screens, and silences in ways that acknowledge the changes in our ability to store, access, and control the past. Does increased access to debates about the meaning of the past necessarily lead to a new plurality of voices? And if so, how are these different voices weighed, combined, debated, and sometimes even co-opted? Who and what gets excluded and by which means? The chapters in this volume address these questions by highlighting new modes of intervention and expression in an age of spectacle without neglecting the new silences that are created in their wake.

One of the major themes that emerges from this volume is that of an absence or an emptiness caused by events in the past that continues to affect the present. As these chapters show, spaces of memory, including former spaces of death, repression, or atrocity, continue to haunt the present across the globe, from Argentina, to Israel, to the United States, to Central and Eastern Europe, to Canada. Sosa draws attention to the ghostly *Siluetazo* campaign of 1980s Argentina; McMillan shows how the complex racial history of the University of North Carolina haunts the symbolic landscape of the campus; Melamed describes the "haunting melodies" of commemorative videos; and both Pearce and Michlic address the absent communities that ache like phantom limbs for parts of Central and Eastern Europe. As these chapters demonstrate: "To study social life one must confront the ghostly aspects of it" (Gordon 2008). The problem of emptiness brings up many questions about how we should think about the past. Do these spaces always need to be filled? Or, should spaces of atrocity be left empty? Is a museum always necessary? In places where the politics of history make the past an ever shifting ground, memory activists worry about leaving former spaces of atrocity empty. This, they fear, could be the first step towards erasure of the past and to forgetting. Instead, the challenge is to present "absence," to combine the spectacular with a reflection on silences and their political meaning.

Another connecting theme throughout the volume is the practice of storytelling and its relationship to social memory. Doerr's article shows how even in settings where storytelling from different historical and national perspectives is encouraged, the space to be heard is not equal, and the result is often a kind of double silencing. In this process the narratives are firstly ignored and secondly drowned out by the voices of more powerful actors. In Melamed's chapter, we see how video testimony allows for the silences, repetitions, and melodies of collective memories to be read on multiple levels, imploding public and private memory spaces. And in Daniell's chapter, the author looks at a more traditional form of storytelling—the state-sponsored museum—but shows how, even in nationally funded spaces, a new reflexivity towards stories about the past is emerging.

Lastly, kitsch or the fear of kitsch runs through many of these chapters. How can the past be preserved for a mass audience without employing some of the tricks of mass culture? Do spectacular museums, souvenirs, and historically themed tours and festivals distort, damage, or silence memory? As Pearce notes, in the former East Germany there is a neologism to define a particular nostalgia—"*ostalgie.*" The sentiments of *ostalgie* and nostalgia, more generally, tend to attach themselves to objects—often mass-produced products only available in certain places at certain times. The objects at the time of their production can now be conceived as pre-souvenirs. In the present, they are available for easy purchase at museum exhibits and themed commercial spaces devoted to these pasts. The question then is, do these objects work as memory triggers? Or, do they run the danger of simply hollowing out the past?

The chapters included in this volume address these pressing questions; they provide not definitive answers but new conceptual tools and new critical spaces for thinking about contemporary issues of social memory as affected by global and local politics, social media, technology, and "spaces of memory," both emerging and traditional. We have attempted to bring back voices of the formerly unheard, while simultaneously addressing the question of what "being heard" and "unheard" can mean, and how they function in an age of the spectacular.

Notes

1. Stewart presented the concept of "slow theory" at a talk at Eugene Lang College, The New School, in October 2010.

References

Ash, Timothy Garton. 1990. *The Magic Lantern: The Revolution of '89 Witnessed in Warsaw, Budapest, Berlin, and Prague.* New York: Random House.

Barthes, Roland. 1981. *Camera Lucida*. New York: Hill and Wang.
Benjamin, Walter. 1968. "Theses on the Philosophy of History." *Illuminations*. Translated by Harry Zohn. New York: Schocken Books, 253–64.
———. 2003. "The Storyteller." *Selected Writings: Volume 3, 1935–1938*. Cambridge, MA: Belknap Press.
Butler, Judith. 2005. *Giving an Account of Oneself*. New York: Fordham University Press.
Crary, Jonathan. 1989. "Spectacle, Attention, Counter-Memory." *October* 50 (Autumn): 96–107.
Debord, Guy. 1994 [1967]. *The Society of the Spectacle*. New York: Zone Books.
———. 1998. *Comments on the Society of the Spectacle*. London and New York: Verso.
Derrida, Jacques. 1984. "No Apocalypse, Not Now (Full Speed Ahead, Seven Missiles, Seven Missives). *Diacritics* 14.2 (Summer): 20–31.
Foucault, Michel. 1986. "Of Other Spaces." *Diacritics* 16.1 (Spring): 22–27.
Freeman, Lindsey A., Benjamin Nienass and Laliv Melamed. 2013. "Screen Memory." *International Journal of Politics, Culture and Society* 26: 1–7.
Goffman, Erving. 1959. *The Presentation of the Self in Everyday Life*. New York: Anchor Books.
Gordon, Avery. 2008. *Ghostly Matters: Haunting and the Sociological Imagination*. Minneapolis: University of Minnesota Press.
Hirsch, Marianne. 2008. "The Generation of Postmemory." *Poetics Today* 29.1: 103–128.
Huyssen, Andreas. 2003. *Present Pasts: Urban Palimpsests and the Politics of Memory*. Stanford, CA: Stanford University Press.
Margalit, Avishai. 2002. *The Ethics of Memory*. Cambridge, MA: Harvard University Press.
Martel, James. 2006. "The Spectacle of the Leviathan: Thomas Hobbes, Guy Debord, and Walter Benjamin on Representation and its Misuses." *Law Culture, and the Humanities* 2.1: 67–90.
Nienass, Benjamin. 2013. "Postnational Relations to the Past: A 'European Ethics of Memory'?" *International Journal of Politics, Culture and Society* 26.1: 41–55.
Nora, Pierre. 1989. "Between History and Memory: Les Lieux de Mémoire." *Representations* 26 (Spring): 2–24.
Olick, Jeffrey. 2007. *The Politics of Regret: On Collective Memory and Historical Responsibility*. New York: Routledge.
Rothberg, Michael. 2008. *Multidirectional Memory: Remembering the Holocaust in an Age of Decolonization*. Stanford: Stanford University Press.
Stewart, Susan. 1993. *On Longing: Narratives of the Miniature, the Gigantic, the Souvenir, the Collection*. Durham, NC: Duke University Press. (Originally published in 1984 by Johns Hopkins University Press.)
Taylor, Diana. 2003. *The Archive and the Repertoire: Performing Cultural Memory in the Americas*. Durham, NC: Duke University Press.
Van Wyck, Peter C. 2010. *The Highway of the Atom*. Montreal: McGill-Queen's University Press.
Vinitzky-Serrousi, Vered, and Chara Teeger. 2010. "Unpacking the Unspoken: Silence in Collective Memory and Forgetting." *Social Forces* 88.3: 1103–22.

Part I

Spectacular Memory

Memory and Appearance in the Age of Information

Chapter 1

Haunted by the Spectre of Communism

Spectacle and Silence in Hungary's House of Terror

Amy Sodaro

The *Terrorhaza,* or House of Terror, opened in 2002 in what was once an apartment building on one of Budapest's most beautiful avenues. Its location, 60 Andrassy Boulevard, is one loaded with meaning and memory: the building was taken over in 1944 by the Arrow Cross, Hungary's National Socialist movement, which deemed it the "House of Loyalty" and used it as its headquarters and prison; after 1945, the Hungarian communist secret police took control of the building and used it until 1963. The renovated building now houses a spectacular, ultramodern memorial museum that is meant to tell the story of these two regimes of terror and to serve as "a monument to the memory of those held captive, tortured, and killed in this building."[1] The past that it remembers is difficult, indeed—a complicated past of collaboration and complicity, suffering and terror under two of the twentieth century's worst totalitarian regimes.

The House of Terror was conceived and paid for (using taxpayers' money) by right-wing Prime Minister Viktor Orban in the midst of the bitter 2002 election campaign against the Socialists, the successor to the Hungarian Communist Party. At the time, Orban was believed by many to have connections to the extreme right-wing and openly anti-Semitic Hungarian Justice and Life Party.[2] Because of the highly political provenance of the museum and the ideological drive behind it, many in Hungary and around the world believe that the museum was and is a political device employed by Orban and Fidesz[3] to vilify the Communist party and implicitly link it to today's left-of-center politicians. The $20-million museum opened in February 2002 to a crowd of tens of thousands, organized by Orban, on the eve of the "Memorial Day of the Victims of Communism"[4] and just two months before the election. Despite the fact that when the Socialist candidate, Peter Medgyessy, won the election, museum proponents feared that it would be closed or turned into a "house of reconciliation," it remains the House of Terror. Orban is today back in power, giving the House of Terror a new life and meaning in the present political landscape of Hungary and in the broader debates and discussions about memory in our contemporary world.

Like other memorial museums that both commemorate and educate about violence, conflict, and atrocity, the House of Terror has an ambitious and complicated mission. It seeks not only to remember the victims of the two totalitarian regimes, but also to serve as a space of history and learning, with its highest function being to morally educate its visitors to reject such totalitarian and dictatorial ideologies in the future. By injecting its exhibitions and portrayal of the past with such a powerful moral message, the House of Terror positions itself as something of a "moral compass"[5] against which contemporary Hungarian society can measure itself. However, its highly political genesis—with an unbalanced representation of the history of twentieth-century Hungary that virtually ignores fascism in its fervent effort to denounce communism—and its sheer theatricality undermine this moral message, making it a highly controversial museum and memorial. It does, after all, claim to be a museum of memory of both regimes and is the only state-sponsored memorial museum; the museum's politics, then, become a reflection of official Hungarian politics, and the museum's silences become official forgetting by the Hungarian political establishment.

In this paper I analyze the exhibition narrative and strategies employed by the House of Terror, in light of Hungary's post-1989 political and social context, to examine the often-conflicting legacies and memories of fascism and communism as they are represented in Hungary's de facto national memorial museum. These conflicts over memory of the past are not unique to Hungary, though, and while the House of Terror is widely agreed to be an overly politicized institution, it also is not unlike other memorial museums in the post-communist world in its tenuous attempt to negotiate the memory of two totalitarian regimes in the service of the newly liberated nation state. Memory projects are usually as much about the present as they are about the past, and the House of Terror is no exception; a close look at its genesis, exhibition design, and the debates that surround it tell us more about twenty-first century Hungary than about Hungary's past. Despite the sheer spectacle of the dramatic museum, silences abound, and in many ways the museum serves as a screen upon which contemporary right-of-center Hungarian politicians project their idealized present and imagined future. Like Freud's notion of "screen memory," the theatrical presentation of a particular version of the past in the House of Terror obscures and silences alternative versions of the past, thus putting present Hungarian politics on display under the guise of an "authentic" representation of Hungary's painful and tumultuous twentieth century.

Post-Communist Politics in Hungary

Even before the fall of communism in 1989, the second half of the twentieth century was marked by an increased interest in memory and a zealous effort to come to terms with the past. While there are many possible explanations for why the past looms so large in our present, what is obvious is that the stakes of memory are high because the past and its memory have the power to make demands on and thus shape our present world (Poole 2010). On the other hand, memory and the past are also shaped by the present and, in the words of George Orwell, "who controls the past controls the present" (1948). Memory and the past become extremely important political, social, and moral tools, especially for regimes emerging from dictatorship and repression.

Communist and other totalitarian regimes of the twentieth century very much understood the high stakes of the past and its memory and so made every effort to have total control over it, often erasing and rewriting memory and history according to the ideological goals of the regime. While private and individual memories were difficult to control, totalitarian regimes were able to dictate what was publicly remembered and how. The hegemonic memory imposed by communist regimes became a powerful means of repressing the population and suppressing difference, pluralism, and independent thought; in the words of Milan Kundera, "the struggle of man against power is the struggle of memory against forgetting" (1978). With the fall of communism in 1989, as with the toppling of other powerful ideologies of domination like fascism and colonialism, a flood of memories that had been suppressed, forbidden, or silenced was released. Pierre Nora refers to this as a "recovery of memory" and describes it as a form of "ideological decolonization [that] helped reunite these liberated peoples with traditional, long-term memories confiscated, destroyed, or manipulated by those regimes" (2002: 5). Upon the fall of communism, in addition to the release of Nora's "traditional" memories, there was also the recovery of memories of the horrors of World War II and the Holocaust as well as of suffering under the communist regime.

Memories of communism were the most recent and acute, and it was a communist regime that transitional governments were most zealously trying to put behind them. In many senses, the recent past of communist dictatorship loomed largest in the sphere of collective memory and became an important political tool for new regimes that were trying to move forward and found themselves with carte blanche vis-à-vis the past.

However, as Tony Judt writes: "the real problem was the temptation to overcome the memory of communism by inverting it" (2005: 824). Thus, while the mostly peaceful revolutions of 1989 may have cleared the way for the development of liberal, open, democratic societies, they also opened the door to heightened nationalism, and with it xenophobia and ethnic tensions. In the void of a dominant ideology to structure social meaning, the countries of the former Eastern Bloc emerged from the ashes of communism with their national identities as the most forcefully cohesive and prevalent ideologies to cling to. Together with a renewed sense of nationalism and identity centered on the nation state, ethnicity and difference also came to the forefront with the recovery of memory, making the world a new place full of numerous "others" with alternative—and often competing—versions of the past and present, as well as differing views of the future. In other words, following the fall of communism there was "too much memory, too many pasts on which people can draw, usually as a weapon against the past of someone else" (Judt 1992: 99).

The communist experience in Hungary following the failed 1956 revolt was arguably different than that of its neighbors. The relatively open and comfortable "goulash communism" of Janos Kadar's regime meant that for many Hungarians, the lived experience of communism was not quite as stifling and austere as it was in neighboring countries, and Hungarians enjoyed relative wealth and freedom. However, the economic compromises of the Kadar regime to keep the people relatively content paved the way for a host of economic challenges that—minimized and allowed to fester under the state-controlled communist economic policy—came to the fore after the fall of communism in 1989. For many in Hungary, the fall of communism most obviously brought the end of economic stability, not necessarily the long-desired freedom and openness that other countries experienced. Additionally, as Janos Kis argued shortly after Hungary's first democratic election, the nature of Hungary's transition—negotiated by the elites and intellectuals instead of resulting from a popular movement of the people—left much of the Hungarian public feeling disenfranchised and disconnected from Hungary's new democracy from its very inception. Because "the overwhelming majority of Hungarians [could] detect little or no change in their lives" (Kis 1991:

5), the perceived success of the post-communist leadership was largely based on the economic situation of the Hungarian people, which was often not better but worse than under communism.

This link between political leadership and the economic situation on the ground has led to major shifts in power back and forth between the political left and right from the first democratic election in 1990 through today in a "left-right musical chairs" that evidences the ongoing discontent of the Hungarian populace (Jordan 2010: 105). At the moments when Hungarians have been most disillusioned, it has become very easy for demagogues to sweep in and offer instant, simple solutions to a population feeling serious economic and social woes. Hence, throughout the twenty years since the fall of communism, extreme right-wing parties have managed to seize on populist discontent and frustration with the establishment. Social and economic conditions in Hungary today offer fertile ground for the nationalist rhetoric and ideology of Hungary's right-wing parties. The economic and political unease has led not only to nostalgia for the security and stability of communism, but, for many Hungarians, has reopened the wound of the Treaty of Trianon, a national trauma for Hungary in which over 50 percent of its lands were taken away in the wake of World War I and the dismantling of the Austro-Hungarian Empire. The right-wing has been able to exploit this memory and speak of a great and powerful "Hungary for Hungarians," and—especially in times of economic crisis—it has turned this exploitation of fear and unease into serious political power (Jordan 2010).

This was especially evident in the April 2010 election. Hungary was one of the worst-hit EU nations in the economic crisis of 2008 and is still reeling from the effects. The backlash of the economic downturn—not to mention the lies of the former socialist prime minister about the economy[6]—has led to a fierce nationalism in much of the country and a reinvigorated vilification of non-Hungarians, primarily Roma, who are viewed as pariahs at the heart of Hungary's problems. The vitriol over the economy, the failures of the Socialists, and the fear and anger toward the Roma and other minority populations has led to such anger and frustration with the establishment that a recent poll found that 46 percent of Hungarians believe that "everything and everyone is bad" (Jordan 2010: 101). Exploiting this fear, uncertainty and anger, Jobbik, a far right-wing, paramilitary party that dons black uniforms reminiscent of the Arrow Cross and is openly hostile to Jews and Roma, won an alarming 16 percent of the vote and 47 seats in Parliament in the 2010 election. While Orban and Fidesz vowed to rein in Jobbik, they also immediately seized on the mood of the country and the nationalist rhetoric of the far right. They promised dual citizenship for all Hungarians,[7] established an annual National Unity Day every June 4 to commemorate and mourn the "national tragedy" of Trianon (Saunders 2011), and put in place a number of laws and policies that are arguably authoritarian, alarming many of their neighbors and fellow EU states and making many nervous that Hungary is currently "transitioning from democracy."[8]

The political, economic, and social upheavals of Hungary following 1989, as in many of its neighboring former Soviet satellite states, have bred a powerful combination of nationalism paired with nostalgia for the simpler and more stable communist past, both of which are evident in the House of Terror. Further, each political party in Hungary has evoked memory of the recent and the more distant past to further its own political agenda. This political use of the past is particularly evident with regard to the House of Terror, which plays both to the nationalist rhetoric of the Hungarian right as well as to the nostalgia for the "good old days." It is an often discomfiting combination and at times is shocking for the non-Hungarian visitor to go from absolute terror inflicted on the helpless Hungarian nation at the hands of the Soviet occupation to ironic and even fond reminisces about Hungary's communist past. But the kitschy rendering of the past in the House of Terror is nostalgia meant only for those who survived communist rule; the real story of the museum is the terror and suffering of communist rule in Hungary as a warning of the evils of totalitarianism, for the present and future, addressed to those who did not live through it.

Memory Politics and the House of Terror

As early as 1997, József Szájer, a leader of the then out-of-power Fidesz party, had the idea to turn the building at 60 Andrassy into a museum of communism.[9] The seed was thus planted and when Fidesz gained power in 1998, with Viktor Orban as Prime Minister, the project slowly began to take shape. In 2000, the beautiful building at 60 Andrassy was purchased by The Public Foundation for the Research of Central and East European History and Society, a government-sponsored foundation under the directorship of historian Maria Schmidt, who was one of Orban's closest political advisors and has been director of the museum since its inception.

According to Schmidt, the primary impetus behind the creation of the House of Terror was the question of what to do with the many perpetrators of crimes committed under the communist regime. Hungary has had an uneasy relationship with "transitional justice," swinging back and forth between calls for lustration, with the opening of the past government's files and criminal prosecution on the one hand, and closing the door to the past on the other by sealing the files and instituting a general amnesty for communist party members and leaders. However, most proposals for any form of transitional justice have been, at their root, only political posturing—none were ever taken very seriously by the Hungarian people and little in the way of transitional justice ever came to fruition (Kiss 2006). In the early 1990s, the Hungarian parliament created a law that would allow perpetrators from the communist leadership to be tried for those crimes committed during the darkest days of Hungarian communism, especially immediately following the crushed 1956 uprising. However, the Hungarian Supreme Court overturned the law as unconstitutional and not fitting the criteria of rule of law (Kiss 2006: 932), essentially placing the "rule of law over justice" in the words of Schmidt. This was not at all uncommon in the region; many countries throughout Central and Eastern Europe struggling with coming to terms with the past and its perpetrators rejected the notion of criminal trials as impractical, divisive, and expensive: the perpetrators seemed too numerous and the peace and democracy too tenuous to risk threatening them with lengthy criminal trials (Rosenberg 1995). Rather, an uneasy amnesty was settled upon and the gaze of the former Eastern Bloc and Hungary was directed toward the future.

However, this was a deeply unsatisfying resolution to such a haunting problem for many people, especially Schmidt and her colleagues in the Fidesz party. Firmly believing that without justice in the form of holding perpetrators criminally responsible, Hungary would not be able to move forward, plans for a museum to expose the truth about the communist past were drawn up. In the words of Schmidt, this was a necessary means of dealing with the past and its perpetrators, as "a new era needs to come to terms with the past." The museum, then, was conceived in large part to be a public forum for holding the perpetrators of communist crimes accountable—if not judicially, then morally.

Further, it was not enough for the museum to serve as a space for those who had experienced communism to come to terms with the past and find some form of reparation in the public exposure of their victimizers. Rather, Schmidt wanted to create a museum for the younger generations. For those who did not live through communism or are not old enough to remember, the House of Terror is intended to portray such a picture of Hungary's past under communism as to make today's youth grateful that they do not live under dictatorship. As Schmidt describes it, following the fall of communism "it was very difficult to have a positive relationship to democracy"; things had not gotten especially better for many people, who found themselves worse off and longing for the stability of socialism. For this reason it was deemed important to create a museum that showed the "reality" of life under dictatorship. By demonstrating how terrible it was, the House of Terror is intended to teach young generations that dictatorship (and in particular communist dictatorship) is bad and democracy is good, no matter how much effort is required to make democracy work.

In order for the museum to effectively tell the story of communism in Hungary for new generations, the museum's creators believed that it needed to first "reach the heart of children and people" before reaching their brains. In this way, it is intended to provoke an emotional reaction first and foremost, with an intellectual response following. It also, for Schmidt, had to be a museum in which her daughter (22 at the time) would not be bored. Having visited other memorial museums in Germany, the Baltics, France, and the UK, Schmidt and her team envisioned something that would be even more interactive, technological, and engaging—more spectacular—than what they'd seen. Hence, the museum is a dramatic, experiential, and haunting experience for the visitor, with numerous audio, visual, and interactive components that attempt to engage the visitor and seek to provoke an emotional, guttural, deeply affective response to the horrors of communism and, to a lesser degree, fascism. It is clear that evoking spectacular memory was the goal of the design of the House of Terror from the moment of its conception—the past made into pure spectacle.[10]

Inside the House of Terror

The drama of the House of Terror begins before one even enters the building. The graceful nineteenth-century façade is dominated by striking black "blade walls" that separate it from the building next to it, warning the visitor of the militarized nature of what is inside. Jutting from the roof is a stark black overhang with the word "TERROR" spelled backwards,[11] the communist five-pointed star, and the Arrow Cross symbol cut out of it. It is claimed that at precisely noon, the sun shines so that the shadow of the word "TERROR" fills the sidewalk below (Rev 2008). But at any time of day, the blade walls make clear the dark and sinister past contained within the building. Designed by award-winning architect and scenic designer Attila Ferenczfy Kovacs, who also designed the museum's interior, the dramatic façade not only spells out the museum's dominant theme, but is a prelude to the theatrical experience that lies within.[12]

Figure 1.1. House of Terror façade with blade walls. (Photo by Amy Sodaro.)

Greeted by the word "TERROR," the experiential rendering of the past begins before even gaining entrance to the museum: the museum's entrance is small and cramped, meaning that visitors often must stand in long lines to buy tickets, echoing the bread lines that dominate popular imaginaries of life under communism. Once inside, the visitor is greeted by an ominous and foreboding soundtrack that will haunt her throughout the entire museum.[13] Rising up over the music is a sobbing victim of communism asking *"why?,"* seeking to understand the senselessness of the terror one is about to witness. Like the façade and long lines to get in, these theatrical elements set up the entire experience for the visitor, which is as carefully narrated, framed, and rendered, just as the glaring, cut-out word "TERROR" is angled for the proper effect.

Past the ticket counter is a courtyard dominated by a huge Soviet tank, resting in a reflecting pool against a wall of photographs, presumably of victims. The tank symbolizes the arrival of the Soviet occupiers in Hungary, who, in 1945, promptly took over the graceful but menacing building. Already well-oriented toward the narrative the museum will tell, the visitor is directed to an elevator to the third floor where the journey through the two totalitarian regimes begins with a sign bearing the words "Double Occupation." The very name of the room indicates that Hungarians were victims, pawns of the Germans and then the Russians—any collaboration was forced upon Hungary, as these two regimes forced themselves upon the Hungarian people. Dramatically arranged with a wall splitting the room into fascist and communist occupation, what is immediately striking—and what will remain true throughout the rest of the museum—is the sacrifice of information and documentation in the form of text, labels, photographs, and video to spectacular, theatrical renderings that blur concrete, historical fact with symbolism and imagi-

Figure 1.2. Entrance to House of Terror exhibit. (Photo by Amy Sodaro.)

nation. Each room is dominated by a quote, which is intended to "say it all" and make clear the purpose of the particular room's installation —in the case of "Double Occupation," the quote is "Last night I dreamt the Germans left and no one stepped into their shoes," Imre Kovacs—and make up for the lack of other text and information. However, the quotes are in Hungarian and no translation is provided in other languages. An information sheet accompanies each room, but otherwise the museum is striking in its lack of textual information, especially for the non-Hungarian visitor.

The next two rooms, "Arrow Cross Corridor" and "Arrow Cross," constitute the bulk of the museum's representation of fascist occupation, the Holocaust, and Hungary's complicity with the Nazis. Through the vilification of Hungary's fascist leader, Ferenc Szalasi, some of the horrors of the Holocaust and the destruction of Hungarian Jewry are touched upon, though with scant reference to the home-grown anti-Semitism that brought the fascist movement (and the Germans) to power. In the Arrow Cross Corridor, which is dripping with symbolism and arranged as a kind of "Last Supper of hatred" (Mathe 2010), the alternating Nazi and Arrow Cross uniforms remind one that it was the German infiltration of Hungarian politics that led to the Holocaust's devastation in Hungary and underlines the museum's message of victimization at the hands of the occupying regimes. It is also in this room that the House of Terror's disregard for authenticity first becomes apparent, though not necessarily to the casual visitor; the uniforms and Arrow Cross plates on display are not actual artifacts, but reconstructions, like much of the museum, with no labels indicating their provenance one way or the other. As the layers of symbolism and dramatic interpretation become obvious in the museum, the departure from traditional museological principles becomes ever more striking and troubling. Blurring the lines between museum and movie set, the House of Terror challenges notions of museums as houses of history, collection, and documentation, and instead turns memory into spectacle and history into mere symbolic representation of the past as imagined by the present.

Following these two small rooms that are the only ones to focus on fascism, the visitor is taken to the "Gulag," representing the far reaches of Siberia, and from there into the small transitional room, "Changing Clothes," which shifts the focus of the exhibit to the heart of the museum's message. In "Changing Clothes" members of the Arrow Cross are depicted as switching sides after the war and joining the communists; it is clear that while their uniforms and politics may have changed, this small minority of "bad" Hungarians shifted sides to remain in their role as tormentors of the innocent Hungarians. The implication from here on is that they learned from the Nazis how to be especially evil, which was a skill that they would develop to its greatest potential under the Soviet occupation. From here, the visitor is immersed in the terror of the communist "occupation" of Hungary.

Beginning with the "darkest period" of communism, the exhibit takes the visitor through "The Fifties": the front of this room has red-curtained "poll booths," which at once ironically reference the "perfect democracy" that communism purported to be, but also the stolen election of 1947,[14] and which allow visitors a moment to sit down and listen, on the period-style phones that are placed throughout the museum, to archival speeches from the era.[15] Behind the façade, though, the visitor finds the "reality" of life under communism in the shape of surveillance devices, propaganda speeches, and the proscriptive Socialist Realist paintings of the period. This depiction of "Life under Communism" reminds the visitor that communist principles and ideals permeated every aspect of life, even the most private corners of existence. However, lest one be tempted to interpret this as complicity of the Hungarian population through everyday life under communism, the next two rooms, "Soviet Advisors" and "Resistance," emphasize the foreign nature of the communist regime and the effort—at all levels of Hungarian society—to resist the totalitarian occupation. Again, reconstructed props and heavy symbolism that, according to researcher Aron Mathe, all Hungarian visitors who lived through communism will understand immediately, underline the message and plotline of the museum, which might remain obscure to the casual international visitor.

From here the horrors of communism persist, with "Resettlement and Deportation" depicted by a veiled Black Maria, the ominous black car used to transport prisoners in the middle of the night that is recognizable even to those who do not have a direct experience of communism, and a completely reconstructed torture cell that may or may not have existed at all in the building; on the wall hang imagined instruments of torture. Nowhere in the museum is it clear what kind of violent acts actually took place, though violence is suggested everywhere. Two rooms about the "Hungarian Political Police" follow, and deliberately name the individual police officers in the higher echelons. To the outrage of family members (Schmidt 2010), on the wall hang photographs of the officers, in the public shaming that Schmidt envisioned the museum enacting. Next, the room titled "Justice" depicts the theatrical nature of the communist show trials, complete with audience seating, a stage upon which the action would take place, and a tiny room cut into the wall for the "prompt" to feed the defendant the lies the Party wanted him or her to tell as a confession. This pretend courtroom/theater is entirely papered with bureaucratic dossiers and documents related to trials, indictments, sentences, appeals, and investigations.

However, tucked into these rooms that depict the brutality and arbitrary terror of communism are several rooms devoted to everyday life under the regime that are nostalgic, ironic, and pure kitsch. A room devoted to Hungarian peasants is a maze of one kilogram blocks of lard, complete with a papier-*mâché* pig, intended to evoke memories of the 1969 satiric Hungarian film *The Witness,* the plot of which centers around the illegal act of slaughtering a pig, and to evoke humor and irony in visitors for whom one kilogram of lard was precious under communist rationing. There are two rooms devoted to propaganda, which alternately depict the vibrant colors of propagandistic posters and advertisements and black and white photographs of the reality of everyday life; however, the empty food tins, old radios, newspaper cutouts, round, vinyl settee, and fake plant are nothing if not nostalgic for what was. Immediately recognizable to those who lived under communism, these rooms belie the horrors that are implied in the other rooms to have so completely pervaded the population through their comforting depiction of the mundane everyday experience for the vast majority of the population under communism. Another room, completely aluminum with eerie blue lighting, pokes fun at this precious "Hungarian silver" made from the bauxite mines of Hungary, again using kitsch to almost fondly recall life under communism.

Departing again from nostalgia and kitsch, the exhibition moves on to a dramatic, dark, and uncanny cave-like room with a lighted cross cut out in the floor and a disembodied priest at its head. Though there is no text to explain the room, most visitors know that it refers to communism's war on religion in Hungary. Dark, brooding music plays in the background and cut-out lighted shelves in the walls depict small religious artifacts, though again whether these artifacts are authentic or not is left undocumented. Haunting music continues to provide the soundtrack—here for the communists' war on none other than God himself.

Nearing the end of the exhibit, the visitor finally finds herself in an elevator descending painfully slowly to the (completely reconstructed) torture cells in the basement, while on video a former execution assistant describes the process of hanging political victims. In the basement, visitors are encouraged to enter the torture cells, which have been recreated, as no records remain of what the cellar of 60 Andrassy actually held. There are cells too narrow to sit down in, or too low to stand up; cells that forced the prisoner to stand in icy water for hours on end or to sit in complete darkness. There are small cells in which prisoners would have lived, arranged "thematically" with photographs of famous dissidents, clergy, anti-fascist activists, and others who may or may not have been imprisoned in 60 Andrassy. And there is the execution cell in which a gallows is erected, though if one pays attention closely she learns that no executions took place in this house of terror. The blank slate of the building's cellar thus serves as a screen upon which an image of a past of Hungarian victimization that suits the museum's creators is able to be theatrically and chillingly projected.

The torture and "execution" cells open onto a moment of short-lived triumph, with the "Hall of the 1956 Revolution," which is followed by a haunting memorial, "The Hall of Tears," that is dedicated to "those who were executed for political reasons between 1945–1967." The names of these victims are inscribed in light on the room's four walls, and in the center, a "graveyard" of wobbly, tall crosses, each affixed with a flash-light memorialize these victims.[16] At last, emerging from the horrors of the Soviet totalitarianism, the final room, "Farewell," assures the visitor that the Soviets are forever gone, and that Hungary has been justly liberated. Hungary and her innocent people are now free and independent to pursue their pure, moral agenda—which is, of course, in direct opposition to the communist agenda. The visitor is brought to the edge of the abyss then led out of the torture chamber and into liberty. Passing a wall of photos of the perpetrators,[17] the visitor is reminded that liberty has prevailed and that those who committed such atrocities will not be allowed to go free.[18]

Memory, History, and Authenticity in the House of Terror

As director Maria Schmidt told me, the purpose of the House of Terror is to help Hungary come to terms with its past in order to start a new era of freedom and democracy. This needs to begin with holding the perpetrators accountable and teaching the younger generations the dangers of totalitarianism. Like similar memorial museums, this intention is noble and most would agree that totalitarianism amply demonstrated its evils throughout the course of the twentieth century. However, the ways in which these goals play out in the House of Terror is questionable at best and deeply troubling at worst.

The House of Terror website describes the exhibition as follows:

> The exhibition is structured within a framework: that frame is provided by the rooms called "Double Occupation" and "Farewell." The frame-like structure indicates that the Nazi occupation of the country on March 19, 1944 enabled the introduction of an autocracy modeled on foreign examples, while the Russian withdrawal, which ended on June 19, 1991 guaranteed—and made irreversible—the independent, national, democratic evolution of the new Hungarian Republic.[19]

Clearly, the purpose of the museum is to depict the terror of foreign occupation, and to juxtapose it against Hungarian independence, democracy, and nationalism. In essence, this is a highly nationalistic and propagandistic museum. Istvan Rev, a historian and political scientist at Central European University, summarizes the story of the museum:

> After the long decades of degeneration—starting with the German occupation on 19 March 1944 and terminating with the humiliating retreat of the Soviet troops on 19 June 1991—the new era has begun. The leader [Orban] and his native people [...] have finally found each other, and are ready to embark on a smooth road leading to the future. (2008: 72)

Issues of past collaboration are lightly touched upon (and cannot be avoided when dealing with the Arrow Cross and communism), but ultimately in the museum's portrayal, virtually all true Hungarians were innocent victims and pawns of German and Soviet occupiers. And now that Hungary is liberated and reunited, the future is at last in the hands of real Hungarians. This sort of nationalistic narrative is understandable in a country that emerged from nearly a century of occupation, and as Tony Judt points out, it is prevalent throughout a region that shared similar sociopolitical experiences (2005). However, this nationalistic effort to define *real* Hungarians and put the future in their hands is dangerous in a country like Hungary, where exclusion of minorities (Roma and Jews, especially) is central to the politics of the far right and is seemingly a central part of Orban's own party platform. One sure lesson that emerged from World War II and European fascism is the danger of nationalistic, exclusive ideologies.

However, just as troubling, and the subject of much of the controversy surrounding the museum and the highly political context of its creation, is the utterly imbalanced representation of fascism and the Holocaust versus communism; unfortunately, like the nationalistic tenor of the exhibition, this imbalance reveals much about Hungarian politics and society today. Out of more than two dozen rooms, just two are devoted to the Arrow Cross, the Holocaust, and the German occupation of Hungary, and even these two emphasize the German influence and control over Hungary's actions and how short-lived fascism in Hungary was, while barely touching upon Hungarian complicity or Hungary's already-complicated relationship to its Jewish population. Nowhere is it clearly stated just how devastating the Hungarian Holocaust was, nor is the homegrown build up of anti-Semitism in Hungary that paved the way for the Holocaust and Nazi collaboration addressed. In many senses, the loud and spectacular memory of the terrors of communism in Hungary that is on display in the museum serves as a convenient "screen memory" in the sense employed by Freud, to block what is possibly the more disturbing and difficult memory of fascism, the Holocaust, and extremist right-wing politics in Hungary's past. The museum effectively silences Hungary's fascist past in the cacophonous memory of communism that it displays.

In a country in which anti-Semitism seems to be on the rise or at the very least not going away, this imbalance is troubling, as are the two responses that the museum has to critiques of its portrayal of the two totalitarianisms. The museum's first response attempts to turn the critique around and criticize what Schmidt and others describe as the taboo in Europe over the equation of communism and fascism. For her and others involved with the museum, fascism and communism are two sides of the same totalitarian coin and the museum is simply attempting to portray communism as truly evil and terrible as it was—an equivalent to fascist totalitarianism. The Holocaust has received enough attention, they believe, and the horrors of communism deserve to be represented and commemorated equally. While there may or may not be such a taboo, the museum's portrayal is hardly *equal,* undermining this as a valid response to the criticism. Instead, memory of communism drowns out and almost completely silences memory of fascism and the Holocaust, the only possible reason for which appears to be to protect Hungary's current right-wing, nationalistic political orientation.

The second response claims that this criticism is actually a veiled complaint that the House of Terror is not a Holocaust museum. Those at the House of Terror respond easily that it is not and should not be a Holocaust museum, as there is a new Holocaust museum in Budapest to fulfill this role. As Schmidt puts it, the fact that some people are not happy about the House of Terror's inattention to the Holocaust is actually the fault of the Holocaust museum, which was funded and conceived at the same time as the House of Terror, but did not "do it" as fast and as well as the House of Terror, in the words of Schmidt. The Holocaust museum's mistake, according to Schmidt, in addition to opening late and generally lacking the sort of dynamism and excitement of the House of Terror, is that it is a "Jewish institution." Because of its "Jewishness," she argues, it isolates itself from Hungarian society, which sees the Holocaust not as a Jewish event but as Hungarian. She speaks as if these two institutions were always intended to be complementary and the Holocaust museum simply did not live up to its side of the partnership.

The Holocaust Museum opened in 2004, two years after the House of Terror, and tells the story of the Hungarian Holocaust. Visually striking, with hauntingly dark corridors cut through with blades of light and eerie music and sound effects in the background, Hungary's Holocaust museum clearly has taken some inspiration from the House of Terror and is attempting a similar sort of immersive experience. However, its emphasis on Hungarian complicity and the scale of devastation seems to be a direct answer to the House of Terror and Schmidt's arguments for why the House of Terror all but ignores the Holocaust. Though sometimes heavy-handed in its execution, the Holocaust museum insistently conveys Hungarian complicity, the deep roots of Hungarian anti-Semitism, racism toward the Roma population, and racism more generally, as well as the systematic disenfranchisement, dehumanization, humiliation, and ultimate murder of Hungary's Jews, and the wide-reaching, devastating consequences of the Holocaust on all of Hungarian society. Its exhibition stops where the terror of House of Terror's exhibition picks up and in many ways does complement the House of Terror, but the two institutions remain highly incompatible, primarily because the House of Terror claims that it is a place of memory for both regimes of terror; its extremely bold but troubling execution does not fulfill this vision.

Furthermore unlike Budapest's Holocaust museum, the House of Terror purports to use the authenticity of space—of this terrible, beautiful building on Andrassy Avenue that for much of the twentieth century was a symbol of supreme repression, fear, and totalitarianism—to portray the evils of *both* totalitarian regimes. But not only does it do a strikingly uneven job of telling these evils (and in so doing exposes its deeply political roots and objectives); it also sleekly packages "history" with little regard for authenticity in its exhibit installations, compromising the power of place that it attempts to harness. The House of Terror attempts to use the site-specificity of 60 Andrassy to tell its story of horror and bolster its historical claims, but in its flagrant use of reproduction, guesswork, artistry, and emphasis on symbolism at the expense of authenticity, it is more of a communist crimes theme park than museum. While memorial museums in general have departed from the traditional museological focus on collecting and displaying to emphasize a more experiential approach to making meaning of the past, the extremely minimal use of authentic artifacts and primary-source documentation[20] in the House of Terror marks a new era of experiential exhibition strategies. It is pure memory spectacle, but the past and history that lie behind the theatrics are completely elusive—overwhelmed by the clamor of the heavy-handed exhibition.

The House of Terror is intended to "tell the truth" about what happened under the communist totalitarian regime (and to a far lesser degree, under fascism) as a warning to the future about the dangers of dictatorship and totalitarianism; however, if the museum itself is so careless with truth, in the form of the many reconstructions and recreations that do not explicitly state their provenance, and offers so little in the way of explanatory text, what are we to make of its claims of authenticity and telling the truth about the past? While we know that the building itself is saturated with history and memory, what is authentic and could reveal something "true" about what happened there has been stripped away and covered with fancy paint, dramatic wallpaper, faux silver, stylized reproductions, and kitschy humor, and no longer can "speak" for itself. And knowing the political origins of the museum, we must wonder about what words are being put in 60 Andrassy's mouth and what words are completely silenced, perhaps never to be heard or remembered.

The Moral of the House of Terror

The House of Terror, like most memorial museums from which it takes its inspiration, is intended to play a moralizing role in society, in addition to telling and teaching twentieth-century Hungarian history. This is evident in its intent to not only reveal the "truth" about communism in Hungary, and so hold perpetrators accountable on a moral level, but also to use the memory of the past in a way that will morally educate Hungarians (and non-Hungarian visitors) about the evil of totalitarianism so that they will embrace democracy. However, the overt politics behind the museum, the scant and imbalanced nature of its narrative, and the reckless theatricality of its exhibitions seriously undermine its role as any kind of moral authority. Yet the drama of the visitor experience and the forceful story that the museum tells make it extremely compelling, especially for a visitor without much background knowledge of these historical events, or one whose opinions are reinforced by the House of Terror's message. Visitors expect memorial museums to be sources of history and truth about the past, as impossible as such a quest for truth may be, and the House of Terror plays with this power of memorial museums in a way that is deeply disturbing. In a country like Hungary that, since 1989, has struggled with right-wing extremism, ethnic tension (between ethnic Hungarians and Hungary's Roma population), and economic hardship, perhaps more subtlety, inclusivity, and openness should be expected of a prominent public memory institution.

In many ways, like the communist regimes that gripped Hungary and Central and Eastern Europe for much of the twentieth century, the House of Terror tells a hegemonic version of the past that leaves no space for the flood of alternative narratives that emerged after 1989. It minimizes to the point of almost silencing the experience of the Holocaust and Hungary's own dangerous brush with fascism, and wields the past and its memory as a weapon in the service of present day politics. Though memory projects today seem to be growing more self-reflexive and introspective, with careful attention to inclusivity, pluralism, and even-handedness (Bickford and Sodaro 2010), none of this is evident in the House of Terror. Rather, it is one-sided and brash in its representation of the past, and its creators too easily disregard legitimate criticism and the potential for democratic debate that nuanced discussions of the past and its representation could provoke. For a museum intended to portray the glories of democracy over dictatorship, it ironically takes a dictatorial approach in its execution. The curators have chosen to dictate a moral to Hungarian society, rather than create a space for reflection and debate, undermining the important moral role in Hungarian society that the museum has set for itself. Hungary's past is filled with divisiveness, ideology, and violence; in order to truly derive a moral lesson from the past, perhaps the House of Terror should look inward at the politics that divide Hungarian society today and how these politics are using, and abusing, the memory of the past. If indeed the museum wants to promote democracy and democratic principles, a good place to start would be using Hungary's complicated past to challenge the present undemocratic principles and practices of the Fidesz regime that divide Hungarian society and threaten its fragile democracy.

Notes

1. http://www.terrorhaza.hu/en/museum/about_us.html (accessed June 20, 2012).
2. Orban again became Prime Minister in April 2010 as his Fidesz party regained control of the Hungarian Parliament; while today he denounces Hungary's radical right wing in the form of Jobbick, nevertheless Orban remains an extremely controversial figure to many Hungarians and, increasingly, to the international community.
3. Fidesz, Viktor Orban's political party, was founded in 1988 as *Fiatal Demokraták Szövetsége,* the Alliance of Young Democrats by anti-communist youth in the opposition movement. Since the end of communism in Hungary, however, the party has become more and more conservative and today is the main conservative political party.
4. According to Istvan Rev, this commemorative date was "initiated by the right-wing government to compensate for and balance 'Holocaust Memorial Day,' which had been introduced by the previous government" (2008: 80).
5. These are the words used by the U.S. Holocaust Memorial Museum, one of the most sophisticated and prominent memorial museums in the world; quoting director Sarah Bloomfield, that museum serves as "a moral compass to keep us [America] on course" (qtd. in Linenthal 2001: 65).
6. Ferenc Gyurcsany, Prime Minister from 2004–2009 and leader of the Socialist Party, admitted to withholding information about the actual budget deficit in Hungary during his 2006 election campaign. In 2006 Gyurcsany gave a speech to his party that was filled with obscenities and revealed the lies he and his party told in order to be reelected; the speech—which was supposed to be closed—was leaked to the

press and sparked protests throughout the country and the resignation of Gyurcsany. Excerpts from the speech in English are available at: http://news.bbc.co.uk/2/hi/europe/5359546.stm (accessed April 1, 2011).

7. When Hungary's borders were redrawn under Trianon, many ethnic Hungarians remained outside, and it is estimated today that over 2 million ethnic Hungarians live in the states neighboring Hungary: Austria, Slovakia, Ukraine, Romania, Serbia and Montenegro, and Croatia. This is a relatively large number compared to the roughly 10 million living in Hungary today, and under the 2011 dual citizenship law, there are now no residency requirements to gain Hungarian citizenship; one must just prove Hungarian ancestry and speak Hungarian. Those suspicious of Orban and Fidesz's motives suspect that granting dual citizenship to any or all of these ethnic Hungarians is not only bolstering the demand for Hungary for Hungarians, but could also potentially be used to challenge the borders of young, more fragile states like Slovakia and Ukraine.

8. See Andras Bozoki, "The Hungarian Shock: Transitioning from Democracy?" http://www.deliberatelyconsidered.com/page/2/?s=hungary&submit_x=0&submit_y=0&submit=Search (accessed April 1, 2011).

9. Much of the background and details about the House of Terror come from interviews conducted by the author with Maria Schmidt, director of the museum, and Aron Mathe, researcher at the museum, in July 2010.

10. Schmidt anecdotally tells the story of the opening of the museum when a group of "survivors" of communism visited with a group of youth, aged 6 to 16. The "survivors" were quite unhappy with the museum, instead expecting something more "traditional"; however, after visiting the exhibit with the youth, their minds were completely changed. They loved the museum because they believed it to effectively convey their experiences under communism to this younger generation.

11. The word "terror" is the same in English and Hungarian.

12. It was also a fierce point of controversy because Andrassy Boulevard is a World Heritage site, and such an alteration was passionately contested. However, Schmidt happily asserts that the controversy over the façade gave the museum more publicity than it could have hoped for and ultimately backfired for the museum's detractors (Interview by author with Schmidt, 2010).

13. The museum's soundtrack was composed Ákos Kovács, http://www.terrorhaza.hu/en/museum/about_us.html (accessed June 20, 2012).

14. In the parliamentary election of 1947, the Communist Party used widespread election fraud to boost their representation, before ultimately eschewing any attempt at democracy in 1948–1949 when, under orders from Moscow, the communist Hungarian Working People's Party ultimately seized power.

15. The phones throughout the museum also play testimony from victims and survivors, but none of the audio is translated into English.

16. The concept of the memorial comes from a story told to Kovacs, the exhibition designer, by his grandfather, who fled Hungary under communism by affixing torches to bamboo poles that waved in the wind and distracted the border guards, allowing him to cross the border undetected (Interview by the author with Aron Mathe, 2010).

17. The perpetrators are defined as those "who took an active part in establishing and maintaining the two Hungarian totalitarian terror regimes … as well as those who held responsible positions in the executive orders of these two regimes" (Exhibition Guide).

18. This wall of perpetrators is highly controversial, especially as many are still alive and have indeed gone free. Maria Schmidt, director of the museum, told me the story of a man who came to her and begged her to take down his photo because his second wife,

whom he had recently married, did not know that he had been a member of the political police and would divorce him if she found out; his children had already found his photo in the museum and were not speaking to him.

19. http://www.House of Terror.hu/index3.html (accessed June 21, 2012).
20. Aron Mathe showed me the artifact storage room, which was hardly larger than a closet with only a few dusty volumes and several mid century artifacts on its shelves.

References

Bickford, Louis, and Amy Sodaro. 2010. "Remembering Yesterday to Protect Tomorrow: The Internationalization of a New Commemorative Paradigm." In *Memory and the Future: Transnational Politics, Ethics, and Society,* edited by Yifat Gutman, Adam Brown, and Amy Sodaro, 66–86. New York: Palgrave Macmillan.

Bilefsky, Dan. 2010. "Hungary: New Leader Assails Far-Right Party's Rise." *The New York Times,* April 12. http://www.nytimes.com/2010/04/13/world/europe/13briefs-Hungary.html?_r=1&scp=11&sq=hungary percent20roma&st=cse (accessed September 1, 2010).

Bohle, Dorothee, and Bela Greskovits. 2009. "East-Central Europe's Quandary." *Journal of Democracy* 20.4: 50–63.

Jordan, Michael. 2010. "The Roots of Hate." World Policy Institute Blog, October 1. http://www.worldpolicy.org/blog/2010/10/01/roots-hate (accessed November 5, 2013).

Judt, Tony. 1992. "The Past is Another Country: Myth and Memory in Postwar Europe." *Daedalus* 121.4: 83–118.

———. 2005. *Postwar: A History of Europe Since 1945.* New York: Penguin.

Kis, Janos. 1991. "Postcommunist Politics in Hungary." *Journal of Democracy* 1.3: 3–15.

Kiss, Csilla. 2006. "The Misuses of Manipulation: The Failure of Transitional Justice in Post-Communist Hungary." *Europe-Asia Studies* 58.6: 926–40.

Kundera, Milan. 1980 [1978]. *The Book of Laughter and Forgetting.* New York: Alfred A. Knopf.

Linenthal, Edward T. 1995. *Preserving Memory: The Struggle to Create America's Holocaust Museum.* New York: Viking.

Nora, Pierre. 2002. "Reasons for the Current Upsurge in Memory." *Transit* 22. Available at http://www.eurozine.com/articles/article_2002-04-19-nora-en.html (accessed July 31, 2013).

Orwell, George. 1949. *1984.* New York: Harcourt Brace and Company.

Poole, Ross. 2010. "Misremembering the Holocaust: Universalist Symbol, Nationalist Icon or Moral Kitsch?" In *Memory and the Future: Transnational Politics, Ethics, and Society,* edited by Yifat Gutman, Adam Brown, and Amy Sodaro, 31–49, New York: Palgrave Macmillan.

Rev, Istvan. 2008. "The Terror of the House." In *(Re)visualizing National History: Museums and National Identities in Europe in the New Millennium,* edited by Robin Ostow, 47–89. Buffalo: University of Toronto Press.

Rosenberg, Tina. 1995. *The Haunted Land: Facing Europe's Ghosts after Communism.* New York: Random House.

Saunders, Doug. 2011. "Hungary's Strongman Spooks Europe." *The Globe and Mail,* Toronto, January 29, F5.

Tismaneanu, Vladimir. 1998. *Fantasies of Salvation: Democracy, Nationalism, and Myth in Post-Communist Europe.* Princeton, NJ: Princeton University Press.

Chapter 2

Making Visible
Reflexive Narratives at the Manzanar U.S. National Historic Site

Rachel Daniell

> Our nation's ability to honor democratic values even in times of stress
> depends largely upon our collective memory of lapses from our
> constitutional commitment to liberty and due process.
> —*Personal Justice Denied: Report of the Commission on*
> *Wartime Relocation and Internment of Civilians*

Perhaps the last book one would expect to find at the bookstore of a U.S. National Historic Site is one that chronicles gross historical inaccuracies and pro-government propaganda at official sites of memory. But just such a book—*Lies Across America: What Our National Historic Sites Get Wrong* by James Loewen—is not only available in the bookstore at the Manzanar National Historic Site in Owens Valley, California, it is positioned prominently, face out on the central display shelf, featured alongside Ansel Adams's National Park photographs.[1] On a recent visit, as I passed through Manzanar's bookstore and into the interpretive center describing the site's former role as a camp for Japanese American incarceration, I found other evidence demonstrating this same kind of implied critical distance; it became clear that this openness to critique and engagement was not the whim of an individual bookstore employee, but a conscious effort on the part of the designers of the Manzanar site toward a form of site-based reflexivity. This reflexivity did not develop by chance. It grew out of specific historical conditions: the grassroots activist involvement in its designation as a U.S. National Historic Site and the political struggles involved in the official recognition of this history. It is these conditions that make Manzanar a unique case study in the tensions between the present and the past, between the power of the state and the power of community activism.

If reflexivity means that something "bends back" on itself, acknowledges its conditions of production and authorship, and attends to its position in the larger social world, how then might reflexivity at historic sites potentially contribute to public discourse on past state violence? The question of what kinds of knowledge official sites of memory can produce has been a subject of heated debate among both scholars and activists. For example, the human rights group the Asociación Madres de Plaza de Mayo in Argentina has pointed to the destructive potential of official sites of memory to reconfigure events in time by putting them into a circumscribed past, "closing" them, and effectively allowing governments to more easily evade responsibility or acknowledgment of how these pasts live on in the present (Crossland 2000; Robben 2000; Brodsky 2005). Since the creation of state-sponsored historic sites is embedded in the interests of the present state at the time of official designation (Young 1992, 1993), we must always ask ourselves what interests of the present are being served by this particular rendering of the past. We must also recognize that the creation of these "official" historic sites is often the result of ongoing negotiations between diverse state interests at different levels of government (Verdery 2002) along with various social actors, including those relatively external to state decision-making, such as activists and local community groups. Traditionally, the factors leading to the creation of U.S. official memory sites have rarely been included in a site's presentation to visitors. By making these factors, negotiations, and tensions visible, historic sites have the potential to contribute to what Andreas Huyssen has called "productive remembering" and "usable pasts" (Huyssen, 2003: 27, 29): ways the memory of the past can activate a productive politics in the present. The Manzanar site offers interesting examples of site reflexivity through which to examine reflexivity's potential as part of a productive form of remembering.

Manzanar occupies a curious position—one it shares with many other sites of memory—in that it commemorates the repressive actions of the same government that is its primary funder and architect. The U.S. government manages this piece of land through the National Park Service, a bureau of the Department of the Interior. It is the same democratic government (although of course not the same administration) that in 1942 mandated the rapid incarceration of all Japanese Americans in the westernmost states, ripping people away from their homes and businesses and confining them in tarpaper shacks under armed guard. During World War II, Japanese Americans were treated as enemies of the state solely based on racialized categories. They were shipped off to live in federally run camps, such as Manzanar, Tule Lake, or Heart Mountain, regardless of the absence or presence of any specific evidence of their support for Japan or the Axis powers and regardless of their citizenship status.

Just forty years later, the U.S. government held a Congressional Commission investigation into this mass incarceration, which declared the actions of the government a violation of Japanese-American citizens' rights. In the aftermath, the Civil Liberties Act of 1988 was passed, resulting in an official U.S. government apology and associated financial reparations. Now the Manzanar site itself and the site's narrative recounting of these repressive state actions have become part of the official discourse of history of the U.S. national park system, part of the heritage visitors are invited to experience by the National Park Service with their trademarked marketing tagline, "Experience Your America.™"[2] Tensions between the present and the past are inherent at any site of the memory of violence, but nowhere does this tension make its presence felt more acutely than at a place where the perpetrator and commemorator stem from the same system of government.

Getting the state to recognize its own past acts of violence is only possible through pressure, as "only rarely does a nation call on itself to remember the victims of crimes it has perpetrated" (Young 1992: 270, 270fn). At Manzanar, this pressure came in the form of community activism. Manzanar is very much an example of a negotiated site, where different interests came together, fought, clashed, and compromised, resulting in an official recognition of a particular history of state violence. It is through this negotiated aspect of Manzanar's history that heightened forms of reflexivity have been made visible in its historical narrative: a reflexivity that emerges from the way some of these struggles have shaped the tale the site tells and, moreover, in the way it incorporates the present in its display of the past.

Manzanar's History

America's Camps

Manzanar is located in a wind-swept patch of desert at the base of the Sierra Nevada Mountains in Southern California. Several miles from the nearest town, the site features a single building surrounded by a vast expanse of land enclosed in barbed wire. This lone building is the interpretive center—filled with the artifacts, models, videos, photographs, and narrative text that tell the story of the forced incarceration of thousands of Japanese and Japanese American persons during World War II.

Figure 2.1. Exterior view of the Manzanar Interpretive Center—housed in the sole remaining original building on the site. (Photo by Rachel Daniell and Maury Botton.)

After the bombing of Pearl Harbor in December 1941, Franklin Delano Roosevelt issued Executive Order 9066 on the advice of General John L. DeWitt.[3] This order mandated that all persons of Japanese ancestry living in the three western continental states (Washington, Oregon, and California) immediately dispose of all their property holdings and possessions beyond what could be carried on their person and report to the War Relocation Authority (WRA). This effectively dispossessed the western Japanese-American community of all of its businesses, homes, and farmland, forcing people to sell at drastically low prices or to abandon their property altogether. With only the few possessions they could carry, they then gathered at WRA "assembly centers" as the first step in their incarceration, before being shipped off to long-term camps such as Manzanar.

Manzanar was part of a network of ten camp locations set up by the federal government during World War II under the euphemistic designation of "War Relocation Centers." In fact, these were locations of mass incarceration—a form of concentration camp, created to forcibly confine and control a population—where the government forced over 120,000 people into confinement based on their ethnicity.[4] The majority of these persons unjustly confined were Japanese-American citizens, with approximately two-thirds holding U.S. citizenship and approximately one-third being non-citizen immigrants.[5] German Americans and

Italian Americans, by contrast, were not rounded up en masse, but were generally confined only when more specific bases for incarceration were determined; the majority of the several thousand detainees of German and Italian heritage were also non-citizens.[6] The treatment of persons of German ancestry and Italian ancestry during the war was unjust as well, but the treatment of persons of Japanese ancestry was more widespread and based on the principle of confining an entire community.

What awaited detainees at Manzanar was a stretch of desert land outfitted with tarpaper and wood post shacks. There were minimal work opportunities and little privacy in the barracks, toilets, and showers. Living conditions have been described by witness testimony as spartan and disruptive of family life:

> People were housed in tar-papered barrack rooms of no more than 20 by 24 feet. Each room housed a family, regardless of family size. Construction was often shoddy. Privacy was practically impossible and furnishings were minimal. Eating and bathing were in mass facilities. Under continuing pressure from those who blindly held to the belief that evacuees harbored disloyal intentions, the wages paid for work at the camps were kept to the minimal level of $12 a month for unskilled labor, rising to $19 a month for professional employees. Mass living prevented normal family communication and activities.[7]

Beyond the difficulties of living conditions, privacy, and compensation, detainees were kept under constant watch and their activities were restricted.[8] A watchtower loomed over each corner of the Manzanar site, with mounted searchlights and armed guards. Several of the ten camps

Figure 2.2. Reconstruction of guard tower. (Photo by Rachel Daniell and Maury Botton.)

experienced incidents resulting in shooting injuries and deaths, including two deaths at Manzanar in early December 1942, when military police who had been called in to assist with a detainee protest opened fire after the crowd refused to disperse and the detonation of tear-gas and vomit-gas grenades caused members of the crowd to run toward the soldiers in a panic. Despite facing these harsh conditions, Manzanar detainees managed to grow food, run an internal newspaper, create goods for the war effort, and even build small gardens in the desert, up until their eventual release from confinement.

After the war ended, the detention camps were closed. Almost all of the Manzanar structures were given away for scrap materials and the land reverted back to the Los Angeles Department of Water and Power. By the late 1950s, Manzanar was mostly open land again, except for the auditorium building, which had been built by the internees themselves to hold high school graduations, dances, funerals, and assemblies. That building began to be used for maintenance vehicle storage and repair by the Inyo County Roads Department. At this point, the site was in a state of near-abandonment and there was little to indicate its history—only the remaining auditorium building and a monument left standing in the camp's small graveyard, bearing the inscription *I Rei To* ("Soul Consoling Tower").

Manzanar's Recognition as a Site of Memory

Judith Herman, in her writings on trauma and recovery, has argued that the realities of past traumatic experience only come to light publicly under contemporary political conditions that make such exposure possible

Figure 2.3a–b. The monument at the graveyard site at Manzanar: middle distance and close up views. (Photo by Rachel Daniell and Maury Botton.)

(Herman 1992). In a similar vein, there is evidence that it was the political context of the late 1960s that helped facilitate a grassroots effort by survivors and activists to recognize Manzanar and the detention experience. Without the efforts of these activists, it is unlikely that Manzanar would ever have been declared a historic site and even more unlikely that the Manzanar interpretive center would give the kind of narrative of history that it does today.

Sue Kunitomi Embrey was a former detainee who led the way, along with a group of Los Angeles-based professors and students. Inspired by Cesar Chavez and the United Farm Workers' march from Delano to Sacramento, they organized the first community Manzanar pilgrimage in late December 1969 to the detention camp site.[9] That action was the spark that generated an annual large-scale pilgrimage ritual that led to the formation of an ongoing, active community organizing project.

A subgroup of the pilgrimage activists called the Manzanar Committee was established by the early 1970s. They looked for further recognition of the rights violations that had occurred and further redress from the government. Starting at the state government level, they requested state historic status for Manzanar from the California State Department of Parks and Recreation; their actions and the support of a few key government actors led to Manzanar's designation as a California Registered Historic Landmark in early 1972. By going from smaller-scale direct action to sustaining a movement-building process that took action in the formal political realm, Embrey and other activists were able to stake a claim on the historical significance of the site that state officials found hard to deny.

Later in the 1970s, another fight for official government recognition began, this time in the halls of Congress. Senator Daniel Inouye and Senator Spark Matsunaga and Congressman Norman Mineta and Congressman Robert Matsui all pushed for recognition of the mass incarceration through formal political channels. In fact, this development at the legislative level had also stemmed from community activist initiatives. It was representatives from the Japanese-American Citizens League (JACL) who requested a meeting with these congressmen in 1979 to advocate for better redress for Japanese-American people for their treatment during the war.[10] As a result of these efforts, in 1980, Congress passed bills proposing an investigatory commission, the Commission on Wartime Relocation and Internment of Civilians (CWRIC) Act, which President Jimmy Carter signed into law. The Commission conducted an investigation, gathering testimony from over 750 witnesses, and released its report, *Personal Justice Denied,* in 1982. The report contains a damning account of the words and actions of General DeWitt, as well as recommendations for acknowledgment of the violence done to Japanese-American lives and forms of financial reparation. President Ronald Reagan signed the Civil Liberties Act of 1988 based on the report's proposal: acknowledging that a grievous mistake had been made by the government and offering reparations and an official statement of apology.[11] President George H.W. Bush then issued apology letters during his term the following year. As funds began to be allocated for the recognition of these events and the need for an official historic site began to emerge, the federal government once again turned its attention to Manzanar.

The process of transforming Manzanar from a state historic landmark into a federal-level historic site with a more inclusive and detailed official historical narrative brought tensions between different interests to the foreground. The National Park Service started to create a management plan for the site and held four public hearings for community members to weigh in on the plan. Attending the hearings were survivors, local businesspeople, farmers, and representatives from local Native American communities. The interests voiced in the hearings resulted in a different plan for the historical narrative than had been anticipated either by the federal representatives or the Manzanar Committee organization. Many local residents wanted the earlier history of the area be represented, predating the World War II era. Farmers wanted representation of the agricultural industry in Owens Valley. The Paiute-Shoshone (*Numa* and *Newe*) tribal nations, who had been dispossessed of massive resources by government actions in the early twentieth century, wanted recognition of their own losses of life, land, and water access at the hands of the U.S. government—Owens Valley Tribal Elders cautioned Inyo County Supervisor Wilma Muth to acknowledge the "painful memory of our people when a great number of our ancestors were slaughtered along the way through and near Manzanar at the hands of the U.S. government while being driven south on foot to an unknown destination."[12] They and others in the region also particularly wanted documentation of the area's widespread water rights issues (the Los Angeles Department of Water and Power still owns much of the land and water rights in the region, despite being a four-hour-drive away, and the long-standing usurpation of that resource via local and federal government agreements have shaped the history of the Owens Valley region).[13]

There was also a small but vocal minority against any use of the land for a memorial site, particularly among veterans of World War II. Local resident Bill Hitchens published a number of newspaper editorials protesting the idea of creating a memorial, arguing that U.S. camps were more humane than the camps housing American prisoners of war in Japan and thus did not need to be recognized as repressive. These comparative arguments were countered by Japanese Americans further explaining their position and the need for the site. Veterans who had served in World War II as part of regiment 442—an Infantry Regiment comprised solely of Japanese-American soldiers that fought during the latter part of the war—came in uniform to talk directly to the other veterans about why they felt it was so important that the site be recognized. The contributions of regiment 442 were respected by the other veterans groups, and the coming together of these veterans, along with the community interactions that took place as a result of the public discussions, changed the overall dialog about the site. Concerns expressed in the hearings were taken into consideration in the site's planned narrative, which led to increased local support.

Manzanar was officially designated as a National Historic Site by congressional legislation in 1992. Today the site consists of a large area of land where the archeological foundations of the camp's living quarters, group latrines, factories, and kitchens can be seen, as well as re-creations of a guard tower and a dining hall shack. The site's cemetery monument serves as the focal point of the yearly pilgrimages and a place where visitors leave offerings, but the bulk of the historical narrative is presented in the interpretive center that opened in 2004 in the auditorium building. It is here, in the interpretive center, that we find three pivotal examples of reflexivity in the site's presentation of history.

Figure 2.4. Foundation remains of Manzanar women's latrine and two reconstructed mess hall shacks. (Photo by Rachel Daniell and Maury Botton.)

Making Visible—Forms of Reflexivity

Origin Stories

The first example of reflexivity at the site is the way in which the Manzanar narrative includes its own origin story as a central part of its overall historical timeline, framing the site's larger history for the visitor with its own trajectory of becoming an official site of memory. Spanning multiple narrative panels, the interpretive center depicts the history of the pilgrimages, Sue Embrey, the Manzanar Committee, and multiple other advocates for the recognition of detention camp history, as well as past arguments against its recognition. Furthermore, the National Park Service is careful not to take credit for originating the Manzanar National Historic Site project. Unlike some off-site depictions that leave out the role of community activism in spearheading the campaign for Manzanar to be recognized (or for Congress to designate an investigatory commission),[14] origin stories in the interpretive center at Manzanar make it clear that the site was started by grassroots activism, describing Manzanar's official designation by Congress in 1992 on a timeline panel as the result of "years of grassroots campaigning by former internees and others."[15]

This narrative of history highlights the fact that official sites acknowledging repressive state action can be established through the demands of social movements and notes for the visitor that the site they are experiencing would not have existed as a National Park Site without the work of community activism. These aspects of the site's narrative might cause

1955 - 1995 The auditorium is used as a garage and shop by the Inyo County Road Department.

March 3, 1992 After years of grassroots campaigning by former internees and others, Congress designates Manzanar National Historic Site, a unit of the National Park Service.

1996 The National Park Service purchases the auditorium from Inyo County.

2002 - 2004 The auditorium is adaptively restored. Exhibits and film are developed.

April 24, 2004 2,500 guests and dignitaries celebrate the rebirth of the auditorium as Manzanar National Historic Site's Interpretive Center and park headquarters.

ceremony
NPS Photo.

Figure 2.5. Interpretive Center narrative panel showing acknowledgment of the grassroots activist origins of Manzanar's historic site designation. (Photo by Rachel Daniell and Maury Botton.)

the visitor to consider which other sites of state repression remain unacknowledged and what kinds of past state violence might potentially be formally recognized as public history in the future.

Official Language and the Limits of Reflexivity

The second form of reflexivity evident at Manzanar involves language and terminology—the choices of official language to describe the camp.[16] The use of euphemism to cloak state actions is a well-documented phenomenon and is of particular concern in the history of the World War II period around U.S. racialized imprisonment. In the past, the federal government has often referred to the Japanese Americans displaced by Executive Order 9066 as "evacuees," with implications that the move was for their own protection, and referred to the camps as "relocation centers." After years of criticism by activists and historians, however, the words "evacuee" and "relocation center" have been generally acknowledged as language that served to obscure repressive state action.[17] The issue of U.S. government language was explicitly addressed in the Congressional Commission's report, *Personal Justice Denied:*

> The Commission has not attempted to change the words and phrases commonly used to describe these events at the time they happened. This leaves one open to the charge of shielding unpleasant truths behind euphemisms. For instance, "evacuee" is frequently used in the text; Webster's Third International Dictionary defines an evacuee as one "who is removed from his house or community in time of war or pressing danger as a protective measure." In light of the Commission's conclusion that removal was not militarily necessary, "excludee" might be a better term than "evacuee." ... We leave it to each reader to decide for himself how far the language of the period confirms an observation of George Orwell: "In our time, political speech and writing are largely the defense of the indefensible. ... Thus political language has to consist largely of euphemism, question-begging and sheer cloudy vagueness."[18]

Still, though the terms "evacuee" and "relocation" may now be falling out of regular usage, debate continues over what to call the camps in historical narratives: Internment camps? Incarceration camps? Concentration camps? The camps met the technical definition of concentration camps—designed to concentrate, confine, and control a population—and were organized via state-mandated groupings of persons based on racialized identities, yet, the association of the term "concentration camp" with the torture, mass murder, and genocide under the Nazi regime has led some to argue against its use for the U.S. World War II domestic camp context. Utilizing the standard definition of "internment camp," however, risks not adequately capturing the extent of the detainee-excludee experiences and risks obfuscating the U.S. state's massive violation of human rights.[19] How, then, do the authors of the historical narrative at the Manzanar site handle the questions of language and representation of the government's actions?

There are two instances where the interpretive center brings up language controversies explicitly. One is near the beginning of the exhibit, on a panel of historical narrative: "ever since the U.S. army enclosed this one square mile with barbed wire in 1942, people have debated how to accurately describe Manzanar." The panel goes on to describe the various wording that was used during World War II—from "War Relocation Center" to "concentration camp" to "Jap camp." Here the site text's recognition of these conflicting representations during the war begins to seed the issue of disputed historical accounts for the visitor and points to the question of how meaning is shaped through language choices.

The second instance is where the site tells the story of the battle over terminology that would be used on the California State Historic Landmark plaque before the site became managed at the federal level. The activists of the Manzanar Committee and JACL debated with the California Parks Department over how to describe what Manzanar was and the origins of the events that happened there. The Parks Department objected to the strong language demanded by activists. The battle between the California Parks Department and the Manzanar Committee activists, along with various government and non-government supporters, is described in detail in the National Park Service Historic Resource Study publication on Manzanar:

> On three occasions, representatives of the Manzanar Committee and the Japanese American Citizens League traveled to Sacramento in an attempt to get their wording accepted by state officials. After the state found other words, such as "hysteria" and "greed," objectionable, the Manzanar Committee enlisted "community support" in "the form of letters and petitions." State Assemblymen Alex Garcia ... , Ralph Dillis ... , State Senator Mervyn Dymally ... , and Assembly Speaker Robert Moretti entered the fray on the side of the Japanese American groups. After a stormy 90-minute confrontation with William Penn Mott, the Director of the state Department of Parks and Recreation ... a compromise was worked out.... [T]he state would write the first paragraph on the plaque. The second paragraph [was] to be written by the Manzanar Committee and the Japanese American Citizens League.... The third paragraph incorporated compromise language.[20]

These heated negotiations ultimately led to the California state landmark sign reading:

> In the early part of World War II, 110,000 persons of Japanese ancestry were interned in relocation centers by Executive Order No. 9066, issued on February 19, 1942.

> Manzanar, the first of ten such concentration camps, was bounded by barbed wire and guard towers, confining 10,000 persons, the majority being American citizens.

May the injustices and humiliation suffered here as a result of hysteria, racism and economic exploitation never emerge again.

The interpretive center includes this language struggle on a panel where the California plaque is reproduced and the portions of text central to the debate are highlighted. The old California plaque is even still on-site along the exit road, keeping the traces of these stages of struggle visible. Through its direct citation of language controversies, Manzanar brings in a reflexive outlook, which highlights the conflicting interests involved in determining the official language and then implicates how that language shapes our perception of history.

However, what Manzanar does not include is its own struggle with the terminology that would ultimately be used on its site interpretive panels. This is another story about language use that could have been told: Manzanar's entire historical narrative was re-written during the interpretive center design because of language debates such as those that arose for the state-level signage. The contractor designing the site hired a writer to compose panel narratives, but the drafts made the NPS uncomfortable; in it the camps were called "concentration camps," WRA staff called "prison guards," and internees called "prisoners." The NPS discarded

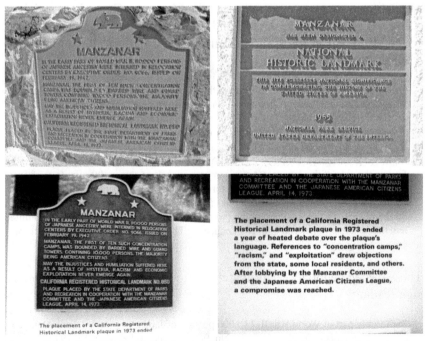

The placement of a California Registered Historical Landmark plaque in 1973 ended a year of heated debate over the plaque's language. References to "concentration camps," "racism," and "exploitation" drew objections from the state, some local residents, and others. After lobbying by the Manzanar Committee and the Japanese American Citizens League, a compromise was reached.

Figure 2.6a–d. California Historic Landmark signage versus National Historic Landmark signage and representation of signage language controversy at the Interpretive Center. (Photo by Rachel Daniell and Maury Botton.)

those versions of history and hired a new writer to redo the entire narrative using the terms "internment camp" and "internee." Although the on-site Parks Department staff will readily discuss the process with visitors, the making of this language choice itself is not directly referenced in the site's narrative.

There is some degree of reflexivity here because the site's need to make a terminology choice is implied by its own inclusion of other terminology choice stories—but it only goes so far. The site is reflexive enough to draw attention to the war-period euphemisms, and even reflexive enough to reproduce the site's own earlier, more strongly worded State Historic Landmark sign; but it is not reflexive enough to directly address its own language choices in the interpretive center narrative. This issue of language and representation is an arena where Manzanar reveals the limits of its reflexive practices and the tension inherent in its position as a state-funded, state-run site commemorating state violence.

Making Racialized Government Policy Visible in the Present

The third and, perhaps, most striking reflexive feature of the Manzanar interpretive center is not on a panel that addresses history, but on a panel that addresses the political present in which the center was created. This is where the site bears witness not only to the particular abuses of state power that resulted in the World War II camps, but also to the problems of state power itself and racist oppression as a structural recurrence. There is a picture featured on a panel toward the end of the exhibit that shows a group of protesters holding signs. The caption reads: "Demonstrators protest the mandatory registration of Middle Eastern men, San Francisco, California, January 10, 2003."

What is so startling about seeing this image in the context of a federally funded, federally run site is that the visitor is being invited to draw a comparison between the forced registration and incarceration of Japanese Americans in World War II and the forced registration and numerous detentions of many Middle Eastern and Muslim persons under the post-9/11 Bush administration policies, including the National Security Entry-Exit Registration System, or NSEERS. The NSEERS registration order was enacted in September 2002 and the Manzanar interpretive center officially opened in April 2004. Thus, at the time the panel narrative was created, the registration order (and the Bush administration's many other repressive post-9/11 policies) were not safely in the historical past, ascribed to a different political leadership. On the contrary, they were very much in the present. How did a federally run site come to include such a potentially controversial implied critique of federal actions—

Figure 2.7. Image of protestors within exhibit panel context at the interpretive center, referencing the forced registration and numerous detentions of Muslim-Americans under the post-9/11 Bush Administration. (Photo of exhibition display by Rachel Daniell and Maury Botton; photo within display by AP Images/Marcio Jose Sanchez.)

actions contemporary to its implementation? The answer lies in the efforts of ex-detainee activists involved in the Manzanar site.

The Manzanar Committee pilgrimage participants openly called for solidarity with Muslim and Arab communities immediately after unjust treatment of those communities began to be apparent subsequent to the September 11th attacks.[21] As early as the spring of 2002, a statement of support for these communities was part of the central program of the Manzanar Committee's pilgrimage activities, which were described that year as "the 60th Anniversary of Executive Order 9066, honoring Heart Mountain and Rohwer Internees and solidarity with Muslims and American Arabs."[22] Manzanar Committee member Jenni Emiko Kuida stated on the 2002 pilgrimage website: "we can see that targeting, scapegoating, and hate crimes against Muslims, Arabs, and South Asians after September 11th, and the indiscriminate rounding up of people, is the same thing that happened to the Issei."[23] There is an ongoing dialog between activists in these communities regarding racialized state repression. Since 2002, there has been an increased presence of Muslim Americans making the pilgrimage to Manzanar, where these communities come together to share information and advocate for awareness of what happened in

World War II in the context of the treatment of Muslim Americans in the 2000s.[24] It is the representatives of the Manzanar Committee organization who also serve as advisors on the historic site's Advisory Committee who have insisted on making the connections between the two forms of state repression visible at Manzanar.

On this same narrative panel, the text asks the visitor to question whether the forced incarceration and dispossession of Japanese Americans has any similarities to other actions by the U.S. government. Along with the protest photo, there is also a photograph of a whites-only water fountain from the 1950s. Both the protest photograph and this civil rights-era photograph remind the visitor that racialized state repression backed with the force of law has taken place in the United States in contexts other than the specific World War II history of Manzanar. These photographs encourage the visitor to draw connections between past and present, between different expressions of the function of state power. The site's narrative does not attempt to make these particular histories of repression equivalent; but, rather, it juxtaposes them for the visitor to see potential resonances. Here the museum narrative is inviting a kind of productive extension of the politics of memory into other events—something that might fit into Huyssen's previously mentioned concepts of "productive remembering" and "usable pasts" (Huyssen 2003).

Visibilities and Invisibilities

There are a number of important critiques that need to be made of the Manzanar National Historic Site, particularly with regard to its use of language and the invisibility of other histories relating to state power and this piece of land. A state-funded, state-run site of conscience will always be constrained in the kind of history it can tell about past actions of the state. As noted by James E. Young, Michel-Rolph Trouillot, and other scholars whose research has examined the production of history, memory sites are always as much about the politics and power dynamics of the present as they are about the past (Young 1993; Trouillot 1995); Manzanar is no exception to this. Examining the provenance, administration, and funding procedures of such sites reveals even more textured detail about how the contours of historical representation are shaped. We need to ask of this site: Why is its own language debate not made more transparent? What other issues have been left out of the narrative? Significantly, for the Owens Valley area that Manzanar is a part of, why are certain questions involving state power around the experiences of local Native American communities voiced predominantly as stories of the "past" and not extended into the politics of the present as actively as other issues in the exhibit? Why, in particular, is the question of Paiute tribal communities' and other local communities' control over water resources—though diligently covered in its earlier historical period in the "Layers of History" portion of the exhibit—not brought more up to date with ongoing struggles over resources and recognition? In these instances, critiques have been raised about the ways in which sites dedicated to the memory of state violence, especially those run by the state, can allow governments to evade responsibility by pushing events into a "closed past" or letting one set of historical events overshadow others that are still relevant to the Manzanar site.

At the same time, Manzanar does make an important attempt to grapple with its own constraints as a state-funded site and points to perspectives that might undermine its own position of authority. It achieves this through its reflexive elements: in its presentation of its own history and its allusions to linkages with present-day state actions, both of which highlight the very fact that historical narratives are written in a particular context of competing authorships and specific social conditions.[25] The tensions inherent in these conditions, when made visible, have the potential to generate a more productive relationship to the past.

Ultimately, what I want to raise through this chapter is the possibility that reflexive narratives of history, particularly in the context of state-sponsored sites, have the capacity to: (1) make visible the ground-level political, personal, and administrative contestations through which histories of repression gain official acknowledgment; (2) evoke, through tensions in narrative representation, similar tensions inherent in being a state-sponsored site dedicated to recognizing criminal actions of the state; and (3) begin to highlight questions of how repression operates that might allow the site not only to articulate the machinations of power in the particular story of important events in the past, but also to contribute to critical outlooks on power both in the present and for the future. Approaches such as this can give the visitor useful tools for critiquing state action and historiography itself. Narratives at sites of memory that reveal their own questions of language, authorship, and changing historical representations over time, that make contradictions visible instead of resolving them, have the potential to open up rather than close off the past.

Note on Terminology in This Chapter

In writing this chapter, I generally chose not to use the term "concentration camp" because of its association with death camps of the Nazi government; though technically accurate, in a transnational memory studies publication it seemed potentially confusing to the reader to use the identical term. "Internment camp" is the descriptor of choice at the Manzanar interpretive center, but I have decided to minimize use of that term because of what "internment" makes less visible—the prison conditions of the site and the inaccuracy of applying "internment" to the imprisonment of citizens—as well as in order to show solidarity with descriptions of the history that underscore that these incarcerations were violations of human rights. I generally use the words "detention camp" or "incarceration camp" to designate the place and "interned" or "incarcerated" to designate the action. My terminology conforms with the "Resolution on Terminology" adopted by the Civil Liberties Public Education Fund: http://www.momomedia.com/CLPEF/backgrnd.html (accessed July 1, 2012) and the nonprofit organization Densho's analysis of terminology and language choice recommendations, http://www.densho.org/default.asp?path=/assets/sharedpages/glossary.asp?section =home (accessed July 1, 2012). It should be kept in mind when reflecting on U.S. government actions during World War II, however, that these camps fit the definition of concentration camps.

Notes

I would like to thank the NSSR Interdisciplinary Memory Studies Group for their generous comments on drafts of this chapter, as well as David Janes for his careful and detailed review, NPS staff members Richard Potashin and Alisa Lynch for their thoughtful responses to my questions, Ida Susser for her encouragement and support, and Elizabeth White and Maury Botton for their insights, probings, and pushes to take my writing further.

1. My observations at the site are from a visit in 2009. Consistently since that time, the book has continued to be featured prominently in the Manzanar online bookstore, operated by the Manzanar History Association, a partner organization of the national historic site: http://www.manzanarstore.com (accessed June 28, 2012.)
2. "Experience Your America" is a trademark of the National Park Service.
3. DeWitt's entire argument for the recommendation was later heavily criticized by the Congressional Committee for both its baseless and its racist nature.
4. Looking reflexively at our own role as scholars, we might also note that several anthropologists worked on behalf of the U.S. government in these detention camps. While some government anthropologists spoke out against the camps, others supported the detentions and some even gave names of detainees to the FBI, effectively singling out those detainees for further incarceration and suspicion. There is currently a call out to the American Anthropological Association to consider issuing a formal apology for the role anthropologists played in supporting detention. For more on this topic, see David Price's 2008 book *Anthropological Intelligence: the Deployment and Neglect of American Anthropology in the Second World War.*
5. Due to the restrictive (and racist) immigration laws of that time (the Exclusion Act of 1917), the first-generation immigrants (Issei) would not have been able to become citizens.
6. See *Personal Justice Denied.* The treatment of German Americans and Italian Americans was also unjust, though it took a different form and citizenship was more of a deciding factor in whether persons were sent to incarceration camps. There have been subsequent government inquiries into the particular violations against German Americans, Italian Americans, Jewish refugees, and others during the war, including

the Wartime Violation of Italian American Civil Liberties Act and the Wartime Treatment Study Act. The state of California has issued an official apology to the Italian American community for treatment during World War II, but not yet to the German American community.

7. As described in the summary section of *Personal Justice Denied.*

8. For example, they could not take photographs or own radios or vehicles. In addition, the camp newspaper that they formed could not print anything critiquing the camp conditions.

9. See the NPS *Historic Resource Study Report.* It should also be noted that there were other, smaller pilgrimages before 1969. Two survivors, Rev. Sentoku Maeda and Rev. Soichi Wakahiro, had begun visiting the site on a yearly basis even earlier, from the mid 1940s, but their actions did not directly lead to this community action on a larger scale.

10. Edison Uno was a particularly active leader within JACL who pushed the organization to move for recognition and redress.

11. In addition, in 2011, the Acting Solicitor General of the United States, Neal Katyal, issued an official, legal Confession of Error in regards to the two Supreme Court cases *Hirabayashi v. United States* and *Korematsu v. United States*—past cases through which the constitutionality of the internment policy was questioned but ultimately upheld by the Supreme Court. Katyal's Confession of Error amounts to an official declaration that the government should not have won these two court cases.

12. As quoted in the NPS 1996 Historic Resource Study publication on Manzanar.

13. An area of the exhibit called "Layers of History" came out of these hearings, taking on many of these considerations.

14. In the National Park Service's report *Confinement and Ethnicity,* for example, the Manzanar Committee is not mentioned in the description of the evolution of the Manzanar site, nor is JACL's role in advocating for a Congressional Commission indicated in any way.

15. This text is on a panel describing a timeline of history of the site that includes its designation by Congress as a National Historic Site.

16. See "Note on terminology in this chapter" at the end of the chapter text, as well as the Civil Liberties Public Education Fund's website, http://www.momomedia.com/CLPEF/backgrnd.html (accessed July 1, 2012), and Densho's analysis of terminology and language choice recommendations, http://www.densho.org/default.asp?path=/assets/sharedpages/glossary.asp?section=home (accessed July 1, 2012).

17. See *Personal Justice Denied* and the statements on terminology referenced in footnote above by the Civil Liberties Public Education Fund, http://www.momomedia.com/CLPEF/backgrnd.html (accessed July 1, 2012), and Densho http://www.densho.org/default.asp?path=/assets/sharedpages/glossary.asp?section=home (accessed July 1, 2012).

18. *Personal Justice Denied,* summary section.

19. See statement on terminology at the end of this chapter.

20. NPS 1996 Historic Resource Study publication on Manzanar.

21. More information on this effort is available in the video "Manzanar Muslim Pilgrimage" produced by CAIR-LA in association with NCRR and JACL.

22. See online records of the Manzanar Committee regarding the 2002 pilgrimage, http://www.manzanarcommittee.org/pilgrimages/manz2002/PR-042202.html (accessed July 15, 2012).

23. Ibid. Note that Issei are first-generation immigrants.

24. Drawing connections between past and present politics also continues: in an early 2012 article on the Manzanar Committee blog criticizing President Barack Obama's authorization of the National Defense Authorization Act (NDAA), Bruce Embrey wrote "echoes of the past—hysterical, baseless fears, fueled by racism, [sound] so similar to what our families and friends endured prior to, and during World War II, and, now, in an eerily familiar fashion, baseless fears are leading to the erosion of our civil rights." See Manzanar Committee blog article on the NDAA, January 25, 2012: http://blog.manzanarcommittee.org/2012/01/25/national-defense-authorization-act-nikkei-community-must-redouble-efforts-to-defend-constitutional-rights/ (accessed July 15, 2012).

25. Another interesting example of reflexivity and the incorporation of historic site origin stories can be seen at the African Burial Ground National Historic Monument in New York City. This site's discovery and subsequent management involved many contentious decisions and it took strong community activism to create the historic monument site as it exists today. See "Seizing Intellectual Power" by Cheryl T. La Roche and Michael L. Blakey in the journal *Historical Archaeology* 31.3 (1997) for more on the early years of the process.

References

Books and Reports (Print and Electronic Editions)

Adams, Ansel. 1944. *Born Free and Equal, Photographs of the Loyal Japanese-Americans at Manzanar Relocation Center, Inyo County, California.* New York, U.S. Camera. Library of Congress online archives. http://memory.loc.gov/ammem/collections/anseladams/aamborn.html.

Armor, John, and Peter Wright. 1988. *Manzanar.* Commentary by John Hersey. Photographs by Ansel Adams. New York: Times Books, Random House, Inc.

Brodsky, Marcelo, ed. 2005. *Memoria en construcción, el debate sobre la ESMA.* Buenos Aires: La Marca Editora.

Burton, J, M. Farrell, F. Lord, and R. Lord. [National Park Service, Western Archeological and Conservation Center, U.S. Department of the Interior.] 1999. *Confinement and Ethnicity: An Overview of World War II Japanese American Relocation Sites.* Publications in Anthropology 74.

Commission on Wartime Relocation and Internment of Civilians. 1982. *Personal Justice Denied: Report of the Commission on Wartime Relocation and Internment of Civilians.*

Crossland, Zoe. 2000. "Buried lives: forensic archaeology and Argentina's disappeared." *Archaeological Dialogues* 7.2: 146–59.

Garrett, Jessie A., and Ronald C. Larson. 1977. *Camp and Community: Manzanar and the Owens Valley, Fullerton Oral History Program.* Fullerton: California State University.

Herman, Judith. 1992. *Trauma and Recovery.* New York: Basic Books.

Hirabayashi, James. 1994. "'Concentration Camp' or 'Relocation Center'—What's in a Name?" *Japanese American National Museum Quarterly* 9.3: 5–10.

Huyssen, Andreas. 2003. *Present Pasts: Urban Palimpsests and the Politics of Memory.* Stanford, CA: Stanford University Press.

Manzanar Committee. 1998. *Reflections in Three Self-Guided Tours of Manzanar.* Los Angeles, CA: Manzanar Committee.

National Park Service, Pacific West Region, U.S. Department of the Interior. 2006. *Cultural Landscape Report: Manzanar National Historic Site.*

National Park Service, U.S. Department of the Interior. 1996. *The Evacuation And Relocation Of Persons Of Japanese Ancestry During World War II: A Historical Study Of The Manzanar War Relocation Center.* Historic Resource Study/Special History Study. Vols. 1 and 2.

Okamura, Raymond Y. 1982. "The American Concentration Camps: A Cover-Up Through Euphemistic Terminology." *Journal of Ethnic Studies* 10: 95–108.

Robben, Antonius. 2000. "State Terror in the Netherworld: Disappearance and Reburial in Argentina." In *Death Squad: The Anthropology of State Terror,* edited by J. A. Sluka, 91–113. Philadelphia: University of Pennsylvania Press.

Schiffrin, Deborah. 2001. "Language and Public Memorial: 'America's Concentration Camps.'" *Discourse & Society* 12.4: 505–34.

Trouillot, Michel-Rolph. 1995. *Silencing the Past: Power and the Production of History.* Boston: Beacon Press.

Verdery, Katherine. 2002. "Seeing Like a Mayor: Or, How Local Officials Obstructed Romanian Land Restitution." *Ethnography* 3 (March): 5–33.

Young, James E. 1992. "The Counter-Monument: Memory against Itself in Germany Today." *Critical Inquiry* 18.2: 267–96.

———. 1993. *The Texture of Memory: Holocaust Memorials and Meaning.* New Haven and London: Yale University Press.

Video Sources

Embrey, Sue Kunitomi. 2002. Video oral history interview conducted by the Manzanar National Historic Site. National Park Service. http://blog.manzanarcommittee .org/2009/12/06/2002-manzanar-national-historic-site-oral-history-sue-kunitomi-embrey-parts-10-12/.

Manzanar—Never Again. The Untold Stories Project. Produced by WETA and Florentine Films. http://video.pbs.org/video/1184937107/.

Manzanar Muslim Pilgrimage. Produced by CAIR-LA in association with NCRR and JACL. Hosted by LinkTV. http://www.linktv.org/programs/manzanar-muslim-pilgrimage.

Chapter 3

The Everyday as Spectacle
Archival Imagery and the Work of Reconciliation in Canada

Naomi Angel

> It was on June 11, 2008, in front of millions of Canadians, that words of
> sorrow and profound regret resonated in the heart of Parliament … And I
> remember quite vividly the images brought to mind by those words.
> —Michaëlle Jean, Governor General of Canada, October 2009[1]

On October 15, 2009, the Governor General of Canada, Michaëlle Jean, participated in a truth and reconciliation event in Ottawa. The event marked a new beginning for the beleaguered Indian Residential Schools Truth and Reconciliation Commission (IRS TRC). Established in 2008, the commission had already experienced the resignation of the first three commissioners. Having regrouped one year later with three new commissioners, this event marked a fresh start in addressing the Indian Residential School (IRS) system in Canada. In brief, the IRS system took Aboriginal children away from their families, often forcibly, and placed them in church and state-run schools. Having stripped parental rights from Aboriginal men and women, the schools represented the paternal logic of the colonial system. In addition to being removed from their kin and intimate support networks, the children were forbidden from speaking their own languages and practicing their religious and cultural beliefs. In operation for over a century, the system represented a powerful colonial drive toward assimilation, and it reflected and perpetuated ideas of Aboriginal peoples as "savages" and "uncivilized." Over 150,000 Aboriginal children attended the schools and many survivors have now spoken out about the physical, emotional, and sexual abuse that occurred there.[2]

In her opening address at Rideau Hall in Ottawa, Governor General Michaëlle Jean spoke of Prime Minister Stephen Harper's official apology to survivors of the Indian Residential School system and the images brought to mind by his words:

> I thought about the devastating archival photos that I saw for the first time in the Tr'ondëk Hwëch'in First Nation Cultural Centre, which welcomed me in June 2007, in Dawson City, Yukon.
>
> Those photos were heartbreaking, infinitely sad, showing Aboriginal children forced by the dozens onto the backs of trucks, eyes wide with alarm, terrified.
>
> You know what I am talking about.[3]

Her last sentence reverberated through the grand conference room at Rideau Hall: *You know what I am talking about.* Here, she addressed her audience in Ottawa, those watching via live web streaming, and people who access the now archived speech online. The implication is that Canadians know this history, and know it through its visual representation, particularly through the proliferation and circulation of archival images from the schools. Although she mentions a specific set of images, for the purposes of this paper, it is of less importance which particular photographs she references. What is important is the body of archival images that have circulated from these schools, the ways they have circulated, and the ways they are now imagined. Michaëlle Jean suggests that it is unnecessary to see the images, because they can be imagined. As Roland Barthes has written, "in order to see a photograph well, it is best to look away or close your eyes" (1981: 53). Barthes suggests the photograph not only circulates as an object, but as a memory. As one looks away from a photograph, its contours and colors may fade but the mind remembers its essence. Or as Susan Sontag explains, "Memory freeze-frames; its basic unit is the single image" (2002: 22).

Far from static entities, photographs, like memories, are ephemeral. Their meanings and readings change with time. In effect, images and imagination are intertwined. This chapter takes this entanglement as its starting point. In particular, it focuses on the ways in which photographs from the Indian Residential School era in Canada have been used as evocative tools in representing both the "everyday" experiences of students at the schools and something more "spectacular," a history of colonial oppression that is only now coming to light.

For the purposes of this chapter, I use the words "spectacular" and "spectacle" to signal "a social relation among people, mediated by images" (Debord 1995: 12). The images from the schools have circulated in ways that represent a sort of social life. They have made their way through personal scrapbooks, to church pamphlets and the state press, and have often eventually settled in church or state archives. Originally, they spoke to the efficacy of a system designed to "kill the Indian in the child."[4] Now they speak to the subtle and not so subtle violence of that system. In many ways, the photographs from the IRS system can be read as a "self-portrait of power" (Debord 1995: 19), where a colonial and/or institutional gaze is produced and maintained. But this is not the only way in which they can be read. The photographs from the IRS system reveal complex social relationships, between students and staff, between colonized and colonizer, and between the students themselves. This chapter focuses on how Aboriginal children in the schools were constructed as visual subjects through these photographs, and how they may be re-constructed through the reconciliation process.

Contrary to the images evoked by the Governor General, ones where children were sullen or scared, my research focuses on those that show the "everydayness" of the schools. The images of daily activities show children posing for the camera, framed in ways that seem familiar: standing at the chalkboard, as part of team photos or school plays. Often the children are doing chores or learning a trade. Young girls are sewing or cleaning. Boys are learning carpentry or doing yard work. In the residences, rows of beds line the dormitories. Young faces peer back at the camera, sometimes smiling, often not.

Figure 3.1. R.C. Indian Residential School Study Time [Fort] Resolution, N.W.T. (Library and Archives Canada, PA-042133.)

Figure 3.2. Students practicing penmanship, Red Deer Institute, Alberta, circa 1914. (UCC Archives Toronto, 93.049P/850N.)

The last Indian Residential School was still in operation as recently as 1996. This school, White Calf Collegiate in Lebret, Saskatchewan was torn down in 1998. A small group of former students gathered to watch the wrecking ball reduce the school to dust. Former student, Michael Starr stood in the crowd. "It's a very emotional day," he said. "Some of the history is gone … in a lot of ways the people who have been hurt by the residential schools have had some of that pain taken away by knocking it down." For many the destruction of the school was a symbolic end to some of the suffering they endured there. But Starr also added, "At the same time there were a lot of good memories in the school" (quoted in LaRose 1999). Starr's words mark the difficulty in constructing a single narrative about the schools, and they reveal the tangled nature of the traumatic and the everyday.

The Archive and Its Afterlives

In her discussion of cultural memory in Chile, Macarena Gómez-Barris discusses the use of two related terms: "aftermath" and "afterlife." She uses *aftermath* to describe the "political economic legacies" of state-sanctioned violence, and uses *afterlife* to signal "the persistent symbolic and material effects" of this violence (2009: 6). The aftermath and the afterlife of violence help to set the stage for an ongoing entanglement between the past and the present. It is my contention that the archive too has an aftermath and an afterlife, and that the political and the symbolic nature of archives make them a productive space for examining the social relations they represent. The following pages explore the afterlife of one particular image. I have chosen this image not because it stands out as extraordinary, but rather because of its ordinariness, because it both leaves me searching for speech yet calls for a cascade of words. I have chosen it because it reveals traces of both the familiar and the uncanny, and it speaks to the dialectical relationship between the everyday and the spectacular.

The above image was taken at Fort Simpson Indian Residential School in 1922 and is now housed at the National Archives in Ottawa. Although photographs and documents from the schools are scattered across the country in smaller archives (church, municipal, and school archives) and personal collections, the National Archives houses the largest collection of materials related to the Indian Residential School system. In the photograph, two girls and five boys stand in a row, spelling out "Goodbye." In top hats and dresses, the children look prepared for an event; perhaps they are putting on a play or attending a graduation ceremony at the school. Throughout the course of my research, I have come to call this picture "the long goodbye." The boy second from the left is turned away from the camera. The letter "o" hangs low in his hands as he moves towards the door of the building. This movement disrupts the "goodbye," prolonging and delaying a farewell, drawing out its conclusion. By capturing a seemingly innocuous moment, of children dressed for a

Figure 3.3. Fort Simpson Indian Residential School, 1922. (Photo by J. F. Moran. Library and Archives Canada, PA-102575.)

celebration of sorts, it reminds us of the everydayness of the oppression inflicted. School administrators, in reporting to the government on the efficacy of the schools, had kept records of attendance, grades, visits to the nurse, and a long list of other experiences that mark the schools as part of a system working under the guise of benevolence. The schools supported the idea of Canada as a tolerant and benevolent nation, a concept that has long been a central aspect of the national narrative (Thobani 2007; Mackey 2002 [1999]). Rhetoric about the schools touted them as places for learning and upliftment, and a picture of the ideal Canadian citizen was constructed around and through the schools. Church pamphlets targeted towards recruiting new staff proclaimed: "Good food and kindly care build healthy bodies. Christian teaching and character-forming activities develop worthy Canadian citizens."[5] The idea of who constituted a worthy Canadian citizen did not include Aboriginal children. They were seen as subjects to be molded.

If, as Roland Barthes writes, "Photography is subversive not when it frightens, repels or even stigmatizes, but when it is pensive, when it thinks" (1981: 38), this image allows for that thoughtful moment. It asks us to look closer, and when we look away, it stays with us. For Barthes, photographs attain meaning through the studium and the punctum. The studium is the cultural meaning of a photograph. It is "of the order of liking, not of loving; it mobilizes a half desire, a demi-volition; it is the same sort of vague slippery, irresponsible interest one takes in the people, the entertainments, the books, the clothes one finds 'all right'" (1981: 27). The studium evokes the photographer's intent. The punctum, however, is an accident. It disturbs. It is a wound, and it bruises (1981: 48). It is often a detail, perhaps not noticed at first. As I look at this photo, I first assume that it is the boy with the letter "o" that would be Barthes's punctum, that thing that wounds, that leaves its mark on the viewer of the image. But with another look, my eye is drawn to the boy who stands third from the right, the only boy without a top hat, the only boy who looks directly at the camera. He holds the "b" in "goodbye." His direct gaze back at the camera, unsmiling, seems to span the time between the moment of the photograph's taking and the moment of its viewing.

Of course, there are many ways to read a photograph. Elizabeth Edwards characterizes the photographic image as an "ongoing entanglement," part of a larger project that engages "multiple histories and thus multiple trajectories" (2001: 22). The photographic image, in other words, signifies without end. In some ways, the long goodbye may be the photographic equivalent to Sigmund Freud's concept of "screen memories." According to Freud, screen memories are seemingly innocent recollections from childhood. Often vividly remembered vignettes of everyday activities, they mask a more traumatic memory that remains repressed below the surface. In these memories, "what is important is suppressed and what is indifferent retained" (1973 [1962]: 306). The screen memory acts as a memory substitute in order to protect the individual from the traumatic past. "A wealth of meaning lies behind their apparent innocence" (1973 [1962]: 309). Unlike the hazy, dream-like nature of some memories, screen memories are generally sharply recollected, even though their content is misleadingly mundane. On the individual level, screen memories allow people to continue on with their lives after experiencing an emotional wound. They are memory stand-ins, an innocuous trace of the original trauma. "The long goodbye" may act as such a memory stand-in, masking the brutality of the schools with images of the everyday.

Representations of the IRS system generally capture moments that may also fill personal albums: pictures of classrooms, school plays and sports teams. In fact, some of these personal albums are now in the archives. In the course of my research I have looked through many scrapbooks and albums. Clearly thoughtfully prepared, the worn pages with carefully placed photos and handwritten captions reveal the intimate relationships engendered through colonial systems. In representing the quotidian nature of colonial domination, the everydayness of the photographs is part of what make them spectacular. As their hair was cut and they were dressed in school uniforms, the children learned particular values and beliefs, becoming subjects of a "colonial alchemy" (McMaster 1992).

As Ann Stoler has written, "matters of the intimate are critical sties for the consolidation of colonial power" (2006: 4). By managing relationships between parent and child, brother and sister, as well as extended family relations, the schools became a site for the regulation and surveillance of the intimate.

The Photograph, the Archive, and Visible Trauma

The evidentiary role of photography has framed it as a tool to provide proof of past events. Even when one recognizes the constructed nature of photography, it is still difficult to deny that the camera captures some kind of truth. Marianne Hirsch elaborates on this difficulty:

> As much as I remind myself that photographs are as essentially constructed as any other representational form, that every part of the image can be manipulated and even fabricated, especially with ever more sophisticated digital technologies, I return to Barthes's basic "ça à été ("this has been") and an unassailable belief in reference and a notion of truth in the picture. (1997: 6)

Hirsch recognizes that any "notion of truth" that is found in the picture is mediated, but that within the mediation, there are still traces or representations of the real, which call for a more engaged, dynamic reading of photographic images. The image may indeed represent a moment that occurred, but the context of that moment (whether or how it was staged for example) remains difficult to ascertain.

In settler states ideas of indigeneity have often been formulated through the lens of the camera.[6] For example, the photographic work of Edward Curtis produced iconic images of Native Americans that seemed to offer non-Native Americans a glimpse into Native culture and traditions. But Curtis is himself a controversial figure, having taken images of sacred ceremonies and staging photographs for effect, romanticizing the idea of indigeneity and casting indigenous peoples as passive subjects of a colonial gaze (Lippard: 1992).[7] In a sense, one must look past these images, beyond what is shown in order to understand more fully the relationship between what is visible and what is hidden. Christopher Pinney explains: "'Looking past' suggests a complexity of perspectival positions or a multiplicity of layers that endow photographs with an enormously greater complexity than that which they are usually credited" (2003: 4). Pinney goes on to discuss how the indexicality of images has often been taken as a given. He challenges this idea, suggesting instead that "we might understand photography's indexicality to be the guarantee not of closure and fixity, but rather of multiple surfaces and the possibility of 'looking past'" (2003: 6). In other words, one can productively negotiate the indexicality of an image through re-readings and resignifying practices.

In the Canadian case, indigeneity is keenly tied to issues of visuality. For as much as visuality is about what can be seen, it is also about what cannot (Mirzoeff 2011). Aboriginal peoples and their cultural symbols play an important role in constructed ideas of the Canadian nation, but the politics and struggles over land and Aboriginal sovereignty remain marginalized from public discourse. The treatment of Aboriginal peoples in Canada remains a central, often unspoken shadow in narratives of Canadian history. At one and the same time, Aboriginal peoples are defined as central to the myth of the Canadian nation while still labeled as Other, demonstrating a "doubled ontological centrality" (Kalant 2004: 4). Processes of reconciliation in Canada bring this "doubled" relationship to the forefront of Canadian politics.

The relationship of photography to traumatic memory is very much entangled with ideas of the visible as truth and the tangible as evidence. Where language may fail in capturing the traumatic past, visual representations are often relied upon to be a silent witness. Indeed the discourse of trauma is often "predicated upon metaphors of visuality and image as unavoidable carrier of the unrepresentable" (Saltzman and Rosenberg 2006: xi). For example, "the long goodbye" may be read in relation to the myth of the "vanishing Indian." This is a theory that was widely believed at the turn of the century when settlers assumed that the Indians would die off, be bred out, or for whatever reason, not survive late in the twentieth century. This was a myth so ingrained that Aboriginal peoples felt its reverberations too. As Tantoo Cardinal (Metis/Cree) has said, "I remember feeling that to be Indian was to be a part of the past. There was no future for us."[8] Charles Wood (Cree), a former student at the Blue Quills Indian Residential School shared his experience of watching classic Western films while a student. "They would gather all of us kids up for a treat, to watch a movie," he explained. "And when the cowboys killed those Indians, we all cheered."[9] The indoctrination at the schools ran deep. Students couldn't recognize themselves in the Hollywood Indians portrayed on screen, nor could they see a way out of the systemic form of violence that was taking place at the schools. This image, "the long goodbye," captures a moment in Canadian history when the myth of the vanishing Indian was not only believed, but active policies for assimilation predicted its success.

In Avery Gordon's work on haunting in the sociological imagination, she explores the role of apparitions or shadowy manifestations from the past in the construction of the present. She writes, "Haunting recognition is a special way of knowing what has happened or is happening" (1996: 63). The myth of the vanishing Indian is powerful not when the Indian *vanishes,* but because it is always and forever *vanishing.* Images like "the long goodbye" capture this haunting recognition. Both the child who turns away and the one who gazes back at the camera can symbolically be read as a disruption of this myth. The image is a visual representation of both the myth of the vanishing Indian and its disruption; it is representative of both the drive to assimilation and its resistance.

Images from the Indian Residential School system require the viewer to see them as a negotiation. In my understanding of this negotiation, I draw on Rancière's "distribution of the sensible," where what (or who) is seen and heard is delimited by an access to shared understandings of the political and cultural landscape. For Rancière, politics revolve "around what is seen and what can be said about it, around who has the ability to see and the talent to speak, around the properties of spaces and the possibilities of time" (2004: 13). The distribution of the sensible refers to the ways in which a prescribed realm of perception excludes or includes particular forms of understanding through the senses. In regards to the aesthetics of photography, Rancière writes: "the ordinary becomes beautiful as a trace of the true. And the ordinary becomes a trace of the true if it is torn from its obviousness in order to become a hieroglyph, a mythological or phantasmagoric figure" (2004: 34). "The "long goodbye" is an example of Ranciere's "traces of the true." It is torn from its obviousness in that its original referents are no longer known. "The long goodbye" becomes a hieroglyph, a symbol to be read but disconnected, like the traumatic break itself. Yet the "distribution of the sensible" has changed since the photo was taken, for the cultural and political landscape has shifted from an emphasis on assimilation to one of reconciliation.[10]

The power of the image is linked in many ways to the structures that led to its rise. Through processes of modernization and growth of the modern capitalist state, photographic documentation played an important role in the formation of subjects. The camera, far from providing a neutral lens for society, is embedded within certain structures of power, and exerts control over the time and space of a subject, locking him/her into one particular pose or role. In other words, entangled within the mechanical nature of the camera is a whole other set of apparatuses, involving the social order of a culture and the state's need for documentation (Tagg 1988).

The images taken at these schools represent the institutional gaze. "The school photographer's camera, as such, is one of the technologies of socialization and integration of children into a dominant world-view. By staging the school's, and the society's, institutional gaze, class photos both record and practice the creation of consent" (Hirsch and Spitzer 2011). The institutional gaze continues as these photographs make their way through state archives. But the afterlife of the images does not end with the archive.

Reconciling the Archive

In the context of reconciliation, images from the IRS system circulate in new ways and new pathways of looking may begin to form. From June 28 to July 1, 2011, the Indian Residential School Truth and Reconciliation Commission hosted a national gathering in Inuvik, Northwest Territories.[11] At the event, former students were given the opportunity to share their stories through many means including artwork, dance, song and the giving of testimony. It is estimated that 1,000 survivors attended the event, traveling by boat, car and plane to the small town of Inuvik (population 3,500). The days of the national gathering were very long. In the summer months in Inuvik, the sun does not set. In the evenings, under the still-brightly shining sun, the activities moved outside. In comparison to the intense emotions of the days of testimony, the evenings focused on song, dance and entertainment that often went late into the night.

At the Inuvik national gathering, several state and church archives sent binders full of photographs taken at the schools. As former students of the schools looked through the binders in an effort to identify themselves, friends, or loved ones in these often unidentified images, the institutional gaze was negotiated and challenged. The images, while still representing a colonial system, also spoke to a more personal and intimate relationship. When a former student recognized a family member or friend, the archivist dutifully made a copy of the photograph. While the original remained with the archive its copies now move through new, more personal pathways. These images may no longer be "torn from their obviousness." In a sense, they are returned to the everyday. Having made a journey through personal collections, to the shelves of archives and now back again, these images carry with them new meaning. Representative of not only years of oppression in the schools, they now also signal the resilience and strength of Aboriginal peoples in spearheading a reconciliation process. No longer a trace of a forgotten past, the image and the subjects in them are now firmly rooted in a present.

"The long goodbye" was one of the images in the large black binders brought to Inuvik by the Catholic Church. As one of the hundreds

Figure 3.4. Survivors look through archival images at the Catholic Church area in Inuvik. (Photo by Naomi Angel.)

of images contained within these binders, the ordinariness of the long goodbye becomes clear. Unfortunately, no former students have identified any of the children in the image. The lack of knowledge surrounding their identities marks a profound absence. The photograph reminds us that "visible invisibility," and absences and misrepresentations can be productive (Gordon 1996: 16). By drawing attention to some of the limits of the archive, it demonstrates that the archives speculate. They suggest histories but don't write them. The archive is incomplete, containing absences that cannot be filled. As Pierre Nora writes, "Modern memory is, above all, archival. It relies entirely on the materiality of the trace, the immediacy of the recording, the visibility of the image" (1989: 15). But one must also recognize that the archive can only tell us so much, because "the production of traces is always also the creation of silences" (Trouillot 1997: 29). Although the Indian Residential Schools Truth and Reconciliation Commission calls for an end to such silences, "the long goodbye" reminds us that silence is also part of this history.

I began this chapter with Governor General Jean's speech and her recollection of archival images from Dawson City, Yukon. In evoking these particular images she also conjured a larger body of archival images. Similar photographs from across Canada help to tell the history of the IRS system. In this chapter, I have used "the long goodbye" as a starting point to discuss how visual representations of the schools can act as reminders of this past, while also allowing for their resignification in the present. In this resignification, I have argued that the subjects, although often still unidentified, experience a sort of return. In representing the quotidian aspects of the Indian Residential School system, archival images act as reminders that the everyday and the spectacular go hand in hand.

The process of reconciliation in Canada is a complex negotiation of not only a contested past, but a contested future. Discourses of reconciliation often focus on leaving the past behind and moving towards a new, unified future. The goal is consensus, an understanding about what happened in order to construct possibilities for what may happen. In many ways, reconciliation is about the shifting of boundaries, where the borders once thought rigid—between inclusion and exclusion, visibility and invisibility, everyday and spectacle—become more malleable. "The long goodbye," far from representing a static image, can be read as one illustration of these shifting boundaries. The spectacular nature of this image, in that it not only represents but mediates social relations, continues to evolve.

Notes

The research for this chapter was generously supported by the Canadian Social Sciences and Humanities Research Council.

1. The archived webcast of this talk is available through the IRS TRC website, www.trc-cvr.ca.
2. The Indian Residential School system was established through the passing of several legislative acts including the Gradual Civilization Act (1857) and the Indian Act (1867). For more information on the history of the Indian Residential School system see Miller, Milloy, Younging, Dewar, and DeGagné.
3. www.trc-cvr.ca.
4. This phrase, "to kill the Indian in the child," has been used by several government officials in describing the goals of the residential school system. Prime Minister Stephen Harper, in his official apology, quoted these now infamous words.
5. Anglican Church of Canada pamphlet. 6575-104, Box 54 9-14.13.
6. In many colonies, natural and human resources have been the driving motivation for colonization. In settler states, it is land. In other words, settler societies are those where the colonizers have "come to stay," where "invasion is a structure, not an event" (Wolfe 388).
7. For an interesting example of how Curtis's film, *In the Land of the Headhunters,* has been revisited and resignified, see the work of Aaron Glass, Brad Evans, and Andrea Sanborn. In a collaborative project with the Kwakwaka'wakw (Kwakiutl) in British Columbia, the restored film is being screened, accompanied by a live arrangement of the long-lost original score and a song and dance performance by Kwakwaka'wakw (Kwakiutl) descendants of the original film actors. For more see: http://www.curtisfilm.rutgers.edu.
8. In her introduction to the documentary film, "The Learning Path."
9. Conversation with Charles Wood at the Blue Quills First Nations College in St. Paul, Alberta.
10. It should be noted that the road to reconciliation has been long and has involved many significant milestones. In 2006, the Indian Residential School Settlement Agreement was reached. It resulted from the largest class action lawsuit in Canadian history and included reparations for former students and called for the establishment of the Indian Residential School Truth and Reconciliation Commission. Two years later, in 2008, Prime Minister Stephen Harper gave an official apology in the House of Commons.
11. The Inuvik national gathering was the second of seven proposed national events organized by the IRS TRC.

References

Barthes, Roland. 1981. *Camera Lucida: Reflections on Photography.* Translated by Richard Howard. New York: Hill and Wang.

Debord, Guy. 1995. *The Society of the Spectacle.* New York: Zone Books.

Driessens, Jo-Anne. 2003. "Relating to Photographs." In *Photography's Other Histories,* edited by Christopher Pinney and Nicolas Peterson, 14–22. Durham, NC: Duke University Press.

Edwards, Elizabeth. 2001. *Raw Histories: Photographs, Anthropology and Museums.* Oxford, UK: Berg Publishers.

Emberley, Julia. 2007. *Defamiliarizing the Aboriginal: Cultural Practices and Decolonization in Canada.* Toronto, ON: University of Toronto Press.

Freud, Sigmund. 1973 [1962]. "Screen Memories." In *Sigmund Freud: Early Psycho-Analytic Publications Volume III (1893–1899).* Translated by James Strachey. London: The Hogarth Press.

Gomez-Barris, Macarena. 2009. *Where Memory Dwells: Culture and State Violence in Chile.* Berkeley: University of California Press.

Gone, Joseph. 2008. "'So I Can Be Like a Whiteman': The Cultural Psychology of Space and Place in American Indian Mental Health." *Culture and Psychology* 14.3: 369–99.

Gordon, Avery. 1996. *Ghostly Matters: Haunting and the Sociological Imagination.* Minneapolis: University of Minnesota Press.

Hirsch, Marianne. 1997. *Family Frames: Photography, Narrative and Postmemory.* Cambridge, MA: Harvard University Press.

Hirsch, Marianne, and Leo Spitzer. 2011. *About Class Photos.* Jan.10, 2011. http://www.nomadikon.net.

Kalant, Amelia. 2004. *National Identity and the Conflict at Oka: Native Belonging and Myths of Postcolonial Nationhood in Canada.* New York: Routledge.

LaRose, Stephen. 1999. "Wrecker's Ball Claims White Calf Collegiate." *Saskatchewan Sage* 3.8: 18–19. http://www.ammsa.com/node/13210 (accessed March 28, 2012).

The Learning Path. 1991. Directed by Loretta Todd. Perf. Eva Cardinal, Olive Dickerson and Dr. Ann Anderson. DVD. National Film Board of Canada.

Lippard, Lucy R. 1992. "Introduction." *Partial Recall: Photographs of Native North Americans,* edited by Lucy R. Lippard, 13–45. New York: The New Press.

Lydon, Jane. 2005. *Eye Contact: Photographing Indigenous Australians.* Durham, NC: Duke University Press.

Mackey, Eva. 2002 [1999]. *The House of Difference: Cultural Politics and National Identity in Canada.* University of Toronto Press.

McMaster, Gerald. 1992. "Colonial Alchemy: Reading the Boarding School Experience." In *Partial Recall: Photographs of Native North Americans,* edited by Lucy R. Lippard, 77–87. New York: The New Press.

Miller, Bruce Granville. 2008. *Invisible Indigenes: The Politics of Nonrecognition.* Lincoln: University of Nebraska Press.

Miller, Nancy, and Jason Tougaw. 2002. "Introduction: Extremities." In *Extremities: Trauma, Testimony, and Community,* edited by Nancy Miller and Jason Tougaw, 1–24. Urbana and Chicago: University of Illinois Press.

Milloy, John. 1999. *A National Crime: The Canadian Government and the Residential School System, 1879 to 1986.* University of Manitoba Press.

Mirzoeff, Nicholas. 2011. "The Right to Look." *Critical Inquiry* 37.33 (Spring): 473–96.

Nora, Pierre. 1989. *Between Memory and History: Les Lieux de Mémoire.* Berkeley: University of California Press.

Pinney, Christopher. 2003. "Introduction: 'How the Other Half … '" in *Photography's Other Histories,* edited by Christopher Pinney and Nicolas Peterson, 1–14. Durham, NC: Duke University Press.

Poolaw, Linda. 1998. "Spirit Capture: Observations of an Encounter." In *Spirit Capture: Photographs from the National Museum of the American Indian.* Washington, DC: Smithsonian Institution Press.

Raheja, Michelle. 2011. *Reservation Reelism: Redfacing, Visual Sovereignty, and Representations of Native Americans in Film.* Lincoln: University of Nebraska Press.

Rancière, Jacques. 2004. *The Politics of Aesthetics.* Translated by Gabriel Rockhill. London: Continuum.

Rose, Gillian. 2007. *An Introduction to the Interpretation of Visual Materials.* London: Sage.

Saltzman, Lisa, and Eric M. Rosenberg, eds. 2006. *Trauma and Visuality in Modernity.* Hanover, NH: Dartmouth College Press, University Press of New England.

Sontag, Susan. 2002. *Regarding the Pain of Others.* New York: Farrar, Straus and Giroux.

Stoler, Ann. 2006. "Intimidations of Empire: Predicaments of the Tactile and Unseen." In *Haunted by Empire: Geographies of Intimacy in North American History,* edited by Ann Stoler, 1–22. Durham, NC: Duke University Press.

Tagg, John. 1988. *The Burden of Representation: Essays on Photographies and Histories.* Amherst: University of Massachusetts Press.

Thobani, Sunera. 2007. *Exalted Subjects: Studies in the Making of Race and Nation in Canada.* Toronto: University of Toronto Press.

Trouillot, Michel-Rolph. 1997. *Silencing the Past: Power and the Production of History.* Boston: Beacon Press.

Wolfe, Patrick. 2006. "Settler Colonialism and the Elimination of the Native." *Journal of Genocide Research* 8.4 (December): 387–409.

Younging, Gregory, Jonathan Dewar, and Mike DeGagné, eds. 2009. *Response, Responsibility, and Renewal: Canada's Truth and Reconciliation Journey.* Ottawa, ON: Aboriginal Healing Foundation.

Part II

Screening Absence
New Technology, Affect, and Memory

Chapter 4

Viral Affiliations

Facebook, Queer Kinship, and the Memory
of the Disappeared in Contemporary Argentina

Cecilia Sosa

A New Anniversary: Contesting the Myth
of the "Wounded Family"

On March 24, 2010, the anniversary of the 1976 military coup in Argentina, a virtual campaign on Facebook accompanied the traditional demonstrations in the major cities of the country. The campaign involved having participants remove the pictures from their Facebook profiles, leaving the space empty as a sign of commemoration and resistance in the name of the "disappeared"—that infamous category that accounts for victims of the 1976–1983 dictatorship. The Facebook action generated high levels of participation, and, during the days before and after the anniversary, it was possible to witness a community of *faceless* profiles supporting, from digital space, a speechless demand for memory.

This chapter proposes a critical engagement with this initiative. I will consider the extent to which it can be read in parallel to the *Siluetazo* campaign (the Silhouette campaign), an emblematic artistic intervention in the early 1980s that claimed a role in the ending of the military regime. That pioneer activist venture, which resulted in thousands of life-size silhouettes posted on Buenos Aires' walls, resonated almost three decades later in the Facebook campaign through an alternative identification with the missing. In particular, I will examine how that historical political demonstration reverberated across new generations in what could otherwise have been considered a frivolous intervention in social media. Can the seemingly minor gesture of removing one's Facebook profile picture be conceived of as a local emergence of evolving forms of memory? Could it allow us to rethink the capacity of bodies to act upon others in the digital era (Clough 2007: 24, 312–14)? Ultimately, I wish to explore whether this initiative that spread like a virus among Facebook users might suggest a new technology of memory for Argentina's present.

To do so, I propose a critical engagement with Diana Taylor's well-known study of cultural memory in the Americas (2003).[1] In her seminal research on the activism developed by *H.I.J.O.S.,* the organization founded by the children of the disappeared in 1995, Taylor contended that Argentina's post-dictatorship culture was embedded in what she called a "DNA of performance," a biological and self-repetitive paradigm of public presentation based on biological kinship (2003: 175). Although her analysis, first published in 2003, is rich and provocative, it has also introduced an arguably normative reading of Argentine performativity in the Anglosphere, which has tended to confirm the unwritten rule that stipulates that only those who were "directly affected" by the dictatorship's violence—e.g., blood relatives of those who were detained and killed—could legitimately remember and mourn for the disappeared. By contrast, I will argue that the 2010 Facebook campaign showed how in recent years the "privileges" of blood have been expanded to those who are not usually considered victims. Far from dismissing the pain of those directly affected by violence, I want to explore how seemingly less implicated witnesses can also adopt and partake in loss. In doing so, I attempt to make visible the alternative ties that have emerged out of grief, which, I suggest, could be conceptualized as a queer form of kinship.[2] My use of the word "queer" here functions as a form of critique of the bloodline normativity that dominated Argentina's post-dictatorship period.[3] Similarly, in a recent discussion on queer bonds, Joshua Weiner and Damon Young (2011: 223–41) address these ties as forms of social bonding that appear under diverse conditions of negation and constraint. For them, queer bonds do not occur "in spite of but *because* of some force of negation, in which it is precisely negativity that organizes scenes of togetherness" (2011: 236). Indeed, the authors do not approach queer bonds as necessarily homosexual, but rather "as a way of being-with and a mode of intimacy" (2011: 237). Following this argument, I insist on the power of queerness as a lens of analysis that can help to uncover the non-normative affiliations that have emerged in Argentina's aftermath of violence. Moreover, I contend that the Facebook campaign revealed the extent to which the country has recently witnessed a performance of "blood ties" that largely exceeds conventional family settings. In so doing, the digital campaign sheds light on the emergence of wider forms of being together in the wake of loss.

Many scholars have called attention to the familial inscription of the violent past in post-dictatorial Argentina. From different fields and perspectives, they have engaged with the framing of the local trauma in terms of a bloodline assembly of victims.[4] In fact, when democracy was restored in 1983, the network of organizations created by the victims of state terrorism assumed the form of a peculiar "family": the Mothers of the Plaza de Mayo (*Madres*), the Grandmothers of the Plaza de Mayo (*Abuelas*), the Relatives (*Familiares*), and more recently, the Children (*H.I.J.O.S.*), and the Siblings (*Herman@s*) of the disappeared.[5] All of these kin organizations invoked their biological ties to the missing to make their claims for justice. In the wake of loss, they configured what I call a "wounded family." This biological foundation of the demands for justice has deeply informed the memory struggles in the country and also the human rights concerns, which have tended to be processed as a family issue.[6] As Elizabeth Jelin argues in "Victims, Relatives, and Citizens in Argentina: Whose Voice is Legitimate Enough?," "truth" came to be equated with the testimony of those "directly affected" first and foremost, through the voices of blood relatives of the disappeared (Jelin 2008: 177).

But did the dictatorship leave only bloodline victims in its wake? I would argue differently. Not only because this biological framework cuts off the possibility of understanding the transmission of trauma on a broader basis, but also because the very idea of family evoked by the relatives of the victims is not a traditional one. Although *Madres, Abuelas, H.I.J.O.S., Familiares,* and *Herman@s* have invoked their biological ties to the missing, they have also created alternative modes of support, love, and care that exceed heteronormative formations, and, finally, "queered" the very idea of the family. In fact, these kin-associations seem to fit better with those queer relations that, as Judith Butler suggests, "do not conform to the nuclear family model and that draw on biological and non-biological relations, exceeding the reach of current juridical conceptions, functioning according to non-formalizable rules" (Butler 2005: 102). This peculiar overlap between human rights movements and relatives' associations has ultimately resulted in a curious paradox: a demand for justice inspired by bloodline ties which at the same time requires an expanded conception of kinship.

A New Era of Memory and Happiness

During the period launched by President Néstor Kirchner's government in 2003, the particular shape of Argentina's national trauma was put into an official frame. For the first time a government embraced the position of the victims to assume mourning as a national commitment. During his inaugural speech, Kirchner declared: "We are the sons and daughters of the Mothers and Grandmothers of Plaza de Mayo."[7] By casting himself within the "wounded family," the president presented himself as part of the lineage inaugurated by violence. Taking on the identity of the "son," he showed how the lineage of loss was not restricted to those who had been "directly affected" by violence but rather could be inhabited by anyone. The official discourse implicitly responded to the bio-politics of memory and helped in constituting an alternative lineage of kinship: one that does not rely only on blood but rather is part of a broader political struggle. This process continues today in the hands of Kirchner's wife and widow, Cristina Fernández de Kirchner, who took over as president in December 2007 and has remained in office for two terms.

It is my argument that during the Kirchnerist period, the discourse of blood became a sort of "happy narrative," a new "moral order," strategically championed by the state.[8] The very idea of memory was transformed into a "national duty." Here I borrow from Sara Ahmed, who, in her critique of normative forms of happiness, argues that, "to be bound to happiness is to be bound by what has already been established as good" (Ahmed 2010: 133). Similarly, during the Kirchnerist period, memory was turned into a "happy object": it embodied the figure of the political good. Although this governmental shift involved an important recognition for human rights movements, it also resulted in a changed position for the relatives' associations which, after decades of fighting the state for justice, now had to operate in tandem with the government.

After the politics of forgiveness that had been a central platform of previous post-dictatorship governments, the Kirchnerist administrations provided the political impulse to overrule the laws that granted immunity to the military. From 2006, a massive number of trials began prosecuting those responsible for human rights violations under the dictatorship.[9] The anniversary of the 1976 military coup, March 24th, was transformed into a national day of remembering. In 2004, the official ceremony took place in the emblematic navy school and former detention camp, the *Escuela Mecánica de la Armada* (ESMA), where 5,500 people were detained and tortured during the dictatorship. On that day, Kirchner announced that ESMA was to be transformed into a "space of memory," thereby reclaiming the infamous place for civil society. In front of a multitude, he addressed his speech to his "brothers" and "sisters," and congratulated the *Madres, Abuelas, H.I.J.O.S.* and *Familiares* organizations for their "model of struggle" (Jelin 2008: 195). Yet again, Kirchner subscribed to a line of heritage that was much more political than biological. Despite the fact that a profuse list of family titles still endorsed the presence of bloodline victims within the public sphere, the biological normativity was slightly shifted, displaced. In a sense, the presidential couple emerged as the stepparents of a queer lineage in mourning.

In 2008, with Fernández de Kirchner already in office, another stage in the process of national grief began. New voices established breaks and interruptions in the official duty of memory while staging alternative ways of being "affected" by violence. These emerging narratives unsettled the organic solidarity built by the "wounded family" model. They brought new vocabularies to account for the affective lines of transmission that already permeated wider society. In so doing, they offered a new opportunity for a politics of human rights by showing that it was possible to create a more expanded politics of mourning that moved beyond traditional narratives of blood. This new mood shed light on nonnormative feelings of kinship that had emerged out of the experience of violence. It is my contention that the 2010 Facebook campaign also intervened in this dispute—illuminating a virtual community in mourning, an alternative relation among kinship, memory, and politics.

Viral Feelings of Kinship

On March 24, 2010 I woke up early. As usual, I checked my Facebook page. A strange transformation had taken place overnight: most of my Argentine friends had removed their profile pictures and left the space empty. Where there used to be colorful portraits, there were now just the transparent outlines of a head and shoulders—Facebook's default graphic for representing an empty profile image. In some cases, the shadowy figures were also accompanied by taglines: "Nunca más" (Never Again), "Juicio y castigo" (Trials and Punishment), "No los olvidamos" (We Haven't Forgotten You), or simply an iconic number, "30,000"; all phrases that have been pervasively associated with the fight for accountability for the crimes of the 1976–1983 dictatorship.[10] Between surprised and amused, I noticed that the shadowy outlines that occupied the website seemed to be iterating those other silhouettes—the ones that were part of the famous demonstrations against the military in the early 1980s. The emptied profiles appeared to be mimicking the portraits of absence that the *Siluetazo* popularized as the canonic image of the disappeared. Ironically, the 2010 campaign positioned the global corporation Facebook as appearing to support the local campaign through an insidious collection of blank outlines. Throughout that day in 2010, I remember being completely preoccupied by the initiative, checking the website obsessively, looking for new ghostly profiles to emerge. The same status was iterated over and over again: "Facing March 24 we take pictures out of our profiles. A virtual community in mourning." Many Facebook users living abroad posted bilingual taglines. My former supervisor in London, a British sociologist, also signed up. I felt like weeping.

A seemingly minor debate also took place in the virtual space during those days. While some Facebook users argued that the best way to commemorate the missing was by removing the profile pictures, others resisted leaving the space empty and proposed posting images of the missing instead. "The disappeared had faces, ideas, bodies. I will keep the pictures of them," one Facebook user argued. "They are still with us. They will never disappear. Beyond silence, beyond forgetting," another user wrote, refusing to participate in the blank profiles campaign. *H.I.J.O.S.,* the Children of the Disappeared organization, intervened in the digital campaign by uploading a collection of pictures of their missing parents: beautiful, young, smiling faces frozen in time.

I would like to suggest that the Facebook controversy shed light on a broader dispute that still remains silenced in contemporary Argentina: the question of who bears the legitimacy of remembering in the aftermath of violence. This contentious issue still unsettles not just the politics of memory but also the present political and social life of the country. In order to fully understand this debate, I suggest considering the digital campaign alongside another seminal event that challenged the legitimacy of remembering during the dictatorship: the *Siluetazo.*

Becoming Silhouettes

On the 21st of September 1983, thousands of life-size figures were posted onto the walls of Buenos Aires' downtown area. With the military *junta* still in power, a multitude of ad-hoc activists laid down on sheets of paper on the floor of Plaza de Mayo Central Square, offering their bodies to be traced by strangers and transformed into full-scale posters. The resulting silhouettes remained in public space during the whole night—a theatrical reenactment of loss that confronted viewers with "voiceless screams" of those vanished by the military terror (Longoni 2007; Longoni and Bruzzone 2008). This public performance framed the Third March of Resistance organized by the Mothers of Plaza de Mayo toward the end of the military period. Originally conceived by visual artists, the *Siluetazo* initiative was carried out by *Madres, Abuelas,* and other kin-based organizations.[11] Thereafter, the silhouettes remained glued in the imaginary of civil society as a public niche of contestation and denunciation in the wake of loss.

In an oblique way, the 2010 Facebook campaign revisited that original event. The gesture of offering one's own body to be outlined by anonymous stakeholders also resonated in the emptied profiles that occupied the website for the 2010 anniversary. Both initiatives shared the impulse of adopting the place of the other—the disappeared—and, in a limited way, *becoming* that other. Both performances were inspired by the principle of staging the pervasive presence of an absence. While the *Siluetazo*'s life-size silhouettes enacted the empty space left by the missing, the Facebook campaign proposed a re-enactment of that emptiness: it provided the disappeared with a blank space to re-stage their absence. As the Argentine scholar Ana Longoni argues, the *Siluetazo* gave the disappeared a new body, in which the silhouette became the trace; she writes: "[T]o take the place of the missing person is to accept that anyone could have taken the place of the disappeared, that anyone could have suffered the same uncertain and sinister fate."[12] To some extent, the enthusiastic impulse of transference that occupied the Plaza de Mayo in 1983 also "took over" the social media networks in 2010. The Facebook campaign filled up the digital space with non-kin forms of identification and care. A spirit of the collective infused both performances—they both endorsed the ethical imperative of swapping places as a "non-kin" condition for embracing the absences.

At the same time, both interventions proposed an exchange of places between two disparate corporalities. The *Siluetazo* not only indexed the abstract body of the disappeared but also the body of the activists, who volunteered to make the operation possible in a public space at the main city plaza (Longoni 2010: 5). Yet, the Facebook campaign did not imply offering one's body to be outlined by others, but rather leaving one's profile empty to be *occupied* by others. Although the digital campaign remained as an arguably safe/limited online social space of Facebook users, both gestures involved a passage, a movement of transference, and even of migration. While the *Siluetazo* provided a new corporality—however ephemeral—to the missing, the Facebook campaign offered them a virtual space to be filled. These differential forms of exchange also point out a specific transference of affects. Both performances explored at different times how and under which conditions it was possible to share in the transmission of trauma.

Contested Technologies of Memory

To further address this issue, I would like to consider the visual strategies that have been in play in Argentina to engage with the experience of loss.

Longoni addresses the persistency of the figure of the disappeared in the public domain as following two main matrices of visual reenactment: photographs and silhouettes (2010: 6). While pictures have been traditionally used by those "directly affected" to individualize and personalize their loss, silhouettes worked as a way of "transference" for anonymous others, not related to individual disappeared persons through bloodline ties. These differential strategies of remembering were also present during the Facebook campaign. While some users posted pictures of the disappeared within their profiles, others opted for the collective anonymity of the eerie empty profiles. The former strategy was led primarily by the blood relatives of the missing who have traditionally exhibited pictures of their loved ones as treasured, unrepeatable faces and biographies (Longoni 2010: 7). When their relatives' images came to occupy Facebook profiles during the 2010 anniversary, the initiative seemingly worked as a way of reassuring the feelings of property of those "directly affected" by violence. However, this kin-authority was also undermined by thousands of other users who opted for the emptiness of the blank profiles—the use of the silhouettes implicitly contested the bloodline tradition, rejecting personal entitlements of loss, and opening broader modes of connection with those missing across time.

These differential strategies of intervention ultimately shed light on two conflicting understandings of what constitutes communities of the "affected": one formed by the relatives of the disappeared that remains delimited by the images of a personal loss, and the other a non-kin community of mourners enacted by the empty profiles. This later formation expanded the uneven margins of those "directly affected," and it created the basis for a more expanded form of responsibility against violence. By "disappearing" their own profile pictures, the viral community of Facebook users silently (and in a ghostly, but rapid and contagious fashion) claimed a collective sense of ownership of those political absences. Similarly to the *Siluetazo* decades before, this anonymous community enacted a non-linear and non-kin apparatus of memory (this time a virtual one) that, ironically, made the missing reappear.

Not Only the Family

Even so, the use of private albums during the Facebook campaign was not restricted to "direct" victims. Whereas the children of the disappeared uploaded scenes of their broken families, unrelated users also posted pictures of the missing in their own profiles, as a form of non-kin support for the struggle for justice. This distinctive use of photography within the Facebook campaign invites us to revisit Marianne Hirsch's influential notion of "postmemory" while considering whether her meditations on second generations of survivors can be translated to contemporary Argentina (Hirsch 2008: 103–28). Being herself a daughter of a Holocaust survivor, Hirsch argues that descendants connect so deeply with the previous generations' remembrances that these experiences seem to constitute memories in their own right. She contends that the way in which second generations recall the past is different from contemporary witnesses: for them the past is "not actually mediated by recall but by imaginative investment, projection and creation" (Hirsch 2008: 107). Still, some Argentine scholars have strongly resisted the postmemory framework as the hermeneutical model through which to approach the local scene (Vezzetti 2002; Casullo 2004). In fact, categories such as "second generation" or "second witnesses" do not fully align with the experiences of the children of the disappeared. Although their recollections might be fragmentary, many of these people, now in their thirties, were not "second" but first-hand witnesses of traumatic events as children: they were present at the moment of their parents' kidnapping, were kidnapped with them, or were born in captivity at clandestine detention centres.[13]

It is important to bear in mind that Hirsch's early meditations on postmemory draw on Roland Barthes' famous concept of the "punctum," whose initial example develops the trope of the maternal loss that becomes projected as a sort of "umbilical cord" (Barthes 1981: 80). Stemming from this original inscription, Hirsch's early discussions of postmemory strongly relied on family pictures as a "unique medium" for the transmission of trauma. For her, pictures not only allow the viewer to see but also to *touch* the past. She writes that family photos tend to become "screens" that resemble "spectres reanimating their dead subjects with indexical and iconic force" (Hirsch 2008: 116). Still working within this bloodline framework, Hirsch finally warns that postmemory can also work for new generations as a way "to assert [their] own victimhood alongside that of the parents" (Hirsch 2008: 108). Thus, postmemory as a form of embodied knowledge can also work as a sort of "umbilical cord," which always threatens to fall back on the familiar. Nonetheless, Hirsch's latest ruminations on postmemory have attempted to revise the familial basis of memory transmission and look for other forms of affective engagement that also include non-kin forms of witnessing (Hirsch 2012).

The 2010 Facebook campaign suggested precisely this form of intergenerational transmission beyond bloodline narratives. The affective use of digital technologies at stake within this initiative also touched the past, but in a quite *unfamiliar* way: the de-faced profiles acted not only as "screens" suddenly captured by specters of the disappeared, but also as collective surfaces and media for the production of memory in the present. In this sense, this digital campaign proposed an affective and self-propagated platform of memory for new generations to negotiate traumatic experiences.

A Collective Staging of the Self

The use of photography as the staging of a collective claim has a seminal antecedent in Argentina. Even before the recovery of democracy, the Mothers of Plaza de Mayo transformed personal albums into a common placard of loss. They framed the pictures of their loved ones within an expansive banner, and those hints of private lives became part of a political artifact of intervention. The Mothers' collective gesture, which signposted a foundational moment in the struggle of the human rights movement in the country, was also echoed during the 2010 Facebook campaign. Instead of merely re-establishing a sense of familial property of the missing, the pictures reframed within the website profiles also suggested a shared sense of co-ownership of the traumatic past.

If during ordinary times Facebook profiles provide a magnificent virtual space for deploying all kinds of fantasies in the narration of the self, the 2010 campaign on the anniversary of the military coup queered this elusive space. Friends and relatives, but also unrelated stakeholders, recovered pictures of the missing and uploaded them into their own profiles. This digital operation recalled how the self cannot be considered as an autonomous sphere, but rather as an ambiguous territory always defined in relation to others. It ultimately revealed the plural constitution of the subject or, as Butler has said, "the ways in which we are from the start and by virtue of being a bodily being, already given over, beyond ourselves, implicated in lives that are not our own" (Butler 2004: 29). Far from a flippant gesture, the Facebook campaign showed how loss could be a unique opportunity to connect with others. Thus, it stressed an empowered conception of mourning, which showed how grief could contribute to building new communities of "with-ness" among wider sectors of Argentine society.

Absolute Witnesses

The traditional repertoire of images of the disappeared that are used to recall disappeared persons not only includes family pictures but also government identification: ID photographs required of every Argentine citizen, taken in the bureaucratic offices during the military regime. These official portraits, produced by the same state responsible for torture and murder, also pullulated the Facebook campaign. Once reframed into the website profiles, these ordinary black and white portraits, with no traces of personal features or feelings, no stylish clothes, no makeup, no fancy landmarks or any other recognizable context, also came to be part of a unique apparatus of memory. In the digital context, these normative ID portraits became especially poignant: they undermined their official origin while introducing an unexpected challenge to bloodline normativity.

In her bio-political analysis of contemporary Argentina, the British sociologist Vikki Bell develops a fascinating analysis of a single photograph. She focuses her attention on a portrait of Fernando Brodsky, a young man who was kidnapped in 1979 and taken into ESMA's detention camp (Bell 2010). Although the man did not survive, another prisoner, Víctor Basterra, who was made to work as a photographer inside the clandestine center, eventually smuggled a photograph of Fernando taken at ESMA out of the camp. The image was part of the bundle of evidence submitted by the relatives of the missing during the initial trials of the military *junta* members at the end of the dictatorship. Eventually, it also became part of an art exhibition (in an art piece by his brother, Marcelo Brodsky).[14] Following this curious trajectory, Bell argues that Fernando's image shows a sort of "vitality," which remained untouched. Moreover, she asserts that the way in which Fernando stares at his viewers addresses another form of justice (Bell 2010: 82). For her, this picture looks "beyond death"; it enacts a sort of resistance to "becoming-archival," a resistance "of becoming preserved *as past,* even in the art-space" (Bell 2010: 81). In her essay, Bell also poses the provocative question: "What does Fernando's image *want*?" Her answer is compelling: the picture of the young dead man "*wants* its viewer to feel s/he is gazing at an absolute witness, looking into the eyes of someone who looked with those same eyes at his torturers, his murderers" (Bell 2010: 82).

Drawing upon Bell's compelling analysis, I wish to make the case that the vitality and even the aliveness that she detects in Fernando's portrait were also present in the Facebook campaign. The ID pictures, but also those extracted from family albums and even the silhouette-profiles, managed to emerge as *absolute witnesses.* Similarly to Fernando's picture, the viral, uneasy, simultaneous, and contested collection of digital images also called for another form of justice, one that was not limited to the legal trials that were already taking place in the country. Like Fernando, those ID images resisted becoming part of the past. They stared from the screens with a ubiquitous and pervasive demand. They became unfamiliar friends circulating through digital space, suggesting, through their presence in this post-millennial virtual space, a renewed possibility of being remembered in the future. Staring from the Facebook profiles in the wake of the 2010 anniversary, they assumed the absolute witness role: they had the capacity to affect the viewers through a silent interrogation that exceeded their own time (Bell 2010: 81). Reframed into these digital networks, both ID pictures and silhouette-profiles enacted a silent strategy of reappearance—emerging as unfamiliar, uncanny, and ultimately queer faces of public grief.

Furthermore, it could be argued that in the wake of the 2010 anniversary, those distinctive portraits of the disappeared *wanted* to be posted in foreign profiles. They wanted to be seen by new eyes, by more Facebook users, because they wanted to be remembered. More than this, they wanted to be *smuggled out* from familiar files and spaces. They needed to be removed from family-centered routes to be able to contest the normative sense of who holds ownership over the missing. Uploaded within digital space, the images could develop their subversive potential to undermine not only the military bureaucracy of the murderous state but also the safe privacy of family albums. They wanted to be part of a collective ethics that went beyond the familial status of the victim. They wanted to be "picked up" by non-kin users; they wanted to be mediums; they wanted to be chosen in order to exercise the absolute act of witnessing.

During the 2010 Facebook campaign, silhouettes and pictures infiltrated the digital networks with a call for justice that entangled affective linkages across time. The campaign revealed the extent to which the disappeared were still encrypted in the present, circulating, emerging from different states of becoming. In this way, the digital initiative suggested a community beyond the family, in which the dead gazed at the living through the shadowy gallery that took over the website profiles. Thus, the campaign carried out a concept of memory where memory is always in plural and in the process of becoming; one that gives shape to a collective ethics. As a result, the campaign helped to decouple the idea of memory from both individual and familial grounds: it built an artifact of remembering that circulated through social networks ready to be adopted by a new generation of activists and social media users regardless of their backgrounds, or differential levels of bloodline ties to loss. While posted on the website, this digital collection of pictures managed to reverse the sacred privileges of bloodline victims: they bore witness to a more expanded impulse to share in grief. Moreover, this process of re-framing had a liberating impulse: it made available another line of transmission of trauma to anyone who might feel compelled to post the faces of the disappeared on their own profiles. Thereby, the Facebook campaign showed how feelings of loss could be embraced on a collective basis; not only as a victimizing position, but also as a playful *dispositif* of being "implicated in lives that are not our own" (Butler 2004: 28). Under this perspective, the initiative unseated the hierarchies of suffering still embedded in the official discourses of grief in Argentina. It also showed how postmemory actions of remembrance could be released from "umbilical cords" and become available for what Hirsch has recently called "witnesses by adoption," who can retrospectively identify and partake in loss (Hirsch 2012: 10).[15] In so doing, the Facebook campaign suggested a playful path to dismantle the boundaries of the "wounded family" as the only victim of violence.

A Fleeting Community

In 1983 the *Siluetazo* campaign not only impacted those who took part in the initiative, but also those who demonstrated along the walls covered with the silhouettes near the central square. Displaced from territorial locations, the Facebook campaign similarly constituted a bold, visually based (though digital) movement—one that spread like a contagion. The ghostly profiles reproduced themselves like a virus in cyberspace and threatened to transform Facebook friends into a series of specters. In fact, the gesture of offering one's profile to be occupied by others articulated a quiet statement of horizontality. Like the *Siluetazo,* the online campaign made a voiceless proclamation: that *anyone* could join the initiative since *anyone* could have experienced the sinister fate of being disappeared. From this perspective, the operation relied on an ethical impulse: the conviction of giving oneself over, at least for a while, in order to assume the place of the missing. The emptied profiles had the capacity to address users through a mute gaze, spreading across the website an invitation to join the virtual community of mourners. On March 24, 2010, large portions of Facebook became *faceless* and the de-faced profiles became a (queer) condition to share.

The online campaign also revealed how different strategies of remembering—through pictures and through silhouettes—are all part of current disputes about the present. Through either image choice, the digital performance shaped a non-geographical, mobile, and collective assemblage, one that illuminated more oblique ways of being affected by loss. It could be argued that this alternative form of intimacy brought into being a "fleeting community," a new notion of a "we" that quivered in the affective encounter with a ghostly audience of digital users, the unfamiliar, de-faced friends (Ridout 2008: 221–31). This community of voices called out against violence, not in the name of bloodline ties and personal loss, but in the name of a pervasive, unrelenting demand for justice and remembrance.

Whereas in 1983 the *Siluetazo* campaign broke the military "pact of silence" and helped bring to the public sphere the Madres' impossible claim, *aparición con vida* ("reappearance alive"), by 2010 there was no hope of recovering the missing alive. Yet, massive trials of the perpetrators were already taking place and thousands of military personnel were being judged for human rights violation during the dictatorship.[16] In that new context, the collection of silent and eerie profiles responded to a different set of circumstances. While reversing bloodline inscriptions of trauma, the 2010 campaign challenged the repetitive chain of presentation and representation through which the relatives of the victims managed to inscribe their claim into a "scientific and performatic" line of truth and lineage (Taylor 2003: 175). In this sense, the Facebook campaign managed to queer the DNA of performance.

After all, the plural apparatus of memory that emerged from the digital networks did not rely on blood. Rather, it suggested novel ways in which an experience of memory transmission could travel through bodies, blurring the margins between the self and the other, and inviting alternative forms of being together in loss. In this manner, the Facebook campaign pointed toward an idea of justice that flowed beyond the current trials. It worked as an impulse that could not be constrained into restrictive forms of bloodline ties; rather it reworked kinship while engaging with an expanded collection of "queer bonds." More than a DNA of performance, post-dictatorial Argentina witnesses a broader social struggle about the heritage of loss. The Facebook initiative helped to bring that queer community into flesh.

The Pleasures of Being Plural in Grief

Strangely enough, the 2010 Facebook campaign was not repeated during the anniversaries of the military coup in subsequent years. During the 2011 and 2012 anniversaries, for example, there was some shy removal of profile pictures, but the extent of participation could not compete with the massive enthusiasm reached in 2010. Yet, when former President Néstor Kirchner suddenly died of a heart attack in October 2010, a multitude took over the streets. By that time, the death of the leader worked as a test of the feelings of kinship that had emerged from violence. "He was also our son," claimed the Mothers of Plaza de Mayo recalling the leader's first speech. "Orphans once again," bewailed *H.I.J.O.S.* Precisely, these expanded feelings of kinship, which contested normative conceptions of the family, had been anticipated by the Facebook campaign in March 2010.

Animosities are emerging in Argentina nowadays. A strong polarization has captured the public sphere, and future anniversaries of the coup are likely to take shape in a quite different fashion. This curious fact leads me to a last reflection. Throughout this chapter, I have tried to show how the virtual artifact of memory animated for the 2010 anniversary was not a mere *mise en scene*. Rather, the digital technologies utilized through Facebook fit the demands of memory of that very specific time. The gesture of emptying profiles resonated productively with the expanded feelings of kinship that already circulated in the wider society. This fact speaks to the specificities of the demands of memory and how they intersect and get entangled in particular spaces and times. The Facebook campaign managed to reveal the textures of a particular stage in the process of public grief in contemporary Argentina through a specific use of emergent forms of global technology. The campaign also addressed the different levels of malleability involved in these technologies of remembering, the manners in which digital memories can travel across time, bridging bodies through different surfaces and materials. The shadowy figures that were once part of the *Siluetazo* in the early 1980s came to resonate in the silhouette-profiles that featured the 2010 Facebook campaign. These disparate episodes underscore the conviction that traumatic experiences can be shared. Ultimately, they help to build an affective assemblage of generative forms of memory that eludes official circuits, and rather points toward more fluid and expanded surfaces of the circulation of loss.

My reading of the 2010 campaign has aimed at exploring the expanded capacity of bodies to act upon others and be affected by evolving forms of digital memory. While contesting the exclusive sense of ownership championed by the "wounded family" in post-dictatorial Argentina, the Facebook initiative showed how the desire for memory could not be reduced to a mere property of the relatives, nor a painful duty imposed by the state. Under this light, memory emerges as malleable, always plural, co-constituted, and co-enacted through subtle modalities of attention across time (Blackman and Venn 2010). These messy, overlapping, and also contested operations of memory speak about the capacity of bodies to build new affiliations and attachments in response to violence and loss. They suggest a creative ontology to think the malleability of bodies "in multiple time-spaces, enfolding and unfolding across all the levels of matter," to use Patricia Clough's words (2007: 313). These operations of memory also address the shared condition of vulnerability and corporal interdependency of being together in grief.

In the wake of the 2010 anniversary, the pervasive demands of memory shaped an affective interaction that took over social media. Despite its frivolous appearance, it succeeded in constituting a singular moment of affirmation within an unstable choreography of loss. In so doing, it highlighted a queer system of kinship, which does not rely on blood but on non-normative forms of support, belonging, and care. Thus, the campaign also shed light on the set of unforeseen pleasures of being multiple in grief; mischievous vibrations that inundated the digital space through a voiceless and ecstatic call that invited one to surrender and embrace the place of the missing.

Notes

1. See Diana Taylor, *The Archive and the Repertoire. Performing Cultural Memory in the Americas* (Durham, NC and London: Duke University Press, 2003). In 1996, the Children of the Disappeared founded *HIJOS*, "Hijos por la Identidad y la Justicia contra el Olvido y el Silencio" (Children for Identity and Justice, against Forgetting and Silence).
2. I am indebted to David Eng's recent work to build my approach to post-dictatorial Argentina. See David Eng, *Feelings of Kinship* (Durham, NC: Duke University Press, 2010). For more on a queer reading to respond to Taylor's idea of DNA performance, see also Cecilia Sosa, "On Mothers and Spiders: A Face-to-Face Encounter with Argentina's Mourning," *Memory Studies* 4: 63–72.
3. This is in line with Judith Butler's early account of "queer": "Queer is not being lesbian, queer is not being gay. It is an argument against certain normativity." See Judith Butler, "The Desire for Philosophy," interview conducted by Regina Michalik and Lola Press (May 2001), http://www.lolapress.org/elec2/artenglish/butl_e.htm (accessed November 2, 2011).
4. I am referring to the work of Diana Taylor, Elizabeth Jelin, Judith Filc, Gabriela Nouzeilles, Ana Longoni, and Brenda Werth, among others.
5. The emergence of the organization Herman@s (The Siblings) seems to confirm the productivity of the familial frame as the motor of political activism.
6. See, for instance, Virginia Vecchioli, "La nación como familia. Metáforas políticas en el movimiento argentino por los derechos humanos," in *Cultura y política en etnografías sobre la Argentina,* ed. Sabina Frederic and Germán Soprano, pp. 241–70 (Buenos Aires: Universidad Nacional de Quilmes, 2005).
7. On September 25, 2003 during Kirchner's first speech in the United Nations General Assembly (UN), http://undiavolvimos.blogspot.com (accessed December 13, 2010).
8. In developing the concept of "happy narrative" to challenge conventional human rights discourses in Argentina, I am indebted to Sara Ahmed's recent critique of happiness. See Sara Ahmed, *The Promise of Happiness* (Durham, NC: Duke University Press, 2010).
9. In 2005, the Argentine Supreme Court declared the nullity of the laws of impunity, and prosecutions were allowed once again.

10. While the number of those missing is still under investigation, 30,000 is the number that the local human rights groups have utilized in their main political fight. The number has acquired a collective force within the wider society.
11. The artists were Rodolfo Aguerreberry, Julio Flores, and Guillermo Kexel. See Longoni, "Fotos y Siluetas: dos estrategias en la representacion de los desaparecidos," p. 4.
12. Ana Longoni "Fotos y Siluetas: dos estrategias en la representacion de los desaparecidos," in *Los desaparecidos en la Argentina. Memorias, representaciones e ideas* (1983–2008), Emilio Crenzel (comp.) (Buenos Aires: Biblos, 2010), 43–65. Here, I am quoting from the English version translated by Yaiza Herández in *Afterall* (Autumn/Winter 2010) http://www.afterall.org/journal/issue.25/photographs-and-silhouettes-visual-politics-in-the-human-rights-movement-of-argentina, pp. 1–7.
13. A group of descendants of the disappeared is trying to incorporate the category of "niño desaparecido-detenido" within the current legal framework, as promoted by Angela Urondo, leader of this initiative. See Victoria Ginzberg, "Por primera vez el Estado me está devolviendo algo," *Página 12*, http://www.pagina12.com.ar/diario/elpais/1-178549-2011-10-09.html (accessed October 12, 2011).
14. The exhibition was titled *The Disappeared* and brought together different works about disappearance in Latin America. As Bell explains, Fernando's brother Marcelo contributed to the exhibition with the image of his younger brother, which appeared alongside some video footage and family pictures of Fernando. See Bell, "On Fernando's Photograph," 80.
15. In fact, Hirsch's development of postmemory can be read in parallel with the idea of "prosthetic memory" proposed by Alison Landsberg. After all, they are both strategies to think different forms of transmission of trauma among non-related witnesses. See Alison Landsberg, *Prosthetic Memory: The Transformation of American Remembrance in the Age of Mass Culture* (New York: Columbia University Press, 2004).
16. Today, 1,424 military personnel are involved in cases all over the country (information provided by CELS).

References

Ahmed, Sara. 2010. *The Promise of Happiness*. Durham: Duke University Press.

Barthes, Roland. 1981. *Camera Lucida: Reflections on Photography*. Translated by Richard Howard. New York: Hill and Wang.

Bell, Vikki. 2010. "On Fernando's Photograph: The Biopolitics of *Aparición* in Contemporary Argentina." *Theory, Culture & Society* 27.4: 69–89.

Blackman, Lisa, and Couze Venn. 2010. "Affect." *Body & Society* 16.1: 7–28.

Butler, Judith. 2000. *Antigone's Claim: Kinship Between Life and Death*. New York: Columbia University Press.

———. 2004. *Precarious Life. The Powers of Mourning and Violence*. London: Verso.

———. 2005. *Giving an Account of Oneself*. New York: Fordham University Press.

———. 2009. *Frames of War. When is Life Grievable?* London: Verso.

Butler, Judith, and Regina Michalik. 2001. "The Desire for Philosophy." Interview conducted by Regina Michalik and Lola Press (May 2001). http://www.lolapress.org/elec2/artenglish/butl_e.htm (accessed November 2, 2011).

Casullo, Nicolás. 2004. *Pensar entre épocas.* Buenos Aires: Norma.

Clough, Patricia. 2007. "Biotechnology and Digital Information." *Theory Culture & Society* 24: 312–14.

Eng, David. 2010. *The Feeling of Kinship: Queer Liberation and the Racialization of Intimacy.* Durham, NC and London: Duke University Press.

Hirsch, Marianne. 2008. "The Generation of Postmemory." *Poetics Today* 29.1: 103–28.

————. 2012. *The Generation of Postmemory: Writing and Visual Culture after the Holocaust.* New York: Columbia University Press.

Jelin, Elizabeth. 1994. "The Politics of Memory: The Human Rights Movements and the Construction of Democracy in Argentina." *Latin American Perspectives* 21.2: 38–58.

————. 2008. "Victims, Relatives, and Citizens in Argentina: Whose Voice is Legitimate Enough?" In *Humanitarianism and Suffering: The Mobilization of Empathy,* edited by Richard A. Wilson and Richard D. Brown, pp. 175–201. Cambridge: Cambridge University Press.

Landsberg, Alison. 2004. *Prosthetic Memory: The Transformation of American Remembrance in the Age of Mass Culture.* New York: Columbia University Press.

Longoni, Ana. 2007. *Traiciones.* Buenos Aires: Grupo Editorial Norma.

————. 2010. "Photographs and Silhouettes: Visual Politics in the Human Rights Movement in Argentina." *Afterall* (Autumn/Winter): 1-7. Translated by Yaiza Herández. http://www.afterall.org/journal/issue.25/photographs-and-silhouettes-visual-politics-in-the-human-rights-movement-of-argentina.

Longoni, Ana, and Gustavo A. Bruzzone. 2008. *El Siluetazo.* Buenos Aires: Adriana Hidalgo.

Ridout, Nicholas. 2008. "Welcome to the Vibratorium." *Senses & Society* 3: 221–31.

Sosa, Cecilia. 2011. "On Mothers and Spiders. A Face-to-Face Encounter with Argentina's Mourning." *Memory Studies* 4: 63–72.

Taylor, Diana. 2003. *The Archive and the Repertoire. Performing Cultural Memory in the Americas.* Durham and London: Duke University Press.

Vecchioli, Virginia. 2005. "La nación como familia. Metáforas políticas en el movimiento argentino por los derechos humanos." In *Cultura y política en etnografías sobre la Argentina,* edited by Sabina Frederic and Germán Soprano, pp. 241–270. Buenos Aires: Universidad Nacional de Quilmes.

Vezzetti, Hugo. 1998. "Activismos de la memoria: el Escrache." *Punto de Vista* 62: 1–7.

Weiner, Joshua and Damon Young. 2011. "Queer Bonds." *GLQ: A Journal of Lesbian and Gay Studies* 17.2–3: 223–41.

Chapter 5

Learning by Heart
Humming, Singing, Memorizing in Israeli Memorial Videos

Laliv Melamed

In the sequence that ends *Always Ascending* (*Hemri La'Ad*, Chen Shelach, 2008), a film produced by the Shalev family in memory of their son, Nissan Shalev, the well-known Israeli singer Leah Shabat sits in the family living room with her guitar. At this point we understand that the series of guitar chords heard throughout the film were played by her, and here they are ultimately joined and attuned to a riff that opens one of her most famous songs, *Always Be Waiting for You.* Shalev's sisters sit next to her and tell her that a day before the funeral they heard the song and felt that it talked about their brother, that "it is written about him. *It is him.*" The singer then performs the song, and the sisters join her singing. The song's lyrics are about the anticipation for the return of a loved one, maybe a child, who has gone out to the world, to explore and experience it, and about the longing of the one who stayed behind. The singer's cracked baritone voice has a warm, soulful quality that intensifies the emotionality of the sequence. The sisters' voices stick to hers. They sing the song's refrain: "every plane passing in the sky, every star glowing in the eyes, reminds me of you. A wagtail before it showers, crickets in the evening hours, will always be waiting for you."[1] The sisters sing, laughing and crying at the same time. Their singing bridges a few shots in which Shalev's father and brother speak about his constant presence in their life, even after his death. The sisters' singing, repeating the refrain (and the song's name) "will always be waiting for you," and their simultaneous laughter and crying brings the film to a bittersweet ending. Sweet, since it concludes all the joy and kindness that were specific to Shalev, and bit-ter, because he is now dead.

The sequence has two objectives. First, the few not yet fully articu-lated guitar notes that were played in the background throughout the film are now joined to a theme, which conveys longing, love, and the depar-ture of a dear one. Similarly, this scene, situated at the end of the film, binds together all aspects and memories of Shalev recalled in the film, expressing an ever-growing love and an ever-growing pain. This binding, this bringing to a closure, is manifested not by a last word, the finality of the period or the cut, but by a shared singing that is interrupted by laugh-ter and crying, and the reverberating echo of a musical note. Second, the song registers the specific and private memory of Shalev (it is "written about him") in a public text, a popular song that was played on the radio repeatedly. The song, which is public, general, and shared by all, incites something that for the ears and hearts of Shalev's lovers was singular to him. This emanates from the capacity of the lover to envision his or her loved one in anything or anyone—every plane that passes, every star that glows—the capacity to spot and mark as singular and irreplaceable a specific subject of love. Additionally, this derives from the ability of popular music to sound as if it was directed towards and playing espe-cially for you, accurately voicing what you want to say, providing it with the exact emotional tonality.

The aptitude of this last sequence to implant the very private image of Nissan Shalev in the widely popular song, and thus to render him memorable and commemorated in a public sphere, is emblematic of the film's entire work. Nissan Shalev died in August 2006 during the Israel-Hezbollah War also known as the July War or Lebanon War. He was a helicopter pilot whose helicopter crashed after being hit by a missile. After his death his family decided to make a film. They hired a freelance filmmaker, interviewed friends and family members, sorting through sto-ries and anecdotes from varying perspectives, and collected a variety of visual materials and memorabilia: still images, home movies, voice re-cordings, letters, emails, text messages, and even Shalev's belongings—which with his death became dysfunctional yet sentimental objects. They faced the camera and told about Shalev—who he was, his life story, and his unique charm. They selected musical themes, which were based on Shalev's taste, or themes that became charged bearers of meaning with their loss. The film is a familial production, an intimate project which ar-ticulates love and affinity, in which professional filmmaking is limited to the role of the "for hire" filmmaker, who is ultimately a technical means in the hands of the film's real author, the family itself. The film's topic is the private individual "Nissan Shalev," and the film's subjects consciously draw the line between national and militant slogans and Shalev's authentic and irreproducible sphere of subjectivity ("He wasn't a soldier," they say on a few occasions, "he didn't like the army and didn't want to stay there"). Lastly, the film was meant for domestic use, for the family's own practice of mourning. This situates the film in the sphere of semi-amateur and domestic film production—a definition I will shortly broaden and discuss. Allegedly, the film's speech—its literal act of storytelling, but also its forms of expression and organization—has nothing to tell us about larger social, cultural, and political registers. It is an exchange of memories and feelings among a very intimate, sore collective. However, the film, like many other intimate and domestic memorials, won a form of publicity by being broadcasted on Israeli television Channel 10 during Memorial Day 2008 (and every Memorial Day since).

The presence of such an intimate and personal expression, which insists on being singular and individuated and resists being generalized or summed up by slogans, sheds light on the far-reaching entanglement of affect and politics, subjectivity and ideology. Additionally, it illuminates the ways in which film—its techniques and poetics—enables a certain exchange between the singular and the collective, which is moving, touching and affecting. This is not to say that we can delineate two separate spheres: "private" and "public." On the contrary, close examination of strategies and forms of articulating intimate memories in the ears of the general public exposes the multileveled architecture that mutually designs these two spheres. This chapter focuses on a specific cinematic strategy that is key to understanding the mobilization and orchestration of meaning, one that is crucial in its affect, and, to my view, under-researched in the field of memory studies: the musical soundtrack. I address "music" as cinematic because my analysis situates itself in the indivisible mixing, and the structural matching, of the two, and my interest is directed toward what is cinematic in (specific) music, or what is musical in (specific) cinema. This study interrogates such aesthetic organization as a practice of remembering, employing two levels of analysis: the phenomenological approach, centering on experience and perception, and the ideological approach, dwelling in the larger frames of meaning and interpellation in which experience and perception take place. An amalgamation of features such as tonality, rhythm, pitch, and rhyming, popular music will be addressed here as a practice of memorizing and remembering. Scrutinizing domestic memorial videos[2] produced in Israel during the early 2000s to commemorate dead soldiers, this chapter examines what music summons, voluntarily and involuntarily, how it applies and inscribes specific melodies and sounds to subjects and landscapes, and how it charges them with myth and symbolism. Reorienting the prevalent hierarchy in which music is a background ornament for the image, an amplifier of the image's arrangement and content, this chapter will investigate the use of popular songs as an aesthetic and communicative agent in the text, that is, as a dynamic and multilayered memory practice that imbricates the personal with the political, the non-professional with the official, and the popular with the ideal.

Before delving into the ways in which musical choices in domestic productions play into the politics of memory and forgetting in Israel, I would like to illuminate how the private is separated from the public and how this separation is politically structured. Such a binary system which is at work here is not only a product of socio-political specificities, but is also located in methodological structures in the field of film and media theory and industry.

The Category of the Domestic and the Politics of Affective Memories

In Memorial Day's television programming schedule—a format of public agenda, as well as a platform of publicness[3]—videos like *Always Ascending,* produced by families to commemorate an individual loved one, are exposed to the Israeli public under the category of "domestic memorials."[4] This broadcasting policy has existed since the mid 1990s. A well-established and well-maintained tradition of commemorating individuals has existed in Israel since its earliest decades in the form of memorial albums and films produced either by public television, the Ministry of Defense, or the Israeli Defense Force (IDF). These official productions utilize the life and death of an individual to create a national mythology of heroism, to write a collective biography, to unite the nation, with its different sectors, in death (or mourning), to produce a sense of necessity, and to justify the ongoing militancy of Israeli society through the rhetoric of survival, protection, and high ideals. Memorial videos indicate a historical shift in the discourse of commemoration in Israel, where the production, archivization, and articulation of memory move out of the hands of official authorities and are embraced by the bereaved family itself.

This gradual shift is rooted in a change in the national practice of commemoration, a radical transformation in the Israeli media sphere, and a technological change that has simultaneously affected both the film industry and the field of familial communication and documentation. Following the 1982 Lebanon War and the first Intifada in 1988, two events that are considered extremely controversial in Israeli history, the national practice of commemoration was defined as "a-political." Political debates about the causes and necessity of war, and about the immorality of IDF soldiers that emerged at that time had been denounced as staining the memory of the dead and violating the sanctity of the day. As the historical narratives and the events of war became more controversial, the tone and form of mourning and memory was rendered personal and "private." In addition, a series of training accidents, omissions, and controversies related to the handling of soldiers' corpses and burial procedures, together with waning public support for the IDF's continued presence in the south of Lebanon—a presence that during the 1990s resulted in an increasing number of casualties—fractured the consensus that the Israeli public had toward the place of the army in the social structure of the state. By the early 1990s, Israeli television had shifted from a public- and state-owned single channel to a multi-channel commercial model. This opening up of the media market also changed the nature of the national public sphere produced by television. National publicness was merchandised and individualized. Commercial television's programming rationale and financing structure found the broadcasting of domestic productions which are produced—and funded—by the private sector to be a functional (and extremely cheap) solution for a national day of mourning when advertising or commercial content is banned. Thus, on the side of the transmitting entities, a space and a programming slot had become available for such intimate memories. Lastly, the emergence of video technology on the domestic market during the 1980s, which drastically reduced production costs, made domestic documentation more accessible. A shift in Israel's economic model, which carved a new space for such commodities in the private sphere, as well as a change in the role of the individual as a central agent in society and the rejection of more collective scenarios also affected the extent to which the family had become a documented and documenting entity.

Domestic memorials entail many aspects of the D.I.Y. production.[5] They are assembled through intimate recollection and threads of affinity. What is recalled is not the soldier as an avatar of the larger collective, but the person him or herself, a specific individual, a singular, irreplaceable, particular lost loved one. Such a call for memorialization, invested with intimate feelings, is inseparable from its affiliation with the domestic. The domestic film/video is a product that *allegedly* exists outside the official mechanisms and apparatuses of knowledge.[6] It is a part of the family's internal project of self-documentation. First steps of a baby, a boy in a swimming suit on the beach in summer, family gatherings at the dinner table, graduations, weddings, birthdays, holidays: family documentation documents the family life and adheres only to the interests of the subjects involved. As such, it addresses the mundane, prosaic, and even uninteresting, all obscured by the over-specification, or extra-standardization of the subjects and events. Hence, the documented events, being part of the standard family routine, are to a certain extent uninteresting to those outside the close family circle. On the other hand, if they do offer some interest this remains opaque due to the intimacy and specificity of the act of documentation. In such productions, the documenting drive, which Bill Nichols terms epistephilia (1991),[7] is not about gaining knowledge—in any case, not empirical or historical knowledge. The act of documentation that enables the domestic production is charged with libidinal impulses: to document something or someone in order to capture, to record, to trace and catalogue every movement or expression, to cherish and store moments and phases. This is documentation as an act of love, as a memory that dwells in the heart. We describe such choices—which do not follow a logical formulation but spring from an emotional intensity—as intuitive or impulsive. Marianne Hirsch defines looking at family photographs (even if the viewer is not a member of the family) as affiliative and identificatory, as evolving around the act of recognition: to recognize and to be recognized, "a moment of self-recognition, a moment of self-discovery, a discovery of a self in relation" (Hirsch 1997: 2). Such recognition activates a call to protect and respect precarious throbs of affinity and impulses of feelings that one identifies in the images. Thus, the domestic production is, in its scene of conceiving, an intimate and obscure act, exchanged among exclusive members. When publicly exposed, it bears an affective signature of being in relation, and imparts a sense of nostalgia and sentimentality.[8]

Before subscribing to such sentimental premises, we must first delineate the ideological foundations of the domestic image. Family footage does not necessarily promise an authentic representation of the family, but rather an aesthetic means through which the family is arranged according to social and cultural ideals, and one which is extremely euphemistic, largely omitting difficult feelings. Domestic documentation does not develop separately from the visual commercial discourse of family life; it draws its aesthetic ideas and compositions from magazines, films, and television shows. All depict the family as a space of certain hierarchies and morals, of chastity, order, and specific gender, multi-generational, and economic arrangements.[9] Patricia Zimmermann demonstrates how domestic productions, defined as amateurish, were re-formulated in reaction to professional filmmaking (1995). Zimmermann traces the term "amateur" back to nineteenth-century capitalism, when it was constructed against "professionalism," separating a rationalized form of work from all that is expelled from the workplace: passion, autonomy, creativity, imagination, domesticity, and family life. Consequently, such separation is not a matter of aesthetic or technological determination but bears political implications of what constitutes "public" and what is expelled from it, namely domesticity, familiality, and feelings. Lastly, with the development and standardization of domestic documentation, a vast grey area that lies between the professional and non-professional has emerged. Populated with professionally trained freelance filmmakers who produce domestic, semi-commercial, and industrial films, this emerging industrial and economic category indeed troubles existing typology. Productions administrated by filmmakers who have the training and means are now allocated as domestic. On the other hand, the rapid development of digital media and the increasing accessibility of visual technology in the last three decades opened the field to almost anyone interested in experiencing it. Such accessibility is not limited to means, but also applies to aesthetic knowledge and sensitivities. All this must shed new light on the discursive construction of domestic documentation and its link to the ideological formation of the private domain. However, because of the exclusion of such documentations from official, academic, commercial, and professional discourses of filmmaking, these mutual effects and links between the domestic and the professional are never fully articulated. More importantly, the rendering of a film/video "domestic" situates it outside aesthetic, critical, commercial, and even economical discourses, *hence positioning it outside the political order.*[10] This separation has had a determinate effect on the memory of dead soldiers in Israel—on its production and functioning—over the last two decades. In sum, the category of the domestic must be approached as a discursive construction that entails a political affect.

Melodizing a Lost Loved One: Music as an Aesthetic Arrangement of Feelings, and Politics

After re-orienting the domestic production and uncovering its political grounds, the question of feelings, implied or explicitly expressed by the domestic image and its circumstances of production, still remains. While this work supports the notion that there is an indeterminate sphere of subjectivity and firsthand experience that is informed by an insurmountable love, it is concerned with the ways subjective feelings or biographical experiences are channeled through ideological formations and participate in political acts. As argued, domestic productions have no place in, and bear no interest for, the public, *unless* they are framed and arranged according to larger ideological forms and in relation to official historical narratives. Thus the domestic production is never simply an authentic representation of familial love, assumed to be universal and shared by all. It is always implicated in more specific socio- and geo-political contexts. There is always a form of mediation and aesthetic arrangement that transforms the domestic production from a raw piece of connectedness to a form which bears meaning in larger social spheres. Music is such a mode of arrangement, one which is extremely nuanced and complex.

A common trait of domestic videos commemorating a dead loved one is stitching together talking heads that tell us about the dead with a flow of still or video images, accompanied by popular songs.[11] The marrying of popular songs with materials that were unprofessionally or domestically produced, and indeed belong to the intimate, turns the videos into communicative and affective texts. While such recalling of memories can be fragmentary and sporadic, music bridges the different interviews and images and supports the breaking down of the video into chapters or life phases, creating a smooth transition and bundling all the different memories, thus working as a structuring element within the video.[12] In addition, music produces ambiance, providing a theme and sentiment, illustrating and refining the video's emotional volume, and underscores the tone of each memory. Music is also used to express what language might fail to utter, to "speak" when there are no more words, when the speaker cannot complete the sentence and fails to assemble intense feelings into the concrete rationale of language. On the filmmaker's side, the musical choices stem from a more internal motivation that intuitively connects the musical theme with one's experiences, memories, and feelings of love and loss. Music is a channel of communication: from the private to the public, from the specific to the general, from the emotional to the informative. By not being a-priori verbal, it allows this transformation to be opened up to the affective, associative, and intuitive. The music thus produces a libidinal sphere of connectedness in which spectatorship transcends political implications and is able attend to "pure" feelings. This aptitude is what I wish to unpack.

My interest in the ways in which music arranges and recalls memories has been sparked by my own experience of spectatorship. After a day of viewing all memorial videos broadcasted on channels 10 and 2 during Memorial Day 2008, I realized, while walking home, that I was humming a song.[13] John Mowitt argues that the haunting melody, the non-verbal humming of a song that sneaks in and sticks, is not committed to a conscious memory; it haunts because one actually forgot that one heard it.[14] Thus, the haunting melody is the remembering of forgetting, an involuntary memory that resides in the unconsciousness. This emanates from music's capacity to "speak directly to our unconscious," to communicate something which is beyond language and therefore to suggest a different mode of perception.[15] Arthur Schopenhauer has suggested that music is metaphysic, abstract, beyond words, and affective.[16] The image, on the other hand, is physical, conscious, and constitutes experience and knowledge. In memorial videos the image of the talking head who tells a story and articulates difficult feelings is central. Our interpretive faculties are attuned to empathy, to respond to the image's call to be listened to and to be acknowledged. Such a mode of listening situates speech at the center of a rationalized process of producing ethical bonds, with music as a background tuning of emotional intensity. Considering the non-verbal, the tonal, and the melodic, music is understood as an abstract, formless force that sneaks in. However, the summoning of a melody provides rhythm and structure. Repeating it conjures something familiar, recognizable, and common. The rhythmical repetition that allegedly repeats a non-verbal melody is, by its internalizing and reproduction, a mnemonic act.[17]

Melody No. 1: A Tone of Fatal Destiny and Embattlement

The haunting melody belongs to the song *How Shall I Bless Him* ("Ma Averech Lo"), a song that was played in at least three of the videos I saw that day. The song is related to a very specific moment in Israeli history. It was written and composed right after the 1967 war, which is associated with the height of Israeli imperialism. The song was performed by the Navy Military Band and its soloist Rivka Zohar. It was written by Rachel Shapira as a response to a classmate's death in the war, and was composed by Yair Rosenblum, who was a key figure in military folk-pop ensembles. The song has a cyclic arrangement divided into five stanzas and arranged in pairs (a1-b1-a2-b2-a3-b3 and so on). The musical composition is thus extremely repetitive, presenting one pattern divided into two sections responding to each other, repeated five times until it ascends and breaks at the end. The harmony is simple and diatonic with a basic four on four rhythmic structure. All these aspects turn the song into a catchy and coherent mechanism that is liable to stick or to be remembered.

What is easily recited and rehearsed is the tune. The lyrics, although less memorable, are already implied in the melodic arrangement, carrying with them aspects of rhyming, timbre, and gradation of pitching. In addition, the lyrics are memory-applicable since they are sung by a human voice, which addresses us with its fragility, uniqueness, and subjectivity. The first part of the first stanza is sung by the chorus and tells of an angel asking with what to bless a child. It is answered by the soloist, who sings of the child's curious eyes, heart, and smile. Every stanza opens with the chorus repeating precisely the same question. The soloist sings about the boy's dancing legs and attuning ears, about the youth's strong arms and legs, which handle steel and conquer lands. When it comes to the blessing of a young man, the soloist repeats the blessings, asking what more can one ask, which leads to the fifth stanza and the song's climax. The chorus repeats the question once again, as the soloist's voice ascends and dramatizes, singing "Oh Lord, Oh Lord, Oh Lord, if you only blessed him with life." The lyrics sketch a model of what had become deterministic for Israeli youth. The growing up of a child, full of curiosity and love toward the world, to become a man who channels his physical strength and joyful potency to acts of love and beauty such as dancing, or acts of care and responsibility, such as bravely protecting his nation, which ultimately leads to a tragic end. The song narrates a collective and deterministic tragedy.

The military pop-folk ensemble (Lehaka Tzva'it) filled a musical niche in Israel between the mid 1950s and mid 1970s. Its members were eighteen- to twenty-one-year-old soldiers during their mandatory military service. On the one hand, these ensembles represented the army and the state and worked in the service of the state's ideology; on the other hand they appealed to young audiences as they drew on universal pop and rock culture. The military ensembles had the functional role of providing light entertainment for IDF soldiers. Their less explicit role emerged from the 1950s need to integrate the sons and daughters of recent immigrants into the social texture of the young state while constructing a sense of Israeliness—a collective identity that is organic and relies on a shared and desirable cultural currency (Regev and Seroussi 2004). The military ensembles were renowned for poppy and catchy midtempo ballads that talked about the utopian and naïve hope to end war and to live in peace. The call for peace became a relatively common expression of national aspirations in times when the state of Israel had administrated an oppressive and brutal occupation. In this context, it carried with it late-sixties "hippie" clichés of peace and love. This demonstrates the constant negotiation and, consequently, the epistemological dislocation of national ideology under the guise of universal pop; in other words, the re-dressing of vernacular statements of nationhood with the ornament of foreign tones which seduce the listener with its cosmopolitan decor. Another mode of arrangement that bears ideological and collective significance is the use of the chorus in producing a collective voice. Many of the military ensembles' songs were so catchy and simple that they encouraged people to sing along and thus to identify themselves with the song while joining in a collective act of singing. A musical and theatrical tradition positions the chorus in analogy to the audience, which represents the popular and authentic spirit of the people. Hence, while the main conflict is tossed between high ideals and distinct powers (the state, Gods, morals, humanity), the chorus vocalizes the input of the general public, thus grounding and internalizing an individuated and elaborate story in a social and collective voice.[18]

A notion of universal up-to-dateness is inscribed in the song's composition. The song replicates a popular formula, starting with a rapid organ riff, and the setting up of a half tone midway into the song, which produces a mode of intensification and emotional climaxing, industrially termed "the money note." Lastly, two-thirds into the song, an additional dramatic ornament is presented when the soloist recites the fourth stanza instead of singing it, using a pre-rap mode. However, the song also contains an archaic aspect enabled by its folk elements. It follows a classic and simple structure that allows the song to be shared and to become collective. Such simplicity speaks to the notion of familiarity and tradition. The opening riff has a guitar and flute in it, portable instruments which are associated with folk music and biblical landscapes of hills and meadows. Folk music implies the connection of a people to a place through a coded message of rootedness. Indeed, Zionism aspired to produce a new Jewish pioneer who is implicated in an ancient connectedness to a land. Such an organic connection was structured and formed through cultural means, mainly music and dance, which emphasized physicality (Neumann 2009).

A way to read the political aspect of the combination of folk and pop is granted when associating it with a cinematic genre, which again entails a certain dislocation. The flute solo at the opening riff of "Ma Averech Lo" cites a famous tune known as "Apache" or the "Apache Mode" which was later adopted by early funk and hip hop music.[19] The "Apache Mode" was inspired by the 1954 American Western *Apache,* directed by Robert Aldrich. The musical theme shares many compositional elements with 1960s and 1970s Spaghetti Western soundtracks composed by Ennio Morricone for the films of Sergio Leone. The Spaghetti Western, similar to the folk-pop military ensembles ballad, was a popish and up-to-date version of an established genre, embedded in the 1960s and 1970s cultural climate.[20] The original format, the Western, is a generic model which recalls the myth of populating an unpopulated land, of bringing civilization and order, of the emerging of society according to certain ideals, while negotiating tensions among the wild, the archaic, and the progressive. The Spaghetti Western, also known as "the Italian Western" or the "Continental Western," readopted the myth, while slightly dislocating it, turning the "West" into a multi-continental sign. Going back to

Israel, I have already suggested that, regarding Zionism, what is at stake is the myth of civilization and the emerging of a society organically connected to an archaic landscape. Another aspect to consider here is the growing cultural and political ties between Israel and the United States in this historically critical moment of 1967. If we wish to further stretch this reading, while the popish element in "Ma Averech Lo" evidenced the influences of American pop culture on Israeli youth culture, its opening theme also brought with it scents of American imperialism soon to be adopted by the Israeli state.

This example is illustrative and general. It shows the nuanced ideological implications music brings with it. Such implications are not to be located only in the communicative aspect of the lyrics, of what the song clearly says, but also in the song's forms of arrangement and constructions—in its composition. The melody that uninvitedly sticks brings with it a set of references and citations, entangled in a set of dislocations, so that we forget that we remember them. To add another dislocation or distancing of this theme from its ideological volume, the videos that used the song did not use the original and well-known performance, but a quieter version which further amplifies the song's tragic story. In taming the popish and catchy elements—the organ, the tempo, the chorus—the ideological construction and national theme are further disguised and suppressed. However, I would like to consider two specific examples in which the music is also assigned to images.

Melody No. 2: A Tone of a Place and Displacement

The first example is taken from a video about Tzur Zarhi who died in 2006 in Lebanon. The twenty-minute-long video was simply titled *Tzur Zarhi* and broadcasted on Israeli channel 10 on Memorial Day 2008. It does not indicate its author but briefly thanks Mark Miller, who edited the film. The video has a raw quality. It gives an impression of an immediate, almost unmediated response to death, which resonates with its release shortly after the war. It presents a collection of home movies and still photographs, with no dialogue or narration, arranged in a fragmentary manner, which seem to follow an obscure internal rationale. Watching the film feels like browsing through a family album without knowing any of the subjects involved. *Tzur Zarhi*'s process of production was indeed intimate and domestic. Zarhi's parents collected all kinds of audiovisual materials on their son. Together, they organized, catalogued, and queued the materials. Zarhi's mother, who was mostly invested in choosing the musical themes, perceived music to have "the most affective impact."[21]

Here, music spoke directly to an insurmountable pain, articulating, for the mother, a sentiment that she could not verbalize. Music was doing the work of interviews or narration that the Zarhi family decided to avoid. The video's soundtrack is a realm of shared meaning. While some visual and editorial choices remain obscure or arbitrary, the musical themes are what organize and narrativize the video. Composed of folk songs and encoding a nostalgic sentiment of the simple, earthly Israel, the soundtrack acts as a common ground and provides a sense of typicality that communicates and contextualizes the specificity of the images produced in and for the domestic domain.

The sequence I wish to investigate is the one ending the video. What structures this sequence, as a distinguished thematic unit, is the song that accompanies it—*Fields in the Valley.* The song has a minor sound and ends gloomily with its last chord set down by a tone. The sequence starts with a title of a date—apparently that of Zarhi's death—and a collection of still and moving images of tanks in action and aerial shots that indicate the location of Zarhi's tank on the day of the incident. In addition to the opening notes of the song—deep and dark tones of a French horn—we hear Zarhi speaking on the tank's radio.[22] This mini-sequence fades out to a few still images of Zarhi in uniforms, then moves to a long shot of Zarhi's house, to his farm and the dairy barn. As a form of an epilogue which concludes Zarhi's unfulfilled life, the sequence then lays out a collage of still and moving images: Zarhi as a baby, a bright-eyed child, a young boy who shyly smiles at the camera, at various ages wearing Purim costumes, with his sisters, with his parents, an adolescent, sitting with his family for dinner. The sequence ends with a tracking shot passing by Zarhi's farm. The sweeping, almost directionless, movement of the camera does not indicate any bodily presence, or any point of view. The shot, termed a "ghost ride" in cinematic parlance, portrays the landscape as emptiness and void, as pure movement. This morbid portrayal brings the video to an end, signed with a still image of Zarhi on an agricultural ATV (All Terrain Vehicle).

Before unpacking the kind of work music performs in the video, I would like to attend to its coupling with another affective agency, the amateur family footage. The amateur family footage is signaled here by specific aesthetic characteristics. The quality of the image—the grayish light and interlacing effects (transmitting disturbances) of video—is immediately associated with the texture of the domestic. This notion of rawness, the unpolishedness, or even non-aesthetic signature of the domestic footage often tolerates un-centered framing, jerking camera movements, non-dynamic cinematic language lacking any camera movements or camera angles, unfocused and blurry imagery, and the implications of a lack of planning and directing as well as haphazard and arbitrary aesthetic decisions. The domestic production is often episodic and brief. It has minimal, if any, cuts and draws on a very basic editing or narrative rationale. The succession or sequencing of images is not necessarily a mode of variation or intensification, so that any cut has a role and is distinct from its former. Instead, the editing seems, at times, random and non-linear.[23] As argued earlier, the image can be obscure and, as spectators who are external to the intimate familial scene, we can never gain full access to what it actually says—who are the subjects in the image, what was the specific event. And yet, recognizing it as a family or domestic image brings with it an entire set of emotional references. Indeed, the sequence has many fragmentary images that do not tell a story, but lay out a texture of familial life and love. Even the short depiction of the incident in which Zarhi died, although drawing on non-familial images such as the military aerial shot, is tremendously incomprehensible and non-communicative. I would like to show how the music re-contextualizes such internal sets of memories.

Fields in the Valley was written in 1937 by the poet Levi Ben Amitai and composed by Efraim Ben Haim, both of whom immigrated to Israel during the 1920s as part of a wave of Zionist immigration. The lyrics portray the poet's profound ardor and visceral sense of connection to the Jezreel Valley. The song was written upon the return of the poet to the valley after a period of being away. It expresses his longing and the joy of reuniting with the Valley's landscape, odors, and melodies. The return is described as adhering to a deterministic, spiritual bond. Such spirituality is engraved in materiality: the valley's fields, fertilizers, hay, wheat, water. This joy of reunification with the valley's fields is celebrated by the lover with a hymn. The sentiments depicted are immersed in notions of death and redemption. The land embraces the lover, blesses him, and redeems him. This text is emblematic of conceptions of the land among Zionist immigrants in the 1920s and 30s: the love of the land and its conquering through hard work, through a visceral connection with its materiality, and through dancing and singing. It articulates Zionist aspirations for an emancipated new Jewish subjectivity, which is strong and omnipotent, and which is grounded in, and materialized through, corporeal ties to a land, a place, a reproductive sphere, and a language, represented here by the form of the poem (Neumann 2009).

Zarhi was a third-generation dairy farmer from Nehallal, a village in Jezreel Valley. While such a specific geographic link was not necessarily conscious, a similar notion of connectedness to a land is recalled by the fragmented images of Zarhi that situate him in a landscape—hiking, standing in an open plain overlooking his surroundings, and in the fields on his ATV. This adds to a thematic throb in the video that emphasizes Zarhi's dedication to and love for his work as a dairy farmer. This theme connects him to traditional forms of labor. The conception of landscape as a corporeal and physical sphere of materialization and incarnation is not singular to Zarhi's video. Memorial videos are notably occupied with fetishistic images of landscape. First, as implied by the sequencing of tanks puncturing grassy fields, military aerial shots, and Zarhi on his farmer's ATV, there is an indivisible link between land and life, land and death. The landscape is the same as, or very similar to, the place where the soldier died. However, the landscape is also a synecdoche for everything that is worth dying for: life, belonging, collectivity, identity. It is a site of youth and liveliness resurrecting a space of activity and competency: mountains to climb, rivers to cross, the sea to swim in or play on its beaches, scenery to conquer by gaze. The landscape is a geographical expression of typicality: this grassy hill, or desert crater, is Israel; it is a sentimental sphere of incorporation and containment that creates historical continuity. Lastly, grass, sand, rocks, and water are material, in contrast to memories, feelings, and yearnings. The landscape as setting serves as the means of resurrection and justification. It is a place where memory is registered and possibly materialized. This embodiment of landscape—and the rendering somatic of memory in landscape—claims rights on the territory. Through this organic link and the visceral belonging to a place, ideology is reinforced.

The physical and visceral connection to the land, which is emphasized by the lyrics, positions the song as a hymn to the valley, as a poetic arrangement of the valley's visions and sounds. Thus, the song is conceived as articulating what is indigenous and vernacular. This provokes the question: what is the indigenous sound of the land? Early Zionist folk songs adopted compositional elements or simply entire versions of Eastern European and specifically Russian folk music. This is indicative of the origin of their composers, the Zionist pioneers. The song's composition follows a schema of a modernist art-song, which is presented with a few oriental ornaments that breach the diatonic structure. The mixture of West and East was typical in this genre of songs.[24] This schema of arrangement sums up the way Zionism has constructed indigenousness and vernacularism. Again, the signification of the place as Jewish, Hebrew, Israeli involves a sense of dislocation. The adoption of the oriental ornament exposes the extent to which the link between the idea of Israel and its actual place is non-organic.[25] Structured by music, the memory of the dead Tzur Zarhi resides in a visceral connection between a subject and a place, which recalls the memory of another place, imbricating it in and charging it with a geo-political context.

Being an internal product of mourning that waives any formal and
aesthetic tropes of knowledge production, such as the interview, narration, or structured editing rationale, the video seems to lack any public
register. As broadcast content, it runs the danger of being too private,
too internal. However, in matching the familial amateur footage with the
musical theme, Zarhi's own biography is rewritten here as belonging to
a genealogy and a tradition of Zionist settlements. But, the song is not
the sole bearer of historical volume. Historicity is encoded in the footage
and allows an outside spectator, who saw the video on television, to construct a coherent narrative. The footage shows Zarhi on a trip to Poland
to visit concentration camps,[26] in a Purim costume, in IDF uniform, all
tied to larger cultural typicalities. The short arrangement that portrays
Zarhi's death corresponds with a notion of death that is present both in
the song's lyrics and composition, suggesting that the redemption by the
land can be fatal and self-consuming. Such meta-textual dialogue frames
the individual loss within a larger ideological determinism.

Melody No. 3: A Tone of De-politicizing and De-militarizing the National Death

A significant number of songs used in memorial videos' soundtracks are
in Hebrew, and most of them become associated with a defined sub-cate-
gory of songs played in times of national commemoration and emergency.
Such songs draw on cultural references that condition notions of mourning and urgency. Danny Kaplan notes that this category is not exclusive
to songs that are intimately linked with certain ideological traditions and
highly nationally charged moments in Israeli history but also incorporates
contemporary Israeli pop and rock (2009: 313–45). Pop and rock music,
"with its universalistic, individualistic and in times rebellious" characteristics, becomes a "vehicle for national indoctrination" (319), due to its
systematic broadcasting in days of mourning and emergency. Kaplan, researching Israeli radio broadcasting, terms such systematic broadcasting
"political engineering." Motti Regev argues that although rock music is
associated with a "cosmopolitan orientation," it is "constantly being incorporated into the nationalistic context in a process of 'Israelisation'" (1996:
279). Regev indicates that Israeli rock and pop musicians are marked in
the Israeli public sphere as graduates of dominant socialization tracks.
During the 1970s, and to some extent even today, the military ensembles
served as a training ground as well as a significant arena of networking for
many Israeli musicians. Emerging in the 1970s, Israeli rock adopted elements from Israeli folk music, which was part of the musicians' "musical

biography." Regev also notes that rock composition contains an exchange between rock elements and what is "perceived as personal idiosyncratic and local" (1996: 280), namely traditional Israeli folk.

The last example examines the use of a song that does not dwell on an intrinsic understanding of indigenousness and is far removed from the ideological project of producing a sense of a place, a language, and a locally defined identity. *A Touch of an Angel and His Smile* (produced and broadcasted in 2007), a video about Guy Golan, a navy commando soldier who died in Ansaria, Lebanon in 1997,[27] presents a range of musical themes, most of them released during the 1990s. The video was produced as part of the project *Remember with Love,* initiated by the Israeli television network *Reshet,* in which families organize a collection of queued materials and, together with a network executive, prepare a list of themes, emphases, and musical choices. These are later sent to an editor who edits them together. In some cases the family produces new materials—mainly interviews—especially for the video and collects materials which exceed, or are located outside, its own private collection of albums and home movies. Such materials include news segments which report the incident in which their son died or footage of military training as well as graduation and commemoration rituals taken from military film archives. These materials, which at face value are public, general, and official, become meaningful items in the family album. *A Touch of an Angel and His Smile* is a considerably affective collection of such materials. The video contains a mosaic of still images, home movies, letters, eulogies, family and friends' recollections of their intimate memories of Golan, entwined with television news reportage, and documentation facilitated by Golan's unit, including the launch of an under-water monument for Golan and his teammates who died in the Ansaria incident.

Golan's parents do not address the camera directly to speak about their son or about their feelings of loss. Their personal sense of loss and agonizing pain is vocalized throughout the film in several indirect ways. The music, more specifically the singing in the video's musical themes, is an important cinematic means to facilitate this intermediate "speech." The video uses two songs from the Israeli singer Evyatar Banai's début album. Upon its release, the album was marked as innovative with its bold intimacy and songs that expressed bare impulses of anger, betrayal, desire, desperate love, and fear. The dominant sound of the album is Banai's piano playing and his unique voice. Banai sings with the song and against it, he reaches high tones and then breaks; his voice is strained and tender, suggesting plea and anger. He creates carnal intimacy, an almost excessive closeness. The minimal musical arrangement exposes Banai to the listener; his piano playing is aggressive and passionate. Banai's lyrics con-

note a cosmopolitan existential melancholia of urban life, of self-aware-
ness, and of nuanced emotional scale.

The specific sequence starts with the stiff playing of the few chords that
open Banai's song *Fathers and Sons*. The lyrics depict the dramatic and
complex relationship between parents and children. The visuals show the
spectacular sinking of an old vessel, which now lies at the bottom of one
of Israel's beaches. The vessel contains 12 empty chairs, each inscribed
with the name of one of the soldiers who died in this specific incident.
The footage goes on to show the vessel disappearing beneath the water,
the rippling of the waves, and the marking of the water in which the vessel
is buried with a big arrangement of flowers. Underwater images show the
plaque that announces the incident's details and then cut to Golan's empty
chair with a plaque carrying his name. After this cut, the music is added
with another sound channel of a woman's voice reading a eulogy written
by Golan's father. The footage cuts to a brief image of the Golan family
during the days of mourning that followed Golan's death. It then cuts back
to a poetic image of flowers thrown at the waves and carried by the water.
The female voice says, "I apologize, Guy, if I ever hurt you, if this was so,
it was unintentional, it was only because we loved you. Farewell Guy, my
beloved son, save me a spot close to you in heaven. Love, Dad." The song
takes over. Banai's voice ascends and intensifies. He sings about the difficulty of seeing one's mother in pain. "Who could she blame? Who can I
blame? Father is crying over a son is crying over a father." Simultaneously,
the visuals briefly show Golan's mother and then go back to the spread of
flowers rocking on the waves.

The cinematic language here corresponds with a cinematic melodramatic tradition. The video depicts an injured familial tissue when the bearer
of the melodramatic sensation— of impossible pain—is the mother. Additionally, the sequence is imbued with a sense of loss that aligns it with
the melodramatic temporality of "too late-ness." Like in the melodrama,
certain elements—flowers and water—become instrumentalized in expressing excessive feelings. The reverberating quality of the voice and the
waves, and the ephemeral notion of the flowers, carried by water, work
together to amplify and illustrate longing. A characteristic of melodrama
is the use of music to express an excessive emotion that cannot be grasped
by words. The music provides an irresistible libidinal impulse. It is purely
about feelings. When the album was released it voiced a new kind of masculinity. This masculinity was fragile, bleeding, and emotional. Considering the long tradition of Israeli male singers whose identity as soldiers is
manifested by their biography or song lyrics, Banai was exceptional: he
was neither a soldier nor an emblem of Israeli ideals of masculinity. It is
possible that Golan's family tried to produce a statement by turning their

back on mythological songs and mythological masculinity by subscribing to contemporary and cosmopolitan feelings and themes. It is possible that, by choosing Banai to speak for them, they wished to reproduce the memory of the now dead Golan as a private individual with existential pains rather than the earlier song's child-boy-man who grows up to his death.[28]

In the song's refrain Banai sings about the notion of guilt that is present in a child-parent relationship. Who is to blame, he asks. In the intimate and complex relationship of parents and children the question remains, posing existential dynamics—an exchange of guilt and tears; but here the familial dynamics are already fatally transformed by state power, by national ideology. While the song's intensity affectively pledges the viewer to what is abstract, impulsive, and emotional, the recurring death of soldiers as a result of recurring violence is deeply rooted in political structures and ideological apparatuses.

To conclude, memorial videos can be perceived as a personal item belonging to a stock of familial documentation, an item too fragile and intimate to be addressed or appropriated by formal mechanisms of knowledge production, by aesthetic discourses or even by the official halls of collective memory. However, as argued in this chapter, such a clear cut between what we render as public or what we can protect or obscure as being private is problematic, to say the least. As emphasized throughout this study, it is important to constantly acknowledge and attend the means and gestures through which such videos keep signaling that they belong to and are also conceived *away from* the public. The tension between intimate feelings of loss and memory and the social and collective currency of these videos is what creates their political affect. Such a reading is enabled only by attentively dissecting the videos' modes of production, visual conventions, generic connotations and their use of aesthetic modes and means. Inspecting the use of music as a hyper-emotional, intuitive, or even nostalgic sign in the videos, I have striven to expose the social, historical, and ideological coordinates that guide such intuition, and to demonstrate the ways in which music is a structure—not only of tones and rhythms, but of sentiments, locations, narratives, and concepts. While music can be conceived of as an abstract force which easily travels and which contains a set of dislocated signs, when we forget that we remembered it, we also forget its rootedness in time, in a place, and its politics.

Notes

The author wishes to thank Martin Scherzinger for his insightful suggestions and comments on the compositions discussed in this chapter.

1. All translations of Hebrew lyrics in the article are mine, unless otherwise mentioned.
2. Although the individual product is called a "film" by its producers, I will use the term "video," which points to the domestic sources and the technology which originally enabled these productions.
3. The programming schedule delineates for the media historian a scheme of a general social routine and itinerary while indicating what is at stake, or what are the subjects of discussion (as well as formats of discussion) in a specific society in a specific time, thus creating a sense of the "public."
4. The term "domestic memorial videos" first appears on Channel 8's 2001 programming schedule describing a slot of a few hours situated between the live broadcast of the day's official opening ceremony and the end of the programming day. Although this is the first time such a term appears in the programming schedule, in all channels, it ultimately names a central category that had emerged a few years prior. This research is based on a systematic reading of Memorial Day programming schedules on all channels, as they appear in the popular press (*Ma'ariv, Yediot,* and *Ha'Aretz*) since 1980.
5. In terms of production models many videos are initiated by individuals who have some link to the industry (media and film students and individuals in the film or television industry). In 1998 the television network *Reshet* initiated *Remember with Love,* a project which assists bereaved families with producing their own memorial videos. The Paratroops Heritage Association, a private organization dedicated to maintaining the memory of fallen paratroopers, has produced, since 1994, short videos on the unit's dead soldiers. Additionally, in recent years, as the genre became the norm, bereaved families hire freelance filmmakers to produce more elaborate and lengthy videos. These services are varied in their professional level, prices, and the supply of technical means. Lastly, some of memorial videos are amateur productions administrated entirely by the family with the means available to them.
6. My understanding of the formation of apparatuses of knowledge by ideological designs draws on Louis Althusser, "Ideology and Ideological State Apparatuses," *Lenin and Philosophy and Other Essays,* trans. Ben Brewster (London: New Left Books, 1971). As Althusser shows, the family, as an educating entity, is yet another ideological apparatus. My argument against the de-politization of the videos as manifestations of feelings, and my endeavor to explicate the ways the family works in the service of hegemonic structures, draw on Althusser.
7. See Bill Nichols, *Representing Reality: Issues and Concepts in Documentary* (Bloomington: Indiana University Press, 1991). Nichols explains documentary as driven by a desire for knowledge. The documentary film is defined as a cinematic product which draws on a shared reality and which facilitates an exchange of questions or opinions in the public sphere. On the documentary as a mode of public knowledge, see Michael Renov's *Theorizing Documentary* (New York: Routledge, 1993) and *The Subject of Documentary* (Minneapolis: University of Minnesota Press, 2004); Jonathan Kahana's *Intelligence Work: The Politics of American Documentary* (New York: Columbia University Press, 2008); Brian Winston's *Claiming the Real II: Documentary: Grierson and Beyond* (London: BFI; New York: Palgrave Macmillan, 2008). On the documentary value of the home production, see Roger Odin, "Reflections on the Family Home Movie as Document: A Semio-Pragmatic Approach," *Mining the Home Movie: Excavation in Histories and Memories,* ed. Karen L. Ishizuka and Patricia R. Zimmermann, 255–71 (Berkeley: University of California Press, 2008).
8. Intimate items of memory—such as family footage—constitute, among others, what Marianne Hirsch terms "postmemory" in *Family Frames* (Cambridge, MA: Harvard

University Press, 1997), or Marita Sturken's "cultural memory" in *Tangled Memories: The Vietnam War, the AIDS Epidemic, and the Politics of Remembering* (Berkeley: University of California Press, 1997).

9. See the work of Julia Hirsch, *Family Photographs: Content, Meaning and Effect* (New York: Oxford University Press, 1981), and Richard Fung, "Remaking Home Movies," *Mining the Home Movie: Excavation in Histories and Memories*, 29–40.

10. This is extremely important in the Israeli context in which aspects of costs and pricing are taboo in relation to the memory production of dead soldiers. From the perspective of critical discourse, domestic memorial videos have broadcasted in Israeli television for more than 15 years and yet this genre was never addressed in daily columns of television critics, nor was it addressed in academic discourses.

11. This aesthetic template is widely and universally applied, from the specificity of Israeli memorial videos, activist videos, and even people who upload YouTube videos to commemorate their deceased pets (for example, see http://www.youtube.com/watch?v=Pvn-Y61wyRI&feature=related). On activists' commemoration videos, see Tina Riis Askanius, *DIY DYING—On Activist Memory and the Construction of Martyrdom in Online Commemoration Videos*, paper presentation at the Visible Evidence conference (New York, August 2011).

12. It can be argued that music substitutes for a central cinematic element which is often absent or misused in domestic production—editing. If editing is a core principle of cinematic syntax, music with its rhythm, structure, and elements of repetition and intensification, provides the videos that lack it with a basic editing rationale.

13. This viewing intensity replicates the dense structure of the Memorial Day programming schedule, in which such videos are broadcasted in clusters starting after primetime the evening before and continuing in succession until the day's official ending.

14. The term "ear worm," used to describe a tune that gets stuck in the head, illuminates the parasitic nature of this uninvited remembering and the almost uncontrolled whim to hum. On the haunting melody, see John Mowitt, "Tune Stuck in the Head," *Parallax* 12.4 (2006): 12–25.

15. Arthur Schopenhauer, "On the Metaphysics of Music," *The World as Will and Representation* (New York: Dover Publications, 1966). For Schopenhauer "poetry," or lyrics, is accidental and circumstantial to music. The musicality, namely the metaphysical element in words-as-music—the rhythm, the rhyming, the structure—overshadows the words' speech.

16. Ibid.

17. The experiential link between music and memory still calls for further research. The use of melodizing for didactic purposes such as teaching children the alphabet or basic arithmetic, or the singing of a lullaby to a child, inviting a soothing structure of meaning, are but a few examples that raise questions about the role of music in the production of knowledge or orchestration of meaning.

18. We can think here about the role of the chorus in the Greek tragedy but also the use of the chorus in the Oratorio. On the role of the Oratorio in creating a form of publicness under religious and national orders, see Howard E. Smither, *A History of the Oratorio* (Chapel Hill: University of North Carolina Press, 1977).

19. I would like to thank Martin Scherzinger for pointing at this similarity. The "Apache Mode" was first recorded in 1960 by the British band The Shadows; it was then recorded by early funk project The Incredible Bongo Band, who added to it a bongo drum intro, and later used by early hip-hop artists such as The Sugarhill Gang, L.L. Cool J, and others. The idea that Israeli military pop ensembles and early funk and

hip-hop draw on the same musical riff is indeed intriguing and needs to be further researched. On the role of the Incredible Bongo Band's "Apache" in the history of hip-hop see Will Hermes, "All Rise for the National Anthem of Hip-Hop," *New York Times,* October 29, 2006, http://www.nytimes.com/2006/10/29/arts/music/29herm .html.

20. Interestingly, the musical strategy that guided Morricone was adopting folk elements and satirizing them. Similarly, as Regev and Seroussi note, the military pop ensembles used satire to disguise the ideological valence of their performances. See Motti Regev and Edwin Seroussi, "The Lehaqot Tzvayiot (Army Ensembles)," *Popular Culture and National Ideology.* And Jeff Smith, "Every Gun Makes Its Own Tune: Ennio Morricone, *The Good, The Bad and The Ugly* and 'L'Esthetique Du Scopitone,'" in *The Sounds of Commerce: Marketing Popular Film Music* (New York: Columbia University Press, 1998).

21. Interview with Nahum and Mina Zarhi, January 2012.

22. The recording is taken from a military training exercise that took place several years prior to the event.

23. Family albums are full of numerous takes of the same or similar image. This is a result of the rare use of editing, but also possibly of aesthetically decoding the notion of loving to the extent that one "cannot have enough," endlessly duplicating and reproducing one's image. In this specific case, what I find interesting is that Zarhi's father continues to maintain the practice of documentation-as-an-act-of-love, although his subject of love is gone. After assembling the video discussed here in 2008 he continued to produce more videos that recount his son's death, took an editing course, and kept collecting images of his son from private individuals and public entities.

24. See Motti Regev's discussion of Shirei Eretz Israel, in "Musica Mizrakhit, Israeli Rock and National Culture in Israel," *Popular Music* 15.3 (1996): 275–84.

25. An illuminating discussion that is pertinent in configuring this mode of displacement is the critical work of Ella Shohat on Israeli cinema's eurocentric vision. Ella Shohat, *Israeli Cinema: East, West and the Politics of Representation* (Austin: University of Texas Press, 1989). Shohat's discussion draws on Edward Said's definition of orientalism as the constant structuring and reimagining of the East by the West.

26. These trips are initiated by the Israeli Ministry of Education and are a dominant part of the education system's effort of structuring national hegemony.

27. Golan and another 12 commando soldiers died in an incident near Ansaria, Lebanon in September 2012. The infamous and fatal incident, which was unprecedented in the elite unit's history, is known in Israel as "The Marine Commando's Tragedy."

28. In this case a dramatic conflict between the family and the army is cut out of the video's frames. The Golan family sued the army for mistreatment of their son's body parts and for misinforming the family. For more details on the incident, see Meira Weiss, "Forensic Medicine and Religion in the Identification of Dead Soldiers' Bodies," *Mortality: Promoting the Interdisciplinary Study of Death and Dying* 13.2 (2008): 119–31.

References

Althusser, Louis. 1971. "Ideology and Ideological State Apparatuses." In *Lenin and Philosophy and Other Essays.* Translated by Ben Brewster. London: New Left Books.

Fung, Richard. 2009. "Remaking Home Movies." In *Mining the Home Movie: Excavation in Histories and Memories,* edited by Karen L. Ishizuka and Patricia R. Zimmermann, 29–40. Berkeley: University of California Press.

Hermes, Will. 2006. "All Rise for the National Anthem of Music." *New York Times.* October 29.

Hirsch, Julia. 1981. *Family Photographs: Content, Meaning and Effect.* New York: Oxford University Press.

Hirsch, Marianne. 1997. *Family Frames: Photography, Narrative and Postmemory.* Cambridge, MA: Harvard University Press.

Kahana, Jonathan. 2008. *Intelligence Work: The Politics of American Documentary.* New York: Columbia University Press.

Kaplan, Danny. 2009. "The Songs of the Siren: Engineering National Time on Israeli Radio." *Cultural Anthropology* 24.2: 313–45.

Mowitt, John. 2006. "Tune Stuck in the Head." *Parallax* 12.4: 12–25.

Neumann, Boaz. 2009. *Land and Desire in Early Zionism.* Tel Aviv: Am Oved.

Nichols, Bill. 1991. *Representing Reality: Issues and Concepts in Documentary.* Bloomington: Indiana University Press.

Odin, Roger. 2008. "Reflections on the Family Home Movie as Document: A Semio-Pragmatic Approach." In *Mining the Home Movie: Excavation in Histories and Memories,* edited by Karen L. Ishizuka and Patricia R. Zimmermann, 255–71. Berkeley: University of California Press.

Regev, Motti. 1996. "Musica Mizrakhit, Israeli Rock and National Culture in Israel." *Popular Music* 15.3: 275–84.

Regev, Motti, and Edwin Seroussi. 2004. "The Lehaqot Tzvayiot (Army Ensembles)." *Popular Culture and National Ideology.* Berkeley: University of California Press.

Renov, Michael. 1993. *Theorizing Documentary.* New York: Routledge.

———. 2004. *The Subject of Documentary.* Minneapolis: University of Minnesota Press.

Schopenhauer, Arthur. 1966. "On the Metaphysics of Music." *The World as Will and Representation.* New York: Dover Publication.

Shohat, Ella. 1989. *Israeli Cinema: East, West and the Politics of Representation.* Austin: University of Texas Press.

Smith, Jeff. 1998. "Every Gun Makes Its Own Tune: Ennio Morricone, *The Good, The Bad and The Ugly* and 'L'Esthetique Du Scopitone.'" In *The Sounds of Commerce: Marketing Popular Film Music.* New York: Columbia University Press.

Smither, Howard E. 1977. *A History of the Oratorio.* Chapel Hill: University of North Carolina Press.

Sturken, Marita. 1997. *Tangled Memories: The Vietnam War, the AIDS Epidemic, and the Politics of Remembering.* Berkeley: University of California Press.

Weiss, Meira. 2008. "Forensic Medicine and Religion in the Identification of Dead Soldiers' Bodies." *Mortality: Promoting the Interdisciplinary Study of Death and Dying* 13.2: 119–31.

Winston, Brian. 2008. *Claiming the Real II: Documentary: Grierson and Beyond.* London: BFI; New York: Palgrave Macmillan.

Zimmermann, Patricia R. 1995. *Reel Families: A Social History of Amateur Films.* Bloomington: Indiana University Press.

Chapter 6

Arcade Mode
Remembering, Revisiting, and
Replaying the American Video Arcade

Samuel Tobin

When you first enter one of these places, not the shopping plaza sort with carpets, old fashioned lighting, a more polite volume, and parents holding little kids up to reach the controls, but inner-city versions where the heavies hang out, you know you're in a new species of public place. Strangers of all kinds pack in tight along the walls, intensely engrossed in private behavior while browsers come close up from behind to watch. Rear ends are dark and faces flicker. Something vital is being dispensed.
—David Sudnow, *Pilgrim in the Microworld* (1983)

What is "vital," what Sudnow saw almost thirty years ago, was video game play, in that case in the arcade. That vital body, its posture, its poise and pose returns, is remembered and re-created at the level of bodies, blips, games, gestures, etiquette and tensions by and in current mobile video game play practices. A Nintendo DS handheld player stands, feet apart and planted; arms bent at near right angles and held out at gut level; hands working in rhythm with each other; face illuminated by a soft glow. This posture of play is deployed in two game spaces: that of the current Nintendo DS[1] (and other handheld systems) player playing in public and that of the player of the video arcade standing before a game cabinet.[2] This overlap of bodily technique suggests that there is a fundamental physical link between the DS and arcade player that hints at wider ranging and systematic affinities between the spaces and cultures of DS play and the arcades. To borrow a concept from Paul Connerton, these habits and postures are "incorporating practices" even as they are also play practices (1972). They enact in play a commemoration and mnemonic effect at once. They connect and recall one space of play into another through attitudes, bodies, and ludic modes.

This chapter traces the connections between multiplayer, public, DS play practices and those of the video arcade and how memory (social, cultural, spatialized, designed, and gestural) is used to make these connections. While the video arcade is in deep decline, it was once the dominant space for video game play, and gamer culture, gaming practices, and players' memories still are deeply impacted by the arcade.[3] DS players draw on and recreate many aspects of arcade play in their practices and discourse. Handheld systems like the DS function in ways that are surprisingly similar to the Arcade's hulking arcade cabinets, despite clear technical and practical differences between them. One of their key similarities is that arcade play and DS play each have a capacity for multi-player play. These points of resonance and memory show how we might better understand public and multiplayer DS play by presenting an alternative, multiplayer, public space to use as a comparison and point of reference. This chapter explores the ways in which movement factors into the practices of those who play on the DS and those who play at the arcade. In the arcade the player's body moves around within a more or less stable and static ludic space while the DS the player moves through quotidian spaces, creating unstable and temporary ludic spaces and moments.

I am attempting here to develop a spatialized analysis of video games, focused on the spaces in which they are played rather than on the virtual and diegetic spaces of the video game screen. The space this chapter focuses on is that shared by people, especially strangers when they come together to play games with each other. This space is located, both historically and in player discourse, in the past. I use the space and memory of the video arcade as organizing principle, metaphor, and site of memory to unpack what is at stake in and made possible (or shut down) in the move from fixed arcade space to mobile DS space. Through this principle we will examine how the practices of a past built and social space, in this case the video game arcade, are called upon through new practice, interfaces, and attitudes of players, designers, and actors. In this way a space can become a gesture as play practices and bodily and ludic techniques are drawn upon and reworked in the corporeal memory work of new game players.

Multiple Players, Multiple "Withs"

This section addresses the ways in which DS players connect with and play with other people in public, whether that public is dealt with in person or through networked play. It also offers a corrective to a too-limited view of whom a DS player might be playing "with." This section is meant to provide background for this chapter's larger conceit, which is that aspects of the video arcade might be remembered through current mobile player practices.

First, we need to be clear on what DS multiplayer play is. Without getting too bogged down in technical specifics, it is important first to make clear that there is a difference between "Nintendo Wi-Fi Connection" and what we might mean colloquially by the terms Wi-Fi and connection. "Nintendo Wi-Fi Connection" is Nintendo's name for its wireless service, but this does not mean it has its own Wi-Fi set-ups or that it sells or rents access. When we think of players playing in a group, face-to-face or more likely side by side in the same room, we might assume that they are using a local Wi-Fi signal to link up. However, in the case of multiple-player play on the DS, they are connecting through one player's DS, which acts as a hub.

We might also think about group or "multiplay" more expansively. Even when playing a single-player game, DS players are not playing alone; that is, they often play in settings where they interact with people around them who are not holding a DS. A DS player playing near another person is playing "with them" in that the play is affected by and affects the other people present. I grant that this is an expansive definition of what it means to be a co-player or, to use Nintendo's term, *to multiplay.* I suggest that such an expanded definition is needed to account for the social dimension of mobile players as they negotiate with people who are not playing the same games but are interacting in the play. This idea of expanded co-play is directly informed by James Newman's idea of the co-player as navigator, assistant, and companion in his 2002 essay "The Myth of the Ergodic Videogame."

If we think of the use of the DS as something bigger and looser than mere hand-on-button engagement with the device, then we can see the presence of a range of multiplayers, some who found each other using Friend Codes, some who are just plain old friends, and some who are strangers. For example, we might think of the ad-hoc scrum of active co-players, hangers-on, onlookers, and solo-players who might assemble at a school cafeteria, video game convention hallway, or other rare, but real spaces which read as possible places of DS play and player congregation. Concerned as we are in this collection with memory and how it is created and deployed by different actors, this kind of group play is crucial for developing a perspective that locates practices, and especially media practices, as sites of and paths for memory work.

What this complex assemblage of game systems, people, players, rearranged and appropriated furniture, and deeply charged ludic public space resembles more than any other gaming paradigm is the video arcade. I doubt that those DS multiplayers were consciously thinking about how their waiting for new *Mario Kart DS* matches or the combination of shy and aggressive postures and engagements were arcade-like or referenced the arcade. However, approaching these complex, combative, and cooperative play assemblages from the perspective of the video arcade, we can see what is old as well as new about DS play and more importantly how what is old is expressed or replayed in what is new. I use the figure of the arcade here as a metaphor and organizing principle in order to address multiplayer play in the context of a longer genealogy of collaborative and competitive public game play and to show how instances of such multiplayer play are called upon, recast, and remembered (or as often are forgotten, unremembered, untranslated) in current practices.

What Was (and Is) the Video Arcade?

I am not interested in enshrining the arcade as a sacred site of play, a vanishing home that we ought to long for, or feel the need to protect. Rather I offer this examination of the arcade as a way to provide a historical and comparative framework within which to study handheld play and to connect the handheld game to larger issues of modernity, pleasure, and experience. How these experiences are remembered and not the reality or bare facts of those arcades is what matters, but even if we are "merely" concerned with their memory we still need to begin from a shared image of what these arcades were. These memories and connections are expressed in a host of game and play styles, habits, and practice that I call *arcade mode*. *Arcade mode* is lifted from a common feature in console and hand-held video games that recalls and references an arcade style of game-play, meaning amongst other things: faster, looser, less studied.

I refer to the arcade in the past tense as it is, from the perspectives of a project about the DS and its players, already in the past. For the purposes of this chapter, the video arcade was a dedicated environment for the playing of cabinet or (the somewhat less common) sit-down, "cocktail table" coin-operated video games. The arcade encompassed the space where games were played and the cultures and practices that took root in and grew out of the affordances and limits of that space and its games.

Video arcades were for a time in the United States very successful commercial operations. In the 1970s they expanded rapidly, taking over spaces previously occupied by precursors of arcades at points of travel, waiting, and in threshold spaces. As video arcades were increasingly policed, controlled, and cleaned up, and as younger audiences became their key customers, they increasingly were incorporated into malls and shopping centers, sometimes even anchoring them (Herz 1997: 57). And then, gradually, as these gaming arcades replaced their video cabinets with skeeball and the last drug deal transpired in their bathrooms, they started to disappear, either by being liquidated, or by being transformed into jungle gym-laced children's entertainment centers or animatronic game palace/theme restaurants, such as Showbiz Pizza or Chuck E. Cheese.[4] Today, arcade play barely hangs on, shrinking and hiding in alcoves of bowling alleys, skating rinks, and the entrances to movie theaters, waning landmarks of ludic American space.[5] Spaces such as the self-consciously nostalgic Barcade bar in Brooklyn are evidence not of the arcade's vitality, but of its transformation into becoming a source of nostalgia and symbol of our individual and collective past.

When arcade cabinets are discussed in scholarly and journalistic work on video games, they often are presented as ancestors of home-console systems, just as hand-held games are presented as the home-console system's progeny.[6] Discussion of space/place in game studies recently has moved to studies of pervasive games, mobile phone play, augmented reality, virtual worlds and MMORGS, leaving the arcades far behind. The practices of the arcades and the mobile are not so much at the technical or political economic levels (though both spheres are in play here) as in the ways the arcade is remembered and deployed as an idea, a trope, and a way of playing in current DS culture and practice. The often unseemly, urban, delinquent video game arcade, while at first glance a long way from play on the mobile handhelds, nevertheless shares important features of use, reception, and the potential for transforming public, domestic, and ludic space.

The video arcade space was occupied not just by people actively playing games at any given moment, but also by potential players, people shifting from watching to loitering, looking for games to play and quarters to "borrow," and in general hanging out. Nasaw shows how this kind of hanging out was also a feature of older arcades and was an issue that often concerned arcade owners (1999: 156). J. C. Herz sees the heyday of the arcade (late 1970s, early 1980s) as a loose affair, where management generally had a hands-off approach to loitering and passing time: "People assembled and spoke to each other, but it was the same kind of glancing interaction that takes place in train stations and airports, where everyone is en route" (1997: 58). These were spaces of transition, arcades as "borderlands," with players *en route* to the next game, moving their bodies through the arcade space when not engaged in moving joysticks and pixels (1997: 58). There is something akin to cruising in these movements and spaces; the atmosphere was charged, if not by erotic longings, then at least by desire, nervous energy, and excess.

Charting the origins of this kind of arcade depends on how we define the various elements that constitute video game play in arcades. It is beyond the scope (and constraints) of this chapter in a collection to do justice to the histories and genealogy of the arcades and related ludic spaces. For more information on these spaces see: Steve L. Kent (2001), J. P. Wolf (2008), J. C. Herz (1997), Raiford Guins (2004), and David Nasaw (1999), among others. A longer history of play spaces helps to account for some of the more unsavory associations that have stuck with the figure of the arcade to this day. It is associations to gambling that give arcades their seamy aura, more than the teenage boys loitering in them, the possible drug dealing and other petty crimes, or the sometimes violent iconography and imagery of video arcade game cabinets and their marquees.[7] When the DS player plays in an arcade mode, in a manner that references the arcade, the DS-er is in contact with older public ludic spaces. One link between these spaces is that the games within them, from pinball to *Pong* and so forth, were effectively rented by the coin, usually the quarter or its proxy, the token.

While the economics of play sessions, game cartridges, and ownership are quite different in the case of the mobile player we can see how DS play also harkens back to arcade play by tracing how DS players, depending on the context, still engage in token-sized game play.[8]

Public forms of game play today, as in the age of the coin-op games of the arcades era, are positioned by potential players, game companies, and retailers, as needing to be cheap, or at least cheaper than other forms of video game play (Seppänen 2001).[9] At a cost of twenty to forty dollars, a DS cartridge is not cheap, but it is almost always less than games for home consoles; moreover, the DS device is hundreds of dollars less than a Wii or Xbox. Such economic calculations about the price of a home console or DS game are very different from those players faced in the coin-op games of the arcade, which combined calculations of time and space, as players rented game space for a period of time. The coin of the arcade was originally a penny and only much later a quarter. This neverending need for a coin and the anxiety of running out that characterized the scarcity of the arcade game is not present in modern mobile or home play, where scarcity instead primarily takes the non-monetary (though still economic) forms of limited free time or even battery power that threaten to bring an end to play. Therefore when we talk about the recreation and encapsulation of some aspects of the arcade in new video game spaces or practices, we should keep an eye on how the economic aspects of the exchange change (or do not change, as the case may be).

Quarter begging, extorting, and robbing where common practices of the arcade that are not present in DS play. Your DS might be snatched on the street, but these thefts have more to do with a long tradition of pickpocketing and petty theft and other forms of urban involuntary exchange than with the shared yet still ludic dangers of the arcade. Another kind of violence, a mix of simulated pugilism and actual economically salient contestation is the "who wins stays, who loses pays" mode of play that was sometimes employed in arcade fighting games, such as *Street Fighter, Mortal Kombat,* and *Tekken,* and was also sometimes the practice with dancing games such as *Dance, Dance Revolution.*[10] One of the key cultural features of use of these head-to-head competitive arcade games is that whoever wins plays on, meaning that the loser loses a quarter, or two (or four). These small but meaningful economic tensions, along with the face-to-face interactions, jockeying for a place in line to challenge someone by saying "I got next," or placing your coins on the game to signal your challenge, and, of course, the shame of losing face are all absent in DS play, left behind with the waning of the arcades. Losing on a handheld device is still losing, but if you want to go again in head-to-head play in a game like *Mortal Kombat* on the DS, whether in local Wi-Fi mode or a global gaming lobby, it will not cost you anything but your time and pride: you don't even have to go to the back of the line. However, there are other important ways beyond the particulars of the token-driven economic exchange that such fighters and the cultures that grew up around them are recalled through current DS multiplay.

Here Comes a New Challenger!

Even before there were proper arcades, arcade-style games offered some form of collaborative and/or competitive two player games. *Pong* allowed two people to play against each together, a factor in the initial success of arcades and game rooms (Kent 2001; Herman 2008). Years later, after cycles of boom and bust in the arcade business, Capcom's *Street Fighter 2* would inject new life into the arcades and usher in a period of fighter dominance over that space both economically and in play styles and cultures.[11] Single-player games continued, but the real action was where groups of players and onlookers would gather around cabinets like *Street Fighter 2* (or its many iterations[12]), *Tekken,* and *Mortal Kombat.* In this section I connect this kind of competitive multiplay of the arcade fighter to DS multiplay, showing what remains and what fails to translate, to be remembered from one space to another.

Cooperation is a requirement of competitive game play. In the case of video games, much of this cooperation work is automated; rules and procedures for play are generated by the game system, its programs, design, and hardware, and not by the social interactive work of the players. In the parlance of Bruno Latour, we can say that many aspects of competitive play, most importantly the rules and nature of the game, are delegated to the systems of the game and machine (1992). However, not all aspects of competitive play are shifted onto the game system. As Bernard Suit has demonstrated in *The Grasshopper: Games Life and Utopia* (1978), players must adopt certain attitudes and make social adjustments in order to play games with others. Players in an arcade must still cooperate and work together in order to, in the case of the fighting game discussed here, fight each other. The work of negotiating who is going to play next or at all, how hard or well one might try to play, what kind of interactions are appropriate or not (talking, swearing, bragging, complaining, making excuses, etc.), was carried on outside of the game, and over the years, a set of behaviors became codified into a series of tropes. Protocols of play included the placement of coins on machines to mark who is next in line to play the current champion, the leaving of a station upon defeat and subsequent returning to the back of a line, the nod or "may I?" in joining an unaccompanied would-be combatant otherwise engaged in solo play, and the general lack of gloating after beating or complaining after losing an intense and hard-fought match. What these rituals allowed was a relatively easy and orderly initiation of a match between strangers, a match that has the potential to produce great tension and high affect. These manners and rituals were learned by those who engaged in competitive arcade play and these social codes helped ensure the collaboration necessary to this kind of play (Ashcraft 2008: 94–95).

However, in general, these features have not translated to multiplay with the DS. If the DS were used more often for multiplay amongst strangers in person, then perhaps these kinds of rituals and niceties would develop organically; however, this is not the case. Both at a distance and in-person (or proximity) "multiplay" on the DS has been relatively under-supported and under-utilized. The rare "pick-up game" played in a coffee shop or other local hotspot is charged with the arcade's tensions and rituals around approaching and playing with strangers. However, because most multiplayer play with strangers, where such rituals might be needed, take place not face to face but rather through Nintendo's faceless and bodiless online connection, such embodied rituals of engagement are rendered both unnecessary and impossible.

Cruising for a Bruising

For all their clear differences in spatial orientation between the gameplay
in arcades and on the DS, both arcade players and DS users move as part
of their play. Both kinds of players move even while fixed in one location.
Even when their whole bodies come to rest, standing or sitting still long
enough to play a game, they move while playing; they bob and sway as
their fingers tap and thumbs press, moving rapidly as they engage with
the game's controlling devices. Between games or play sessions, players walk around: DS players walk around their city, town, campus, and
home; and the arcade player walks around in the arcade, along rows of
cabinets, to the bathroom, or to the snack machine, or to the doorway
(Apperley 2010: 40; Guins 2004: 60). They both move to play, to find a
place to play, the right cabinet in the arcade, the right spot for the DS.

The cruising of the arcade cabinets is replaced twice by the DS player.
The first time with the search for a place, even a time to occupy while
playing with one's DS while a small selection of postage-stamp-size game
cards—whole arcade cabinets worth of programs in many cases—are
fingered as tokens and quarters once were in the arcade. The second se-
lection/movement replacement occurs in the DS player's search for online connections to random and friend-code games. The friend-code is a
unique number by which Nintendo means to allow players to find their
friends online and to play with them. This, unlike the DS player's search
for a situation or gap (both temporal as well as spatial) in which to play,
is not the result of the game's mobile qualities but its networked and
single-player screen and control interface.[13] If an arcade player might
walk around the arcade looking for either a free machine or open control set-up and partner/opponent, then the DS player "looks" around as
well, but in a very foreshortened and scripted manner. Part of this stems
from the aforementioned limitation of how friend codes can be shared by
DS players; they must be communicated through systems and networks
outside of the DS to Wi-Fi connection systems, either in local proximity
play, or through the random match capability which some game cards
support. A reviewer at *Gamespot* evaluates the strengths and weakness
of this system: "The friend code, then, is an adequate system for adding
real-life friends to your Mario Kart DS friends list, but it doesn't facilitate the befriending of players you encounter online in any way."[14]

The friend code system does not support the meeting and playing with
strangers that we see in the arcade. We might expect the DS would allow
for more openness and connections than almost any other game system:
it allows a player to be out and about in public space and then to connect
directly to and play with other DS-ers, while at the same time it seems

to allow the kind of free and easy online connection and multiplayer play that is so important to the success of home console and PC games like *Counter Strike* or *Halo*. The DS, in reality, does neither or at least does neither particularly well. Nor does the friend code system call upon memories of or otherwise tap into the habits and practices of the arcade player. That this feature falls flat on these two counts offers us a possible negative example of the importance of arcade memory for game culture and socialization.

Returning to the example of the kind of intricate group play I had observed at the game convention, I think although that kind of multiplay could happen anywhere, it probably would not happen with strangers outside of a setting that already encourages such meeting up and playing. The arcade was such a space. By hosting rows upon rows of cabinets, arcades both actually facilitated video game play through their technical use and also allowed multiplayer video game play to occur, encouraging it by defining that space as one in which you can go up to a stranger and play with him or her. Video game players can't approach strangers on the street or in a café and ask to play with them as there are no cabineted arcade games available in most of these places. However, with the DS, there is this possibility: if we see someone playing with a DS, we could connect with them and play together. It might be that certain settings are the only places where local DS play with strangers happens. These settings are rare but real, such as game or other hobbyist conventions (Comic Con and the like), video game clubs at colleges, and other social settings set up for gaming and game-appreciation in general. These spaces are quite like the video arcade in being dedicated spaces for games, gamers, and game play. What is different is that such gaming spaces cannot be found in every neighborhood, open all day and deep into the night, where a player can walk in and play a game with a stranger.

Thresholds

This chapter has been chiefly concerned with attempting to connect the DS player and the video arcade player, through an analysis of each player's play-spaces as well as through an examination of what aspects of the arcade are drawn on, remembered, and reenacted in DS handheld play. Fundamentally this has been about tracing lineages and lines of public group or multiplayer videogame play. To continue with this approach as well as to make the connections clearer between arcade play and DS play, I now move from the shadows of the arcade to doorways of convenience stores, backs of bars, and the waiting areas of take-out pizza joints, places that housed stand-up and sit-down cabinets as much as arcades ever did, but which are largely missing from histories, geographies, and taxonomies of videogame spaces.

Guins (2004) develops a geography of play in transitory space, which he calls threshold gaming. These thresholds are places where an arcade-style cabinet still might be found, in convenience stores, grocery and liquors stores, family style restaurants, laundromats, and movie theater foyers (Guins 2004: 204). These spaces do not usually register as game spaces, or even distinct spaces at all, and are thus "transitory, nondescript, and virtually invisible." These spaces have much to offer a reading of mobile gaming and its relation to arcade space and cultures, both in terms of language as well as in acting as a kind of bridge between clearly demarcated environments like the arcade and the nomadic and flexible mobile space created in and by handheld players.

Threshold play takes place in fixed spaces, even if those fixed spaces are transitory: they are spaces not *in* transition but spaces *of* transition, as people are coming and going through them. The cabinet game systems (to call them arcade games seems inappropriate), so heavy, so furniture-like in their bulk, are, if not permanent, then certainly soundly fixed in these spaces of coming and going. The uses of such systems, the physical postures, bodily techniques, the games and programs housed within, are quite like those of the arcade. However the rest of the space of threshold gaming, a busy convenience store or pizza shop, is in so many ways not like the arcade; there is a whole different potential array of social interactions, institutional affordances, and more likely barriers found in these mixed-use spaces. In this way much of the comportment of a threshold gamer is as much, perhaps even more, like a DS or handheld player than an ideal-typical arcade gamer.

What the DS play experience is most directly channeling is not the arcades, but the experience of playing a cabinet game in a threshold space, such as a 7-Eleven, pizza joint, or laundromat. Have we failed to recognize or misremembered a collective gaming and even individual gaming past? Perhaps, as Guins points out, threshold gaming is distinctive primarily in its near invisibility; it is "hidden in banality" (2004: 204). Guins's characterization of threshold as liminal space (full of movement, if not in movement itself) and video game play is quite useful for developing a reading of mobile, handheld DS play in public. The DS user shares with Guins's threshold play a strange combination of being nearly ubiquitous, recognizable, and yet hidden in plain sight, and somehow all-too-often left out of studies of video game play. Guins describes this as a matter of flawed data collection, a methodological as well as epistemological problem in game studies.[15] Even the expert nostalgia-merchants of Nintendo and the active, if selective memory-curators of Penny-Arcade and other videogame and pop culture forums, zines, or blogs subsume threshold gaming culture into the figure of the arcade. This erasure, transference, or misremembering has to do with the power of the arcade as shorthand and organizing concept for a range of spaces, modes, and practices. In discussing an earlier version of this chapter with an editor, Byron Kalet,[16] he shared his own arcade experiences with me, animatedly reminiscing about the way he and his friends hung out there, goofing off, smoking bummed cigarettes and the like. He went on for quite a while before he realized/admitted and corrected himself: his "arcade" wasn't an arcade; it was a convenience store with several arcade-style cabinets in it.

This slippage is telling. "Arcade" tends to account for and flow over other spaces of public, coin-op, cabinet play, and while I have just attempted to tease out at least one alternative space of public play, Guins's threshold, we should also respect the power that the term arcade has. The arcade wins out over the threshold because it has come to be the word for that place, culture, and practice. In this way *arcade mode* is a heading used by game players to organize a range of experiences and cultural memories of group play. The point here isn't that players are wrong to place these non-arcade or near-arcade spaces and practices under the category. It isn't that Byron miss-remembered where he played these cabinet games; it's that those experiences in the past as well as those that are current and related (by gesture, by cooperative play, by particular ludic attitude) have become part of a collective video game arcade memory.

What is problematic in the erasure of the threshold for Guins in his work on forgotten or ignored gamers is that these "threshold" spaces were more diverse than was the arcade, particularly along gender lines, and so with the glossing over of pizza shop gamers, we risk also eliding girl gamers (2004). I would add that what we miss and misremember in the victory of the arcade as ur-site of video competition and ludic collective effervescence is just how many people were shut out of it and how hard, difficult, and even dangerous such spaces could be. That the DS cannot reproduce many of the visceral and tense interactions of the arcade might not in fact be such a bad thing for the average player.

Danger Room

Referring to a different kind of arcade, Walter Benjamin says that it is "a city, a world, in miniature" (1999: 36). The city, as expressed in the Parisian arcades that Benjamin describes, is a space that is distinguished by a combination of wandering and lingering as people move through its built environment. The video game arcade player's and non-player's milling about and loitering spills out from the black light and stale smoke of the arcade onto the street corners, waiting rooms, and train platforms in mobile, catch-as-catch-can, time-killing, DS play. The space of video game play is diffused into the urban and suburban landscape,[17] weaker, less concentrated, but seemingly almost ready to solidify into a snatched game anywhere, anytime. What hasn't been remembered as much in DS play is some of the attitude that the kind of concerted ludic loitering and hustling of the arcade involved: a congregation of children, teens, and older adults, seemingly without jobs or better things to do, all coming together to play games, to kill time, to play together, against each other, and to just *be* in that tense space. When DS players do get together to multiplay, they start to perform aspects of that kind of arcade frisson, but it is not the same. DS-ers may experience tension when strangers get too near us who might watch us play, get in the way, and so on, but these strangers are not the potential players that the loiterers in the arcades are. They might play *Super Street Fighter 4* or a "battle mode" game of *Spirit Tracks* against other opponents, but they won't worry about having to deal with the face-to-face issues of that combat, nor will they enjoy the rituals and face-work of dropping in a quarter, siding up to another body, and entering as a new challenger.

These kinds of tensions have not been "ported" by the DS *arcade mode* but we should be wary of confusing their absence with the surfeit of current social tensions and even dangers in the spaces that borrow so much from the arcade. We should also be wary (as game scholars, as critics, and as players) of glossing over, of forgetting, what we left in the arcades. Of course forgetting is exactly one of the means by which we remember, but this forgetting is not neutral, politically or otherwise. The scrum around a *Mortal Kombat* cabinet was rich—yes, but also not necessarily a safe place for everyone. Julian Sefton-Green, in appraising the importance of differently gendered and classed settings of media and youth culture, argues that "precisely what makes these spaces appealing for males makes them inappropriate for females" (1998: 43). As Cunningham suggests in her work on "feminine" play spaces, arcades were not open or safe places for many types of potential players to play, girls being one such group. Desmond Elli's study of teenagers and video arcades suggests that while girls and boys both visited arcades, girls did in smaller numbers and in specific times and generally not at night (Cunningham 2000; Elli 1984). What we might add to Sefton-Green's, Elli's and Cunningham's approaches is the important caveat that a space that is constructed as risky or masculine may not only be inappropriate or even unsafe for women or girls, but for boys as well.

Arcades were places to play games and to hang out, but also sometimes places to buy drugs, to get in fights, and get into trouble. This made them scary and exciting at the time and all too easy to romanticize now. It is all too easy to remember the arcade as a rougher, more dangerous, and somehow more real and authentic space than the slippery and atomized mobile, sedentary domestic, or ironically disconnected network-virtual gameplaying spaces of today. As Cunningham suggests, we should be suspicious of such nostalgic narratives of earlier eras of gameplay, players, and spaces. Arcades were sites of dangers which, at best, kept out many of those who wanted to play and, at worst, had real and permanent consequences. For example, the arcade I frequented most as a preteen, Kaimuki Cue in Honolulu, was the site of a brutal murder, sparked apparently by an encounter at the game cabinets. And still, I mourn the shuttering of *that* arcade, to say nothing of the arcade I frequented while writing this dissertation, the historic and recently departed Chinatown Fair. I am left with my DS; I can play it in public, even on Mott Street, even with other players. I can partake in all kinds of DS practices, some of which include "arcade mode," but these practices are just that—a mode and a style designed to recall but not to offer the video arcade's surprises, innovations, new combinations of people, and its technologies of distraction, interaction, and even joy.

Notes

1. Throughout this chapter I use the term "DS" to refer to the Nintendo DS series of handheld video game systems; these include the DS, the DS Lite, the DS XL, the DSi, and the 3DS. Differences between models are not important to the connections and arguments made here.

2. Both may sit as well—a DS gamer might find a bench, and an arcade player might select a sit-down "cocktail" unit.

3. While hard numbers are difficult to come by, traditional video arcades, that is video arcades which are not Family Entertainment Centers (FEC in industry parlance), are clearly disappearing if not already gone from most cities, towns, and malls. See Hawkins, *Summer Carnival* (and fot90.com) for details of the decline (pre-closing of Chinatown Fair) of arcades in New York City alone. See also The Stinger Report (in particular: Newsletter, October 2, 2010). For coverage of the closing of arcades, including the aforementioned Chinatown Fair and famed Los Angeles Arcade Infinity, see http://arcadeheroes.com/. This chapter is concerned with DS players in the United States. Much of this chapter doesn't apply to the fate of arcade in other countries, nor those arcades' relation to DS or handheld gaming in those same countries. For examination of the arcade scene in Japan, see Brian Ashcraft and Jean Snow, *Arcade Mania* (Tokyo: Kodansha International).

4. Industry publications, such as the Stinger Report support this shift from video arcade to entertainment center, with a shift away from video cabinets as a focus and onto more diverse forms of amusement such as character-themed centers.

5. Raiford Guins calls spaces like this "thresholds," but he focused more on single or perhaps double unit mini-installations such as at the rear of a convenience store or the like and less on the diminished but still discrete and intact arcade spaces (often labeled as "arcade" or "game room" in the case of movie theaters, truck stops, or bowling alleys). See Guins (2004).

6. See Kent (2001), Herman (1997), Wolf (2008) and Poole (2004) for examples of this trope.

7. For background and an immersion in the language and morays of the pre-video game arcade see the work of Rufus King including "The Rise and Decline of Coin-Machine Gambling" (1964). For a historical look at the split between one-armed bandits and early arcade games, see his strident anti-pinball article "The Pinball Problem in Illinois: An Overdue Solution" (1966). For a detailed description of how manufactures, retailers, and legislators came to divide the pinball game from the slot machine and thus amusement games from gambling machines, see the unfortunately anonymous entry, "Gambling," *Annals of the American Academy of Political and Social Science* 269 (May 1950): 62–70.

8. The quarter and the play it could secure was the way "in" for several early attempts at legal suppression of arcades and arcade machines. According to David Goroff, "The First Amendment Side Effects of Curing Pac-Man Fever," *Columbia Law Review* 84.3 (April 1984): 744–74, a law in Illinois was passed making it illegal for minors to put money into machines without parents' supervision, while in California arguments were made that the brevity of arcade play made arcades sites for high turnover and foot traffic, thus "promoting an atmosphere conducive to drug trafficking, pickpocketing, and prostitution" (745).

9. While much of Seppänen's focus is making these games simple, he is also concerned with their being simple to make, use, and buy and thus affordable. See http://www.gamasutra.com/view/feature/3475/designing_mobile_games_for_wap.php.

10. Dancing games follow many of the conventions of so-called fighting games, a relationship perhaps not unlike that between martial arts and teen-dance movies.

11. See http://www.gamespot.com/features/vgs/universal/sfhistory/history.html.

12. See http://uk.retro.ign.com/articles/954/954426p1.html.

13. Both the DS's mobility and single-player interface orientation are clearly related to its small size. It is perhaps obvious that this would be a defining feature, affordance, and limitation of the device but bears repeating.

14. See http://www.gamespot.com/ds/driving/mariokartds/review.html?page=2.

15. Guins calls this a problem of a bias in "Visible Evidence of Who Plays" or "VEWP" (Guins 2004: 202).

16. See http://www.popularnoise.net.

17. And especially what Marc Augé (1995) calls "non-spaces."

References

Apperly, Tom. 2010. *Gaming Rhythms: Play and Counterplay from the Situated to the Global.* Amsterdam: Institute of Network Cultures.

Arcadeheros.com. http://arcadeheroes.com/2011/02/21/chinatown-fair-arcade-closing-wednesday-ground-kontrol-goes-3-0.

Ashcraft, Brian, and Jean Snow. 2009. *Arcade Mania: The Turbo-charged World of Japan's Game Centers.* Tokyo: Kodansha International.

Augé, Marc. 1995. *Non-Places: Introduction to an Anthropology of Supermodernity.* New York: Verso Books.

Benjamin, Walter. 1999. *The Arcades Project.* Translated by Howard Eiland and Kevin McLaughline. Cambridge, MA: Harvard University Press.

Connerton, Paul. 1989. *How Societies Remember.* Cambridge, UK: Cambridge University Press.

Cunningham, Helen. 1984. "Mortal Kombat and Computer Games Girls." *In Electronic Media and Technoculture,* edited by John Thornton Caldwell, 213–226. Piscataway, NJ: Rutgers University Press.

"Gambling." 1950. *Annals of the American Academy of Political and Social Science* 269: 62–70.

Guins, Raiford. 2004. "Intruder Alert! Intruder Alert!' Video Games in Space." *Journal of Visual Culture* 3.2: 195–211.

Hawkins, Matt. 2009. *Summer Carnival.* Self published.

Herman, Leonard. 1997. *Phoenix: The Fall & Rise of Videogames.* Springfield, NJ: Rolenta Press.

Herz, J. C. 1997. *Joystick Nation: How Videogames Ate Our Quarters, Won Our Hearts, and Rewired Our Minds.* Boston: Little, Brown.

"The History of Street Fighter." Gamespot. http://www.gamespot.com/features/vgs/universal/sfhistory/history.html (accessed August 2010).

Kent, Steven L. 2001. *The Ultimate History of Video Games: From Pong to Pokemon and Beyond—The Story Behind the Craze That Touched Our Lives and Changed the World.* Roseville, CA: Prima.

King, Rufus. 1964. "The Rise and Decline of Coin-Machine Gambling." *The Journal of Criminal Law, Criminology, and Police Science* 55.2: 199–207.

———. 1966. "The Pinball Problem in Illinois: An Overdue Solution" *The Journal of Criminal Law, Criminology, and Police Science* 57.1: 17–26.

Latour, Bruno. 1992. *Where are the Missing Masses? Sociology of a Doorcloser.* http://www.bruno-latour.fr/articles/article/050.html.

McLaughlin, Rus. 2009. "IGN Presents the History of Street Fighter: Gaming's seminal fighter, from the first Dragon Punch to the last Hadouken." IGN, February 16, 2009. http://uk.retro.ign.com/articles/954/954426p1.html (accessed August 2010).

Nasaw, David. 1999. *Going Out: The Rise and Fall of Public Amusements.* Cambridge, MA: Harvard University Press.

Newman, James. 2002. "The Myth of the Ergodic Videogame." *Game Studies* 2.1. http://www.gamestudies.org/0102/newman.

Poole, Steven. 2004. *Trigger Happy: Videogames and the Entertainment Revolution.* New York: Arcade Publishing.

Sefton-Green, Julian. 1998. *Digital Diversions: Youth Culture in the Age of Multimedia.* Bristol: UCL Press.

Seppänen, Lasse. 2001. "Designing Mobile Games For WAP." Gamasutra. http://www.gamasutra.com/view/feature/3475/designing_mobile_games_for_wap.php (accessed April 25, 2011).

Sudnow, David. 1983. *Pilgrim in the Microworld.* New York: Warner Books.

Suits, Bernard. 1978. *The Grasshopper: Games, Life, Utopia.* Peterborough, ON: Broadview Press.

Williams, Kevin. 2010. *The Stinger Report* (October). http://www.thestingerreport.com/.

Wolf, Mark J. P. 1997. *The Medium of the Video Game.* Austin: University of Texas Press.

Part III

Silence and Memory

Erasures, Storytelling, and Kitsch

Chapter 7

Remembering Forgetting
A Monument to Erasure at the University of North Carolina

Timothy J. McMillan

In 2001, I began teaching a first-year seminar titled "Defining Blackness." My journey with that class and its descendants is intertwined with my relationship with the memorial landscape, concrete and virtual, of the campus of the University of North Carolina at Chapel Hill. In its initial year, the class decided to take as its focus the idea of how blackness, specifically American blackness, might mediate and alter how people experience the physical campus. In class discussions we surmised that there is a segregation of knowledge and of perception that might become manifest by examining the memorial landscape and that there are aspects of the campus that might be invisible to some but highly charged to others.

Our classroom overlooked McCorkle Place, the oldest part of the campus and a memorial nexus. McCorkle Place includes the first building constructed at a state university, Old East, which opened in 1795 and was constructed, in part, by slave labor. Directly outside our window was a Confederate soldier monument (universally referred to as Silent Sam) that dates to 1913, a gift of the United Daughters of the Confederacy. Recently Silent Sam has become the focus of a group of students (the Real Silent Sam movement) who have staged rallies and teach-ins in front of the statue to highlight current and historic acts of racial discrimination and white supremacy on the campus and in the community. Silent Sam faces Franklin Street (the main street of downtown Chapel Hill) and greets (or confronts) those who enter the campus from the north. Silent Sam is perhaps the most well-known and often discussed memorial on campus and has been the site of a number of campus celebrations and protests.

Figure 7.1. "Silent Sam" Confederate soldier monument. (Photo by Timothy J. McMillan.)

His multiple identities informed our class discussions of how the campus can be read and indicate the disruption within the "Carolina" identity: to be a Tarheel Blue do you also have to celebrate the Confederacy?

Clearly the issue of multiple paradoxical identities has been and continues to be even more manifest at institutions such as the University of Mississippi and the University of Texas.[1] Would a visiting high school student and her parents have a different response to Silent Sam based on their race(s)? Based on geography—would someone from Mississippi read him differently than someone from Vermont? A civil war soldier pointing his gun to the North is a common sight in North Carolina and throughout much of the southern United States, due in good measure to the many gifts of Confederate soldier memorials donated by the United Daughters of the Confederacy in the early twentieth century, clearly as part of the establishment of the myth of the Lost Cause. When the first "Defining Blackness" class explored the campus in 2001 there were no monuments or memorials that specifically emphasized black contributions to the history of the campus, but there were many that memorialized slave owners, white supremacists, and the Confederacy.

The Memorial Landscape

A walking tour emerged out of the first "Defining Blackness" class to engage students with their physical surroundings through a process of explicitly racialized (specifically black) historical analysis. The tour attempts to alter the perceived landscape from its "normative" reading by consciously reinserting omitted and half-told stories. I call this tour *Black and Blue* to problematize the conflicts that can arise from being both a black person but also "Carolina blue" and to emphasize that black people, in a variety of roles, have been a part of the university since its inception. The tour has become a recruiting tool (particularly targeted at underrepresented students and their parents), a community-building event (through groups such as the Black Student Movement, the campus NAACP, and the Black Alumni Reunion), and an educational event (through the libraries, academic departments, and the visitors bureau.) The University has also created a virtual museum which includes a section titled "Slavery and the Making of the University" (UNC, Virtual Museum of University History, 2006). Recently, North Carolina State University has borrowed the model of this tour and modified it to its own history. In 2005, the Unsung Founders Memorial was installed in Silent Sam's shadow, creating a marked change in the memorial landscape since the first "Defining Blackness" class.

The monuments and buildings of The University of North Carolina provide a powerful lens for exploring racial remembering and forgetting in a setting devoted to analysis and introspection. The changing place that slavery and race writ-large have in the institutional memory of the university and the individual memories of its denizens is an important subtext—the common and repeated refrain of the unsung hero, the unknown workers, and the unnamed activists is partially belied in the surviving texts and images from the early history of the University. The cycle of forgetting and remembering, and the transformation of the producers and

Figure 7.2. The Unsung Founders Memorial in the context of the University of North Carolina memorial landscape. (Photo by Timothy J. McMillan.)

consumers of historical texts and monuments are critical in examining the contemporary landscape of the campus and the current debates over the meaning of the place of UNC within Chapel Hill, North Carolina, and the United States. The idea that meaning is being resurrected and recovered from oblivion and that a more inclusive, "more true" story is being told is highly problematic. In a recent letter to the *Carolina Alumni Review,* a member of the class of 1948 wrote about the "Real Silent Sam Movement" that has emerged recently (2011) and its critique of the Confederate Soldier Memorial at the entrance of the campus: "[N]o one today approves of slavery, and the majority of the people didn't approve of it at the time. But it is a part of our history. We cannot change history, we can only report it" (Jones 2012: 18). The idea that there is only one history, the reportable one, is as problematic in understanding the various histories of the slave experience as it is in understanding multiple meanings of the Civil War. Joanne Melish (2006) provides a parallel example in her discussion of the "history wars" at the John Brown House and at Brown University, both in Providence, Rhode Island. Irreconcilable differences in the interpretation of the place that slavery held in the life and economics of John Brown emerged among various constituencies with no effective resolution of these competing histories in sight.[2]

An analysis of the symbolic landscape both monumental and archival reveals a nexus of racial remembering that affects and problematizes again the meaning of slavery and race to the University of North Carolina and to the United States as a whole. This study examines one very specific case of institutional memory and historical erasure written in stone (specifically, marble): the Unsung Founders Memorial.

The University of North Carolina has a well-documented history of slavery that dates to its construction in 1793. Enslaved people were a vital part of the early University both as property of the students, faculty, and trustees, and also as the physical labor that built and maintained the campus. As the village of Chapel Hill developed around the university campus, many enslaved people and a few free black people were vital to the survival of the community. The central notion of the Unsung Founders Memorial, that enslaved Chapel Hillians are unsung, is contradicted by the extensive archives and Southern Historical Collection at the university. Writings of early inhabitants (such as Cornelia Phillips Spencer and William Battle),[3] the legal and financial records of the university (the papers of university president David Swain, for example), and the poetry and other writings of George Moses Horton, an enslaved man who spent much of his time hiring himself out on the campus, are all primary sources and readily available.[4] It was not until 2005 that a concrete symbol of the existence of the enslaved and free black residents of Chapel Hill was erected at the symbolic front door of the campus. The Unsung Founders Memorial provides a case study of memory, memorialization, and the uses of history in an environment filled with academic analysts and interested observers.

The Unsung Founders Memorial fits into rapidly expanding discussions and debates about universities and slavery and the place that the past holds in the contemporary world. Many academic institutions have examined ways to publicly acknowledge their relationships with slavery, slave trading, and the slaveocracy. Generally this acknowledgment has taken the forms of a conference, a physical memorial, and a well-publicized web presence that includes documents and self-analysis exploring the institutional ties to slavery. An ongoing example of this phenomenon is occurring at Lewis & Clark College in Portland, Oregon. The college has attempted to remember York, the man enslaved to William Clark, to problematize the history of its namesake and of American history as a whole. Efforts to memorialize York were hampered by the literal erasure of York's appearance from the documentary record. In 2010 a statue to York was erected on the campus. The campus website explains that "neither the physique nor facial features of the sculpture claim to represent what York actually looked like" (Lewis & Clark College). Ironically, the fact that there are no images or descriptions of Lewis and Clark's Native American guide does not prevent a statue of Sacajawea from being prominent on the campus. Since 2004 a seven-foot tall statue of Sacajawea portrayed as a specific Native American individual resides near the symbolic center of the campus.[5] How to give face to the de-faced, to give memory to the ignored and erased, is a significant aspect of the nascent slavery and universities movement. At UNC this is not exactly the issue, as many enslaved community members are well documented[6] but have been ablated from modern public memory nonetheless (at least from the memories of the elite).

Conferences at Emory, Brown, and Yale, among others, illustrate the growing interest by scholars in the topic and the desire among university administrators to discuss these issues. UNC, like many other universities, markets itself (both intellectually and pragmatically) on its history. On Franklin Street, as one approaches campus, there is a sign that reads "University of North Carolina at Chapel Hill / First state university to open its doors 1795. Chartered in 1789 under the constitution of 1776." On job postings, at business meetings, and in the preamble to the university's honor code, the age and historical significance of the university are emphasized.

Remembering Reconstruction

Since the 1980s there have been periodic, almost cyclical movements among students and other community activists demanding that buildings be renamed and that "corrective" histories be taught and disseminated widely about some of the founding figures in the university. For example, in the 1990s, a group at UNC came together under the name Campaign for Historical Accuracy and Truth (CHAT). Specific targets of these campaigns have included Saunders Hall (William Saunders was a Ku Klux Klan official and recruiter), the Student Book Store (named after Josephus Daniels who was instrumental in reinstating white supremacy in North Carolina in 1898, most notably in Wilmington), and most frequently, Silent Sam.

In 1993, UNC's bicentennial year, the chancellor created an annual award to recognize women who have made an outstanding contribution to the university; this award was named the Spencer-Bell award to honor Cornelia Phillips Spencer. Spencer is deeply enmeshed in the antebellum and reconstruction history of the university, most notably for ringing the bell that announced that the university had reopened after a five-year closure (thus the "Bell" in the Spencer-Bell award). The university had suspended operations during reconstruction for a number of political and financial reasons. Exactly what those reasons were is remembered differently by different modern constituencies of the campus and community. The remembering of the bell ringing and the forgetting of some of Spencer's published statements about race and reconstruction led to several years of rancorous debate.

By 2002, this debate about the choice of Spencer as a namesake for a university award had erupted into a public and heated controversy due to questions about her role in white supremacy, her racial views, and the assertion that she helped to keep the university closed until it was clear that black people would not be admitted. The position that Spencer was active in black disenfranchisement and exclusion was challenged by members of UNC's history faculty as well as alumni and donors and resulted in acrimony and accusations of political correctness on the one hand and historical erasure on the other.

In 2004, UNC hosted a conference titled "Remembering Reconstruction" which was a response to a series of campus discussions about the place that the names of slave owners and white supremacists held in the physical and symbolic landscape of the campus. The center of the firestorm was Cornelia Phillips Spencer. Her name and those of other members of her family are scattered about the landscape. The first woman's dormitory on campus is named Spencer Hall (as is a dormitory at UNC Greensboro, the former Women's College of North Carolina), and the physics and math building is named Phillips Hall (after her father and one of her brothers).

In December 2004 UNC Chancellor James Moeser "retired" the award, due in good measure to the publicity of the conference and the activists. The choice of "retiring" rather than abolishing it was significant in situating Spencer *within* the university community. Cornelia Phillips Spencer's great-grandchildren Spencie Love and Charles Love asked the chancellor to also remove the family name from Spencer Dormitory and to redirect family foundation money that had been earmarked to support Southern Studies at the University. Moeser was able to assuage their feelings and save the name of the dormitory and the money too. In a letter to Spencer's descendants he wrote, "I regret the pain that this controversy has caused you and your family. The last thing we wanted to do in ending the Bell Award was to condemn Cornelia Phillips Spencer or to erase her from our past. The decision was one of practicality because a number of outstanding women on campus said they would not accept the award."[7] "More political correctness run amok at Carolina"[8]—a comment from a letter sent to Moeser—encapsulates the ideas expressed in a number of letters to the chancellor from alumni, donors, and other interested members of the community.

The rift with Spencer's descendants was healed (with great sensitivity as documented in a number of letters in Chancellor Moeser's papers) and on April 21, 2007, UNC's Center for the Study of the American South moved into the historic James Lee Love house which was once the home of Love's mother-in-law, described in the press release as "activist and house resident Cornelia Phillips Spencer." The use of the word activist here can be read in many ways, but it is definitely not hidden, invisible, or "unsung." It seems to be a not so subtle transgression of the usual use of the word by those opposed to celebrating Spencer and "her times." Today Spencer's portrait greets visitors to the Center for the American South, and, of course, she faces north.

The Unsung Founders

The Remembering Reconstruction conference and its aftermath invoked a great deal of symbolic and practical tension on campus and among students, faculty, alumni, and community members. Some thought, as mentioned above, that this was "political correctness" and "historical revisionism"—terms often used in response to the chancellor's choices about the conference and the Bell award. Others—mostly faculty and students—felt the outcomes of the conference to be too little, too late. The latter group suggested a Cornelia Phillips Spencer Day, to annually revisit the university's history and its relationship to issues such as slavery, segregation, and civil rights; however, this proposal as well as a survey of the memorial landscape were rejected by the chancellor. Some activists felt the conference was a necessary but incomplete first step and that much more was left to do, including the renaming of buildings such as Saunders Hall, (re)moving Silent Sam, and increasing "corrective" signage on the campus.

It was on the heels of the "Remembering Reconstruction" conference and the "retiring" of the Spencer-Bell award that the Unsung Founders Memorial was installed. Chancellor Moeser termed the installation a meaningful and substantive response the campus had made to address the issues raised at the conference: the lack of visibility of UNC's historical links to slavery and white supremacy. The planning of the Unsung Founders Memorial began in 2001, when a monument to the slaves who built the university was selected as the gift of the graduating class of 2002. This selection was not without its own controversy, as it came shortly after the attacks of September 11, 2001. There were many students who wished to memorialize the events that had recently shaken them and had directly affected the campus community including the deaths of six Carolina alumni in the attacks. The slate of potential class gifts had been selected before September 11 and it was procedurally impractical to add another option to the ballot. In addition, a monument to enslaved workers, a scholarship for students who were struck by "sudden and unforeseen financial difficulty," and a "marquee for Memorial Hall" (a performance space on campus) were the other proposed class gifts. The historical monument won with 44.9 percent of the vote. University administrators were interested in the symbolic value of this monument to the campus community, and offered to match the funds raised by the class of 2002 to allow the monument to be built in a timely fashion. The senior classes provided close to $50,000 and the provost's office added an additional $40,000.

Memorial Context of the Unsung Founders

When the Unsung Founders monument was dedicated, it did not enter into a memorial vacuum. As at most universities there were already a number of monuments and memorials dating back to the earliest days of the campus.[9] In 1898, the class of 1891 erected a monument to four university "servants" on the grave of Wilson Swain Caldwell in the black section of the Chapel Hill cemetery. The year 1913 saw the dedication of Silent Sam (the Civil War monument) by the United Daughters of the Confederacy at the northern border of the University. In 1990, students formed an organization called CAOS (Community Against Offensive Statues) to protest a public art installation titled *The Student Body* that was installed as a gift of the class of 1985 and which included highly stereotypical images of black and female (and black female) people (and possibly Asian[10] stereotypes as well). In 1991, students at UNC occupied the president's office to demand a freestanding black cultural center to be named after Sonja Stone, a professor in the African and Afro-American Studies Department who had recently died. As recently as 2011, the Real Silent Sam Movement[11] has petitioned the Chancellor to discuss the ways that campus history is presented to the public and taught on campus.

The memorial to the Unsung Founders was installed at the symbolic entrance of the Campus—the site of the original University and close to the old village of Chapel Hill; the monument is somewhat visible from Franklin Street—the old and still most critical thoroughfare. Its location within close proximity to Silent Sam was intentionally chosen to create a dialectic between representations of the Confederacy and of slavery. The Unsung Founders Memorial fits into the victims memorials trope discussed by Kirk Savage (2009) in his discussion of the National Mall in Washington, D.C. The monuments to those who suffered death, defeat, and degradation contrast (both symbolically and structurally) with the heroic monuments that surround them, both on the National Mall and on the UNC campus. The Unsung Founders Memorial also does not pass Savage's "Iwo Jima" test (2009: 276–77) in that it is physically low and relatively small as well as non-representational and not "heroically active," which disrupts its ability to create a powerful and significant memory in the memorial landscape. Savage's "Iwo Jima test" discussion (2009: 261–84) is specifically focused on Maya Lin's Vietnam Veterans Memorial and the criticisms it engendered; the parallels with the Unsung Founders Memorial are multiple, including the setting, the scale, and the ethnic identity of the creator, all of which are discussed below.

The monument was unveiled on May 11, 2005 and officially dedicated on November 5. The monument is a black marble table held up by three hundred small figures designed to represent black workers who built and maintained the campus. Stone stools, modeled on the unmarked headstones (actually rocks) of enslaved people in the Chapel Hill cemetery surround the table affording visitors a place to sit. Other than a stone bench at the Davie Poplar (the mythic site of the University's origin),[12] this is the only "functional" sculpture on McCorkle Place.

The Unsung Founders Memorial was officially dedicated in a ceremony that included Chancellor James Moeser (a white man), the Dean of the College of Arts and Sciences Bernadette Gray-Little (a black woman), student leaders, and some of the descendants of the "unsung" founders including Mildred Council, Fred Battle, and Rebecca Clark. The fact that descendants of the "founders" were known to the administration and were locally available to attend the ceremony indicates a dissonance between the generalized, unsung nature that was at the core of this memorialization and the specific individuals who came to represent these unsung founders.

At the dedication the Chancellor said, "this memorial, I believe, attests to our commitment to shed light on the darker corners of our history. Yes, the University's first leaders were slaveholders. It is also true that the contributions of African American servants and slaves were crucial to its success" (*University Gazette,* Nov. 16, 2005). Notably, Moeser uses the word "servants," which modifies and reduces the impact of the word "slaves." Dean Gray-Little remarked, "[O]ne of the troublesome legacies of slavery is the pall that it casts over the family histories of those who were bought and sold. This monument finally recognizes the many un-named whose toil and talent made the nation's first university possible" (ibid.). In a later interview, reflecting on the dedication, Gray-Little said, "People who were there to listen to the talk, who were family members of some of the very people we were talking about as unsung contributors, appreciated that I spoke of my ancestors, too" (*University Gazette*, Dec. 13, 2006).

Despite the positive reception at the sparsely attended[13] dedication ceremony, the Unsung Founders Memorial immediately had its share of vocal and public detractors who criticized it on a number of pragmatic and rhetorical fronts. The overall critique is based on incomplete and skewed remembering of the racialized past of the university and particu-larly the literal minimizing of the contributions of black people in a me-morial aimed at celebrating and remembering them. This remembering is paradoxical in that it provides agency to those who invoke the (forgotten) black past of Chapel Hill, but in many ways denies agency to the actual black people being remembered. Specifically, the critiques of the memo-rial centered on 1) its non-imposing nature while being surrounded by more "monumental" monuments to the white founders of the campus, 2) its non-specificity, 3) its evasive and self-congratulatory rhetoric, and 4) its creator.

Four days after the dedication, on November 9, 2005, a letter to the *Chapel Hill News* illustrates some of the sentiments that were expressed, particularly among black respondents: "[M]y goodness! UNC has done it again. Another slam against black folk erected on campus. With the help of a Korean artist, advising majority-culture art notables, a cou-ple of students of color and $106,000, a pathetic, demeaning structure midgetizes the enormous contributions of black workers.... Belatedly, some honor is being paid on the mall to UNC black workers. Are we to be grateful no matter what poor manifestation has appeared?" (*Chapel Hill News,* Nov. 9, 2005). And in 2009 at a town meeting on the topic of "What would it take to heal the wounds of racism in Chapel Hill?" a panelist, C. J. Suitt, read a poem titled "My Lovely Little College Town" which included the lines:

A university that has erected a 20 ft tall monument in the civil war SILENT Sam
And less than a hundred yards away is a slave monument that's ... a table
A table that has these 2 ft slaves holding it up
The last time I walked past there was a lovely white family enjoying lunch
What reverence we show still making them be the foundation for the nourishment of this nation
Still no bill for reparations (mschultz *Chapel Hill News* blog, June 14, 2010)

The Figures

In their study of race and representation in Colonial Williamsburg, Gable, Handler, and Lawson (1992) note that slaves are often presented without specificity: generalized figures who are somewhat interchangeable, while whites, lower class and upper class, are particularized and have personal agency and identity. In the Unsung Founders Memorial, the nature of blackness/Africanness, the nature of free and unfree is left unspecified and unnamed, and a more general and amorphous unsung hero exists in contrast to the fully realized and active white/European hero. The mnemonic devices used to instill historical significance in this part of the symbolic landscape of the University of North Carolina posit a general, almost universal, black person; in contrast, they posit a very specific and active white person as demonstrated by Silent Sam or the tall, white, erect obelisk which serves as grave and memorial to UNC's first president, Joseph Caldwell, and which physically dominates the low, black, round Unsung Founders Memorial. The issue of national, racial, and historical identity is collapsed into one general ideal of blackness, while whiteness in its national, cultural, and class variability is marked as particular.

There are three hundred figures surrounding the table and holding it up. One hundred are men wearing jackets, one hundred are men in shirt-

Figure 7.3. The Unsung Founders Memorial—close-up of figures. (Photo by Timothy J. McMillan.)

sleeves, and one hundred are women (all of them the same woman.) That there are only three types of black people is a message that could be gleaned (perhaps one hundred male slaves, one hundred female slaves, and one hundred free black men)—but if this is the case, it is historically inaccurate in the male/female ratio and in the slave/free ratio of antebellum North Carolina; and what of the free women? Particularly as the monumental landscape ages, and the original intents, actors, and debates fade, all that is left is the actual (concrete, marble, or bronze) object, or name, or in this case: namelessness. As discussed earlier, the landscape in which the Unsung Founders memorial exists is filled with specific, individual monuments, memorials, and other remembrances.

The Table

Prior to the official dedication of the Unsung Founders memorial, a University of North Carolina professor declined to participate in the ceremony and included this remark in a letter to the office of University events: "What the monument does is turn unsung founders into unseen little people, down under the lunch table and Frisbee stand. They only exist to serve" (personal communication, 2005). He goes on to say that "[t]he monument does not honor the people it is supposed to honor. It diminishes them, puts them at our feet, and into the shadow of Silent Sam. It does succeed in engaging the attention and interaction of students, but not in a way that honors anybody." A monument that was intended to evoke a reverential and reflective response often provokes a negative reaction among those who interact with it. Or, in the case of many "users," it is solely a place to sit with no reflection on the meaning of the memorial at all.

The functionality of the monument was intended by its designer and celebrated by university officials. The idea that the monument would provide a physical meeting space to discuss issues of the racial divide, to ponder the meaning of history, was asserted. But the way the monument is used as a "mere" table, as a functional but not symbolic space, has caused a great deal of discussion and tension. A student in my Defining Blackness seminar, after studying the history of the monument and the indignities suffered by the enslaved people on campus, came into class one day and said that she was "mad" (personal communication, 2011). She had seen several white students sitting on top of the monument (a routine occurrence), and said she wanted to beat them up. This sentiment has been expressed to me numerous times, and I generally explain that most people do not know what the monument is or is intended to be, and see it as merely a table. On campus admissions tours, the monument is often described as simply "the table." The problem is that others, often black others, view this memorial as not "just a table," but rather as a space that is specifically connected to a past that includes black people. Creating "others" out of members of the student body is not what the artist or the promoters of the monuments stated as a goal; they proposed that the monument would create community, not divide it.

In addition to the size and lack of individuality of the figures, there is also the issue of their position. The figures support the tabletop which places them in easy reach of the feet of those sitting. Mark Auslander (2011: 29) sees these figures as akin to the "blackamoor" figures used in decorative arts, once again objectifying the black body. It is almost impossible to sit at the table without placing one's feet on the figures which results in the wearing of the patina on the noses, knees, and breasts leaving visible markers of the ways in which these representatives of the unsung are being dishonored in practice, while being rhetorically honored on the tabletop. The worn areas are shiny and can be seen heliographing on a sunny day, drawing even more attention to the ways the only black figures on campus are invisible to those who hover above them. Many students (mostly black students) have commented on the disrespect they

Figure 7.4. The Unsung Founders Memorial—close-up of "tabletop." (Photo by Timothy J. McMillan.)

feel when viewing the way the figures and the monument as a whole are treated, without any discernible intent to offend by those who are merely sitting at the table as designed.

The Inscription

The rhetoric of the Unsung Founders Memorial mirrors the ambiguity and forgetting that the physical design of the monument incorporates. The inscription carved on the perimeter of the table top states: "The Class of 2002 honors the University's unsung founders the people of color bond and free who helped build the Carolina that we cherish today." While the intent of the designer and the committee which commissioned and approved the memorial was very clearly to remember the black people who have been so often forgotten in American history, specifically in the history of the University of North Carolina, the inscription equivocates and refers to "people of color," thus including all non-white people, even though there is no documentation of non-black/non-white people being involved in the early construction of the campus. If the intent is to differentiate mixed race people from black people, it was never publicly expressed, nor is it imagined in the bodies that hold up the tabletop. If the intent is to comment on current race issues and the current demographics of UNC, the language is more understandable, but the memorial's message becomes more muddied and its vision of honoring less grounded.

The memorial, which is universally assumed (and often explicitly asserted) to pay homage to the enslaved people who built the ante-bellum campus, does not include the words slave or slavery. In discussions with a member of the team that worked to create the inscription I was told that the word slave was found to be offensive (due to its alienating and dehumanizing aspects that treat a person as property) and thus was purposefully excluded. But by choosing a weaker and less historically precise term, the strength of the monument is also weakened. The rhetorical obfuscation ignores the reality that enslaved people in Chapel Hill (as elsewhere) *were* property that could be rented, sold, inherited, and lost in a bankruptcy, and makes it easy to forget that the vast majority of black Chapel Hillians in the antebellum era were legally slaves under the laws of North Carolina and the United States Constitution. The most well-known free black man associated with Chapel Hill was Thomas Day, who was himself an owner of a number of slaves. Discussing his story would have problematized the rhetoric of the memorial even further and would tie this monument to a sculpture of Day that resides in front of the North Carolina Museum of History, the only black person represented there.

In the official university virtual tour of the campus the memorial is described thusly: "The Unsung Founders Memorial graces the McCorkle Place lawn in front of the Alumni Building. Artist Do-Ho Suh created the memorial, which honors the men and women of color—enslaved and free—who helped build Carolina. The memorial was installed on May 11, 2005" (UNC, Unsung Memorial). The university website rewrites the language of the monument, replacing the more general "bond" with the much more specific "enslaved," but it does not replace the more general "color" with the more specific "black." Even the virtual landscape encodes and enhances the ambiguities of the Unsung rhetoric.

The unwieldy phrase "Unsung Founders Memorial" also harkens to the vague and general notion of black people as portrayed in Colonial Williamsburg discussed by Gable and colleagues (Gable, Handler, and Lawson 1992). While there are many memorials and monuments on campus that specifically remember individuals, this is the only monument that explicitly remembers forgetting, as can be inferred from the trope of the "unsung" as well as from the repeated black bodies beneath the tabletop. At the dedication ceremony the descendants of some of the university's enslaved workers who attended attested to being very content to finally have some recognition of their family history. But just as the figures holding the tabletop lack specificity, so too does the rhetoric that informs the memorial.

Neighboring monuments clearly and unambiguously memorialize specific individuals by name, status, and often occupation. In clear view of the Unsung Founders Memorial (slightly to the west) is the memorial and gravesite of President Joseph Caldwell. To the south, and also visible from the Unsung Founders Memorial, is the Founding Trustees Memorial which lists the names of the 55 first trustees of the University of North Carolina, and carries on it an image of William Davie, a trustee and donor. Directly to the north of the Unsung Founders is the Confederate Soldier Memorial (Silent Sam) which very specifically refers to "the 321 alumni of the University who died in the Civil War and all students who joined the Confederate Army." The names of these 321 people can be found on plaques in Memorial Hall, a five-minute walk from the statue.

Shortly before the dedication of the Unsung Founders Memorial the university library mounted the *Slavery and the Making of the University* exhibit displaying a number of records that attested to the presence of slavery on campus and in the village. In these records were the names of numerous people who worked as slaves on the university campus. The names of many of the individuals who were enslaved do exist in diaries, bills of sale, runaway notices, and other university and town records. Other names have faded from the official university records but persist in the oral and written histories of the descendants of the enslaved: names such as November Caldwell, Rosa Burgess, and Wilson Swain (father, mother, and son, enslaved property of two different University presidents), George Moses Horton (the famous black bard of North Carolina who also hired himself out to President Caldwell), the many enslaved people owned by local judge and UNC law professor William Battle, including China, Harry, and York, and Dilsey and Ben Craig owned by the Phillips family (and well documented in the writings of Cornelia Phillips Spencer). Clearly, the unsung people do not have to be unnamed people, and yet their individual identities are subsumed in the generalized idea of the "unsung."

Why are *these* specific names omitted from the Unsung Founders Memorial when the names of the Confederate dead are carved into the walls of Memorial Hall and the trustees on their monument? Why is the word slave missing from the Unsung Founders Memorial while the names Jefferson Davis and Daniel Boone can be found on neighboring Franklin Street specifying a highway and a trail? Perhaps the Unsung Founders Memorial actually celebrates modern people singing the songs of the unsung and moves the agency from those who built the campus to those who built the monument. And this may indicate something about the recent trend to remember, interrogate, apologize for, and pay respect to those people of color, "bond and free," who worked at universities across the United States.

A final rhetorical point is the use of the word "we" in the inscription. This "we" is suspiciously similar to the first word of the United States Constitution which clearly did not include many people, enslaved and free, at the time it was written. The "we" on the Unsung Founders Memorial indicates that the "we" who honors those who built the campus may not be the people who did build the campus. This othering is a problem that has dogged the monument in that it is sometimes interpreted as a manifestation of white guilt (or subsumed under political correctness), and not a statement of a new, more inclusive body politic which includes the descendants of the enslaved together with the descendants of the slaveocracy. This interpretation is particularly important when examining the legacy of labor relations on campus where the racial make-up of faculty, students, and staff population does not match that of the state, with "people of color" overrepresented among the lowest paid workers and whites overrepresented among the faculty and students. When considering the "we" in the inscription, the racial identity of the subject and the observer comes into question. As all memorials do, the "Unsung Founders" purports to remember the past but actually interrogates its present, in this case 2005. Today, however, the Unsung Founders Memorial is literally lost in the landscape of the campus but also in the memoryscape of the university.

It is worthwhile to contrast the language of the Unsung Founders Memorial with that of the historical marker at the Chapel Hill cemetery. In 2004, the Black Student Movement dedicated a historical marker to commemorate the African American section of the old Chapel Hill cemetery which became the first monument on campus to specifically address the issue of slavery. The plaque reads: "African Americans are buried here in the western section of the community cemetery. Some individuals were enslaved and others were free persons. Many worked for the university. These workers contributed to the growth of the university during its first century and helped Carolina become a leading public university." The wording of this marker is significant in contrast to that of the Unsung Founders Memorial. This plaque both names slavery and indicates that the enslaved and free black people were active contributors to the community. It is important to note that the impetus and design of this marker came from the Black Student Movement at UNC. From its origin in 1967, the Black Student Movement at UNC has had as a primary mission to maintain and promote a black voice on campus, to challenge the dominant paradigm. The differences between the historical marker and the Unsung Founders Memorial present a clear challenge to the unitary "we" in the inscription on the "Unsung Founders."

Race and the Memorial

The choice of Do-Ho Suh as the artist to design this memorial inspired its own set of controversies, due more to his race and ethnicity than his artistic ability. In a number of informal conversations, blog postings, and interviews, questions were raised about the lack of an African American artist, or at least an American artist. Others have seen this as insignificant in terms of public art or as possibly significant in terms of inclusion and/ or color blindness. And, of course, for those who only view or sit on the monument, the backstory is non-existent. Still, local myths have arisen that there were no black artists considered for the commission, and that no black people were involved in the selection of the artist. University officials took great pains to refute these suggestions when they appeared in the press. The vice-president of the class of 2002 is a black man and one of the four members of the selection committee; he also attended the dedication ceremony along with Provost Bernadette Gray Little, the highest ranking black official in the University at the time (the fact of her rank was duly noted in press releases about the event).

An article in the campus newspaper, the *Daily Tar Heel* (May 23, 2002) announced the selection of Do-Ho Suh as the artist to design the memorial: "The gift of the class of 2002, the memorial will be designed and produced by Korean artist Do-Ho Suh. Fourteen artists submitted portfolios of their work to the senior gift committee. Four finalists were invited to the campus, and Suh was eventually chosen." Quoted in the *Daily Tar Heel,* senior class president Ben Singer said, "Do-Ho is a very soft-spoken man—he's very observant. He grew up in similar oppressive circumstances in Korea, where he's from." This connection to the rhetoric of "people of color" and oppression is another manifestation of symbolically tying the memorial more tightly to the twenty-first century than the nineteenth.

An interview with Designboom (Designboom 2007) contradicts the notion that Suh grew up in oppressive circumstances (and the implication that the oppressive circumstances were slave-like is problematic in and of itself). In the interview Suh states, when asked about his childhood, "a unique part of my father and my growing up was actually his practice, although he was a professional painter, he was pretty much the last sort of scholarly painter in Korea. … my grandfather was also a scholar … my mother also loves art, she's a housewife, but is also very involved in preserving Korean heritage and culture." The interview also discusses his significant installations; the Unsung Founders Memorial is absent, as it is from most public discussions about Suh's art. It has vanished from Suh's personal and artistic history; this monument is forgotten, it seems, even by its creator. Four years after the dedication of the Unsung Founders Memorial, the monument (along with its neighbor Silent Sam) served as a metaphor for current racial oppression in Chapel Hill (the city as well as the university). Poet C. J. Suitt argued that the statue offended him in part "because only one black person was on the selection committee. No black artists were considered, and the artist who was chosen specialized in miniatures" (*News and Observer,* Nov. 29, 2009). In response to this published article university officials contacted the *News and Observer* and stated, "Two of the four students on the selection committee were black. One of the three artists who came to Chapel Hill for interviews was black." Later on, it was clarified that "the students sent requests to 70 artists and 11 wrote back. The students chose four finalists and three eventually came to Chapel Hill for interviews: a black person, a Latino person, and Do-Ho Suh, the Korean artist eventually selected" (*News and Observer,* Nov. 29, 2009). The discussion of the race of the artist and his ability to portray a black experience is reminiscent of the recent discussions regarding the Martin Luther King Jr. Memorial that has been erected on Washington D.C.'s Mall. The ethnicity and nationality of the artist, Lei Yixin, from the People's Republic of China, have been called into question in judgments about the meaning of the memorial. Arguments were presented in a variety of forums that King should be memorialized by a black artist using black workers.[14] The discussions that emphasize Yixin's race and ethnicity (and those of the candidates who were not selected) indicate the many layers that the memorial process occupies. As with Maya Lin and Do-Ho Suh, they once again interrogate the "we" that is creating and consuming the memorials.

Remembering Forgetting

What is the function of a monument that does not celebrate the past but problematizes it and examines victimhood? Why would institutions emphasize negative or at least conflicted aspects of their past? Monuments to those harmed by slavery, racism, and other denials of human and civil rights can be read as symbolic reparations and as correctives to institutional memories. In this monument, at least, the harm is not specified, just the honor that now ensues for persisting long enough to be resurrected. In addition to the Unsung Founders Memorial, UNC has also very recently erected a memorial in 2011 to those who fought against North Carolina's Speaker Ban Law, and named a dormitory after famed slave poet and sometime Chapel Hill inhabitant George Moses Horton[15] in 2006. Horton Hall is the first building on a primarily white university campus to be named after a person who was enslaved.

Recent self-examinations of the role of slaves and slavery at Brown University, William and Mary, Yale, Emory, Clemson, and the Universities of Texas, Virginia, South Carolina, Alabama and many others have led to questions about the place of memory and forgetting, and the need for public symbols of remembrance. Many of the discussions have centered on how slave-owning faculty and students[16] are memorialized in building names, scholarships, and awards, while the names of the enslaved who served the students remain obscure. The "Slavery and the University" conference held at Emory University in February 2011 illustrates the great variety of ways in which twenty-first-century universities are exploring their histories with slavery and the ways they are choosing to publicly remember this history. Of course, this is part of a broader societal discussion of slavery and racism in institutions such as the federal government and various state governments,[17] as well as in private institutions including banks and insurance companies.

A 2010 report from the North Carolina Capitol Memorial Study Committee illustrates some of the rationales for transforming memorial landscapes, in this case the grounds of the state capitol in Raleigh. The committee recommended two options to enhance the memorial landscape on the state capitol, the first a memorial to black NC troops in the Civil War. Significantly, in discussing a design for the memorial the committee recommended, "a monument, depicting an African American soldier who fought on behalf of the union ... would take the form of a life-size bronze statue atop a granite base. In that respect, it would be keeping with other memorials already in place on Union Square and would be a counterbalance to the 1895 Confederate monument" (2010: 15). Clearly, this is a very different philosophy than that used in attempting to counterbalance Silent Sam with the Unsung Founders Memorial, where a monument dedicated to the concept of heroism is contrasted with one to victimhood. The second option proposed by the committee was a memorial to U.S. representative George Henry White and to Ella Baker: "In the committee's discussions it was observed that both options ... would commemorate expressions of defiance" (2010: 16). The discussion of memorializing defiance instead of service, agency versus objectification, is a critical difference between the capitol's memorialization approach and that on UNC's campus. As more of the decisions about memorialization are made by those whose race, gender, sexual orientation, and/or class left them disempowered in the past, it seems likely that the nature of memorialization will change in the direction seen in the capitol memorial discussions. The acknowledgment of the new "we" that memorializes is a critical component of this discussion that marks it as a clear departure from the process that created the Unsung Founders Memorial.

It is not the denial or transcendence of oppression that is portrayed by the Unsung Founders Memorial but rather persistence through oppression. The memorial recreates an order in which anonymous little people (metaphoric and literal) stand ready to serve others in mute silence. This disconnect is not artistic but symbolic. The various objections raised—the size of the monument, the visibility in the landscape, the perceived lack of empathy and understanding of the artist, the refusal to name names, the ability to easily misuse the memorial by standing or sitting or changing a baby's diaper on it—are all indicative of the core problem. Who and what is actually being remembered and who is doing the remembering?

On December 3, 2004, Chancellor James Moeser sent a letter to the steering committee of the "Remembering Reconstruction" conference. His letter included the following paragraph:

At remembering reconstruction and afterward, several people said that the University's commemorative landscape should reflect the contributions of all who live, work, and study here. I agree. Students, faculty, and staff ought to see a campus landscape of buildings and monuments that reflect who we are today as well as who we were 100 years ago. I also thought about the comments of people who said that they didn't see women and African Americans in our commemorative landscape. I think that is already changing. Prior to 1990 there were five buildings on our campus named for women but none for African Americans. Since 1992, four buildings have been named for African Americans (two for faculty members and two for staff members) and one more for a woman. In addition, the Class of 2002 commissioned a monument as its senior class gift to commemorate the people of color, both slave and free, who helped construct much of the historic campus. The monument is now expected in 2005 and will be installed on McCorkle Place. (Chancellor James Moeser Papers Box 49)

This demonstrates the view that the Unsung Founders Memorial is intended to be part of the collective process of creating a more inclusive community by using symbols of the past and problematizing a landscape that tends to emphasize the white, male, and powerful.

Mark Auslander in his recent study on remembering slavery at Emory University through the story of Miss Kitty[18] has proposed that the twenty-first century has ushered in an era of "public processes of documented trauma, truth telling, apology, and reconciliation" (2011: 28). He argues that the reparations movements and such new pedagogies as community-engaged research and service learning have opened universities to self-analysis with regard to their slave-owning and slave-trading pasts. He concludes, that "[i]n complicated ways, it has become more acceptable, albeit in fits and starts, to reenvision enslaved persons, so long excluded from the academy's self-conception, as members of the university family" (2011: 28).

David Pitcaithley (2006) discusses similar transformations of policy and pedagogy in the National Park Service in the late twentieth and early twenty-first centuries. He attributes the changes to a growing concern by Congress and historians to create a more inclusive, and a more "explanatory" history to replace a reverential and particular set of stories. Of course, these changes to policy and interpretation were met with a strong backlash from those most invested in the worldview that was supported by the earlier presentation of facts. Pandering, political correctness, and historical revisionism were terms repeated often in the responses to the changes by the Park Service. The same responses can be found in many of the letters to Chancellor Moeser regarding the "Remembering Reconstruction" conference.

I would argue that the new symbolic inclusion in the university family is due in good part to the changing demographics of higher education, both in terms of faculty but more importantly in terms of students, as well as broader demographic changes in the United States as a whole. Including those who might symbolically identify with the subordinated and subaltern in the larger body politic makes perfect sense in a United States where (non-Hispanic) European Americans are declining as a percentage of the total population. Dovidio and colleagues (2001) examine the ways in which racial and ethnic identity affect the ways that students identify with each other and with the institution. Creating symbolic mediators to try to draw people across racial boundaries into a shared identity with a shared history makes simple pragmatic sense. In the case of Chapel Hill, from 2000 to 2010 in the United States census, whites dropped from 77.9 percent of the population to 72.8 percent; Latinos increased from 3.2 percent to 6.4 percent; Asians from 7.2 percent to 11.8 percent; and perhaps most significantly, blacks dropped from 11.4 percent to 9.5 percent, making them no longer the majority minority in the town. Clearly, tying the interests of the demographically declining groups together through a proposed "we-ness" (albeit a shared history of one group oppressing the other) could be a useful political act and may be informing the increasing number of slavery and university discussions across the country.

In 2012, I continued to teach "Defining Blackness," and the "Black and Blue" tour has now become part of the institution, with multiple tour guides taking students and community members through the campus to discuss black histories. The Unsung Founders Memorial is the starting place for most tours, and continues to provoke many conversations about how the past remains in the present and how the past is recreated. The goal of fostering discussion about campus history and racial divides has been accomplished, if not necessarily in the way the artist or the administration originally intended.

Notes

1. Many primarily white institutions (PWIs) in the lower South, such as the University of Mississippi, have explicit symbols of racial segregation and slavery embedded in their cultural fabric—the retirement of Colonel Reb as mascot in 2003, and subsequent attempts (as recently as 2012) to bring him back illustrate an explicit divide rather than the more implicit one at UNC. The recent debate about renaming Simkins Residence Hall at UT Austin (Simkins was a Ku Klux Klan organizer in Florida) also illustrates this point.

2. In her discussions about John Brown and his namesake university, Melish demonstrates how contested histories can become reified and unambiguous to their supporters. On the discussion about John Brown that emerged at the John Brown House, she mentions the conflict between two academics over the legacy of Brown: "[L]obban saw Lemmons as an apologist for slavery; Lemmons saw Lobban as an ahistorical and factually inaccurate zealot" (Melish 2006: 108.) Memorialization often takes one historical perspective and then crystallizes it, even today.

3. Cornelia Phillips Spencer was the daughter of UNC Professor James Spencer and sister of UNC graduates Samuel and Charles Spencer. She is one of the most well-known

writers about antebellum and reconstruction Chapel Hill and an advocate for women's education. William Battle was a local judge and law professor, and the father of Kemp Battle, president of the University during and after Reconstruction.

4. Joan Sherman in the *Black Bard of North Carolina* (1997) provides an excellent overview of the life and poetry of Horton, working from archival sources in the University collection including Cornelia Phillip Spencer's and David Swain's papers.

5. Photographs of both the York and the Sacajawea statues are available on Lewis & Clark's website under the "Visiting Campus" tab.

6. The University Archives, the Southern Historical Collection, and the North Carolina Collection photo archives, all housed in the Wilson Library on the UNC campus (and all open to the public), possess a wealth of primary sources about the enslaved and free black population of the university and the town of Chapel Hill.

7. UNC GAA, Jan. 28, 2005.

8. Moeser Records Box 49 Folder Bell Award February 2005–2006.

9. One of the most visited and photographed memorial spaces is actually the first building of the campus (known as "Old East") which was completed in 1795 and has moved from being only a functional building (it still serves as a residence hall) to a memorial to the longevity of the campus.

10. Criticisms of the student body are well documented in Chancellor Hardin's papers in the University archives as well as in the archives of the student press at UNC. The criticisms focused on five of the seven figures in the statue: the male black figure balancing a basketball on one finger, the female black figure balancing a book on top of her head, a white couple (male and female) where the woman is holding out an apple and resting her head on the man's shoulder while he reads her a book, and a female figure, often viewed as Asian, carrying a violin case.

11. The real Silent Sam Movement is a UNC student- and Chapel Hill community group that formed to explore the relationship between the town/gown racial history and current inequalities in the community. Silent Sam, the Confederate Soldier Memorial, has become a central symbol of this contested history.

12. The Davie Poplar is popularly believed to be located at the site where William Davie chose to locate the University in 1792. Davie's role as "father of the University" is well documented and discussed in local lore; his occupation as a planter and slaveholder less so.

13. Fewer than fifty people attended the ceremony.

14. The debates over the King memorial are reminiscent of the heated public discussions when Steven Spielberg decided to direct the film version of *The Color Purple*.

15. Horton hired his time from his owner and came to Chapel Hill to earn money in hope of buying his freedom. Unlike many of the other enslaved people who served students, Horton wrote poetry for pay instead of performing manual tasks such as hauling water, blacking shoes, and running errands.

16. John C. Calhoun is a prime example at Yale. A residential college named after Calhoun has created controversy and discussion much as Silent Sam has at the UNC campus.

17. In 2007, North Carolina (through bills passed by both chambers of the legislature) issued an apology for slavery and its legacies.

18. Miss Kitty was the enslaved property of Methodist Bishop James Osgood Andrew. Andrew's slave ownership precipitated the split between the northern and southern Methodists in the mid nineteenth century. Mark Auslander (2011) details the various ways that the story of Miss Kitty is told in white and black communities and the con-

flicts these mythic histories create in modern Oxford, Georgia. Auslander's work became central to the Transforming Communities Program at Emory University which sponsored the Slavery and Universities conference in 2011.

References

Primary Sources

Newspapers

The Chapel Hill News
The Daily Tar Heel
University Gazette

University Archives

Records of the Office of Chancellor James Moeser, 2000–2008
Box 49 Folder Bell Award 2004–January 2005
Box 49 Folder Bell Award February 2005–2006

Books, Publications, and Online Sources

Auslander, M. 2011. *The Accidental Slaveowner: Revisiting a Myth of Race and Finding an American Family.* Athens and London: University of Georgia Press.
Designboom. 2007. *Do-Ho Suh.* Retrieved March 31, 2012, http://www.designboom.com/eng/interview/dohosuh.html.
Dovidio, J. S. 2001. "Racial, Ethnic, and Cultural Differences in Responding to Distinctiveness and Discrimination on Campus: Stigma and Common Group Identity." *Journal of Social Issues* 57. 1: 167–88.
Gable, E., R. Handler, and A. Lawson. 1992. "On the Uses of Relativism: Fact, Conjecture, and Black and White Histories at Colonial Willamsburg." *American Ethnologist* 19.4: 791–805.
Jones, D. 2012. "Lessons of Silent Sam: We Cannot Change History." *Carolina Alumni Review* 18.
Lewis & Clark College. n.d. http://www.lclark.edu/visit/features/york/ (accessed March 25, 2012).
Library, W. n.d. *Slavery and the Making of the University.* http://www.lib.unc.edu/mss/exhibits/slavery/ (accessed March 20, 2012).
Melsih, J. 2006. "Recovering (from) Slavery: Four Struggles to Tell the Truth." In *Slavery and Public History: The Tough Stuff of American Memory,* edited by J.O. Horton and L.E. Horton, 103–33. Chapel Hill: Univerity of North Carolina Press.
Pitcaithley, D. 2006. "A Cosmic Treat": The National Park Service Addresses the Causes of the American Civil War. In *Slavery and Public History,* 169–86.
Report, N. C. 2010. *North Carolina State Capitol Memorial Study Committee Report.* Retrieved March 25, 2012, www.ncdcr.gov/capitolmemorial.pdf.
Savage, K. 2009. *Monument Wars: Washington, D.C., the National Mall, and the Transformation of the Memorial Landscape.* Berkeley: University of California Press.
Sherman, J. E. 1997. *The Black Bard of North Carolina: George Moses Horton and His Poetry.* Chapel Hill: The University of North Carolina Press.

University of North Carolina. 2006. *Virtual Museum of University History.* http://museum
    .unc.edu/ (accessed March 10, 2012).
———. n.d. *Unsung Memorial.* http://www.unc.edu/tour/LEVEL_2/unsung.htm (accessed
    March 10, 2012).

Chapter 8

The Power of Conflicting Memories in European Transnational Social Movements

Nicole Doerr

This chapter explores collective memory as a source of democratic conflicts in social movements, with the aim of better understanding the relationship between storytelling and silences in emerging transnational
discursive public spheres. When telling alternative stories on the Internet and in transnational protest summits, activists publicize memories
excluded from national history books (Assmann and Conrad 2010: 2;
see also Olick et al. 2011: 430). However, the publicizing of suppressed
memories and the claims for apology and repair made in transnational
discursive or deliberative publics (Fraser 2007; Daase 2010) should be
examined carefully. When public rituals of memorization in national
public arenas (Olick 1999) take place, the telling of excluded stories not
only risks reproducing trauma but also repeating "defensive storytelling"
by perpetrators and victims themselves (Schwab 2010: 109). How do
conflicting memories related to different social movement groups come
together in emerging transnational discursive publics? And to what extent do silences constrain discursive democracy experiments in the global
justice movement? Asking these questions, my analysis will explore the
conflicting role of silenced memories in the transgenerational context of
storytelling in the European Social Forum.

Created in 2002, the European Social Forum (ESF) was Europe's largest transnational discursive public space for debating alternatives to neoliberal globalization in the global justice movement (della Porta 2005b).
Global justice activists who created the ESF included European citizens

as well as migrants and Turkish activists, traditional leftist organizations and new social movements groups, including many feminists, anarchists and environmentalists (Andretta and Reiter 2009). Many participants remember the first ESF held in Florence in 2002 as an exceptional and inspiring grassroots democratic ritual, which took place after a long period of leftist crisis and factionalism (Wrainwright 2004). However, most also note that the strong enthusiasm and momentum it created soon passed away (Pleyers 2010).

My ethnographic research on storytelling in the ESF shows that the enduring conflict around silenced memories of exclusion better accounts for the seeds of democratic crises and disengagement in the ESF than do other conflicts, such as the social basis of political power related to ideology and identity as such. I studied the democratic crises experienced by the ESF working as a participant observer, interviewer, and discourse analyst of its European-level and national-level Social Forum preparatory assemblies from 2003 to 2006 (Doerr 2008, 2010). Comparing activists' discursive practices at national-level preparatory meetings for the ESF in Germany, Italy, and the UK, my data pointed to an interesting conclusion: across all three countries, the silenced memories of violent exclusion, repeated via present practices of silencing in public discourse, accounted for the intensity and timing of democratic crisis that occurred in each of the national Social Forums. Moreover, the silencing of stories by socially disadvantaged women and/or migrants predicted a future democratic crisis in those cases where there had been no "bad" memories of preceding conflicts. This means that practices of silencing today may, in fact, guarantee the future failure of democracy.

Social movement scholars have interpreted the devastating democratic crises that beset national preparatory assemblies hosting the ESF events as a symptom of differences in political power and the asymmetric resources of the groups involved (Nunes 2004), ideological conflicts (Papadimitrou et al. 2007), and conflicts about political identity (Reyes 2006). Analysts have not, as yet, looked at the impact of conflicting memories and their paradoxical visible invisibility in public discourse (Gilman and Remmler 1994; Olick and Levy 1997). This is surprising, since the "silencing" of experiences of women, workers, and ethnic minorities in national political arenas—including those within social movements—has been a major concern of feminist writers and sociologists interested in political deliberation (Fraser 1992, 2007; Polletta 2002; Young 2001). Feminist discourse theories in particular have examined the exclusionary dynamics of mainstream deliberative publics (Fraser 1992) and the discourse practices of the New Left (Phillips 1993). Moreover, sociologists interested in collective memory have powerfully shown the role of taboo in political discourse as a constraint for present political conflicts, opportunity, and deliberation (Olick and Levy 1997: 922). Jeffrey Olick and Daniel Levy's study of official public debates in place-specific national cultures of political discourse shows that "[t]he relationship between remembered pasts and constructed presents is one of perpetual but differentiated constraint and renegotiation over time, rather than pure strategic invention in the present or fidelity to (or inability to escape from) a monolithic legacy" (Olick and Levy 1997: 937).

Inspired by Olick and Levy, my aim in this chapter is to show the enduring role of *silenced* memories of political conflict in place-specific national settings and how they constrain emerging transnational democracy experiments in discursive public spaces such as the ESF. My comparative focus on conflicting memories and their silencing in the transgenerational public space created in the ESF opens a new question in the literature on democratic discourse in new social movements neglected by previous research. While most scholars have studied social movements' democratic crises in individual national organizing contexts (Polletta 2002) or transnational arenas (Maeckelbergh 2009), I compared democratic crises in three different national contexts across three years of interviewing and ethnographic fieldwork. By studying the ESF I focused on the contentious power of silenced memories in a transgenerational, transnational discursive arena whose organizers include activists from the '68 generation, as well as young global justice activists in their twenties and thirties (della Porta 2005b). I intentionally focused on the *provisional* construction of collective memory (Wagner-Pacifici 1996: 306), in order to show that conflicting memories and the way they are transmitted, embodied, and presented (Wagner-Pacifici 1996: 301, 306) account for the distinct periods and intensity in which democratic crises occurred in the Italian, British, and German national Social Forum arenas. I will discuss this finding after a brief review of the literature on conflicting memories in public discourse and democracy in social movements.

Conflicting Memories and Discursive Democracy in the European Social Forum

Political and cultural sociologists have shown the contentious and contested nature of collective memory at the level of the nation state (Schudson 1992; Olick and Levy 1997), the ritualistic character of public debates on memory in fragmented national political arenas (Straughn 2009), and social movements' powerful symbolic role in the "moments of madness" (Zolberg 1998: 565; Olick et al. 2011: 430). Jeffrey Olick and Daniel Levy, importantly, have shown that collective memory determines what can be said and what remains silent in mainstream arenas of national political deliberation (Olick and Levy 1997). However, we know far less about how collective memories influence voice and silence in the national political discourse arenas created by social movements. In this respect, the Social Forums in Europe are key research sites to compare discursive practices of remembering (Olick 1999) in a progressive setting that brings together individuals and organized social movements as carriers of previously silenced transnational memories (Assmann and Conrads 2010). Although social movements' transnational discursive publics succeed in creating a democratic public space for deliberation about a future transnational narrative of European identity (Eder 2009), little is known about the political inclusion of traditionally excluded groups such as immigrants, women, and working class members in movements' "deliberative spaces" (Doerr 2010; see also Fraser 2007).

Constructed in opposition to national mainstream publics, transnational public spaces in social movements are an exciting arena for exploring the cultural constraints of conflicting memories built in different national, geographical, and social contexts. Created by grassroots global justice activists and not by institutional actors (della Porta 2005a), transnational discursive publics such as the ESF aimed at giving traditionally marginalized groups such as ethnic and linguistic "minorities," women, workers, and migrants a privileged place to tell their stories (European Social Forum 2003). Social Forums trace their model of "discursive or deliberative democracy" (Smith et al. 2007: 31) back to new social movements' "participatory democracies" of the 1960s, 1970s, and 1980s (Polletta 2002). As Francesca Polletta has shown, social movements' "radical democracies" made "free speech" and "deliberative talk" a mark of their own groups' organizing models, rejecting traditional models of representative democracy in "old" leftist organizations (della Porta 2005a; Polletta 2002: 1–12). But while the student movements and '68 movements had an ambiguous relation to the past, today's global justice groups stress their transgenerational lineage—a lineage that includes traditional leftist parties, unions, and feminist, anarchist, and autonomous groups who had been fighting each other since the 1960s (della Porta 2005b). Compared to official media publics and institutional deliberative arenas, the "open speech" setting of ESF is an interesting case through which to explore how those different traditions and groups interact with each other. Moreover, few sociologists of storytelling may have had the chance to observe situations in which the telling of silenced stories within meetings immediately produces stalemates (cf. Polletta et al. 2011). This makes the transgenerational arena of the ESF a unique opportunity to do such work.

My research explores practices of remembering in public discourse within the micro-public sphere created in ESF national-level preparatory meetings. Maurice Halbwachs' narrative approach to collective memory shows that groups' specific practices of oral remembering in narrative form mark cultural "boundaries and define the principles of inclusion and exclusion" in place-specific settings (Halbwachs [1925] 1991: 72; Olick 1999). Interested in the stories of historically excluded ethnic and social groups, Francesca Polletta has shown that memories of tradition- ally disadvantaged groups are an important cultural resource for politi- cal mobilization (Polletta 2006). However, she has also found that such memories fail to make an impact within mainstream public discourse in national political institutions regarding high-stake issues, such as finance or policy-making (Polletta 2006: 106). In combining Polletta's empiri- cal insights with Jeffrey K. Olick's discursive conception of collective memory, I explore how and when silenced memories get transmitted in practices of public storytelling following conflict between different groups, re-creating transgenerational divides (Olick 1999: 334, 347). By comparing the variations between public discourse in different national Social Forum meetings my study demonstrates how collective memory operates in such settings, confirming the converging power of "silenced memories" and their contentious "modes of remembering" in different public contexts (Assmann 2008: 55).

I define silenced memories as consequences of violent conflict whose victims find no arena in which to tell their stories, following Gaby Schwab's cultural approach to collective memory (Schwab 2010: 102– 03). Though silenced officially, such stories nevertheless get passed on in "indirect and implicit ways" and may become fragmented (Straughn 2009) or potentially conflicting memories (Assmann 2005: 10). Follow- ing Abraham and Torok's (1994) psychoanalytical theory of "crypton- omy,"[1] we can understand memories of violence as powerful carriers of conflict, transmitted implicitly and often unnoticeably across generations through the narrative form of "crypts" (Schwab 2010: 103). In her work on transgenerational trauma, Schwab shows that narrative crypts can be traced as they are transmitted through writing and speech in which "bur- ied ghosts of the past come to haunt language from within," as a death atmosphere "threatening to destroy its communicated and expressive function" (Schwab 2010: 102–03).

While scholars have explored the silent transmission of memories of trauma (Hirsch 1997) and of violent political exclusion (Assmann 2005), less is known of exactly how memories of exclusion get processed and included in a way to encourage social repair (Alexander 2006). Aleida Assmann, following Grusin's media theory of memory, assumes that collective memory is necessarily "a mediated memory" (Assmann 2005: 4). She has proposed to look at processes of "re-mediation": communicative practices that facilitate processing the conflicting events and violent histories in which group members were involved (Assmann 2008: 55). Assmann also considers the failure of such remediation processes using Grusin's concept of pre-mediation (Assmann 2005: 3). "Pre-mediation" describes the (negative) impact of violent and traumatic events which can neither be remembered and remediated, nor forgotten, and which are stored in stories foreclosing the future: "the future, which until recently, was considered a resource for innovation, change, hope, and regeneration, has become a source of deep collective anxiety and impending trauma" (Assmann 2005: 3). Assmann shows that narratives about violent exclusion "prefigure" the future in constructing "cultural schemata or templates" for condensed remembering, blocking dialogical interaction across conflicting group identities (Assmann 2005: 4). The prefigurative logic of silenced memories would thus imply that conflict in place-specific meetings would be even more likely to occur if experiences of symbolic violence were previously silenced, without being "remediated" into narratives that give a collectively shared meaning to difficult events.

These critical approaches inform my work here. Officially, ESF organizers explicitly invited women, workers, migrants, and traditionally marginalized ethnic groups and sexual subjectivities, encouraging them to "take voice" within national and European social movement preparatory meetings (Doerr 2008). I found that in many of the national Social Forum meetings, however, stories told by those groups were simply "not heard" or were actively silenced by influential social movement leaders. More specifically, my cross-national comparative approach explores the question of timing: when do silenced and excluded memories of those groups reappear in public deliberation, and when do they trigger conflict in groups?

Cases and Data Collection

For my ethnography of storytelling at the ESF I selected three different national Social Forum publics: the German, Italian, and British national preparatory assemblies. I selected the British preparatory meetings as an adversarial setting for political dialogue through which to explore the continuing impact of conflicting memories of the struggles of the recent decades within the domestic scene of movements and leftist parties involved in building an ESF event in London (Papadimitrou et al. 2007; Wrainwright 2004). In comparison to the UK, the Italian Social Forum preparatory assemblies provided a case through which to explore the conditions for successful remediation of conflicting memories, as it had an advanced practice of mediation that facilitated democratic dialogue during the first ESF in Florence (della Porta and Mosca 2007). Unlike those two cases, the German national preparatory meetings provided a setting to explore political dialogue in the relative absence of conflicting memories: German participants had comparatively fewer previous conflicting interactions and personal contacts than did participants in the other two national cases (Doerr, forthcoming).

My focus on memories as reproduced in these meetings in the immediate context of their telling helps us understand who can authoritatively act as a storyteller of conflicting memories in culturally pluralist social movements, whose memories remain silent, and what the conditions are that shape a story's inclusion into the official stock of narratives institutionalizing the Social Forum's discursive culture.

My data comes from three different sources. First, I tape-recorded and transcribed plenary discussions of ESF preparatory meetings, both national and European, in the original language version of the speakers, and subsequently analyzed the transcripts using Critical Discourse Analysis (Wodak 1996). Second, I refined this Critical Discourse Analysis through a more targeted analysis of narrative forms within deliberation (cf. Polletta 2006). Specifically, I looked at whether and when memories of past conflicts came up in plenary discussions, examining speakers' differing interpretations of the same events and contested narratives. In order to get at potentially "hidden" and encrypted stories—which may be prone to indirectly transmitting silenced memories of conflict—I used a broad definition of what "counted" as a story. While classical narrative analysts define stories as recounting a sequence of events in the order in which they occurred in order to make a point, my analysis also included unfinished and partial stories (Polletta et al. 2011: 3), those potentially symbolizing conflicting, contested, or silenced events.

Third, I analyzed activists' perceptions of discourse practices in meetings. I conducted qualitative, semi-structured interviews with 120 participants in the meetings that I studied, approaching most interviewees and conducting face-to-face interviews during breaks and social gatherings. I selected a balanced sample of interviewees in the meetings studied by taking into consideration the individual, socioeconomic, and organizational backgrounds of activists, as well as their political orientation, gender, nationality, time of participation, and age.

In my analysis of discourse practice and storytelling in meetings and the interviews, I asked two central questions: First, to what extent do stories of past conflict and/or violent exclusion create or repeat conflict in present settings of political dialogue? Second, regarding the transgenerational transmission of conflicts, how do stories told by more experienced activists recall conflicts in *previous* movement generations? Through these two questions, I sought to find out whether and how heterogeneous groups are able to build future cooperation and whether the injection of stories of past conflicts by experienced activists influence newcomers in their narrative dynamics.

Findings: Conflicting Memories as Constraints for Democratic Deliberation

The findings of my research show that conflicting memories help us to understand the timing and intensity of democratic crises in national and ESF meetings. My comparative analysis approach proceeds in three steps. First, I will show that an advanced model of conflict mediation encouraged a relatively long and arguably successful period of political dialogue in the Italian Social Forum preparatory meetings, before such dialog eventually disintegrated. Second, by contrast, without such a model of remediation, silenced memories of previous conflicts in the Left blocked any chance of dialogue and future cooperation in the UK Social Forum preparatory meetings. Third, the silencing of stories by resource-poor groups, women, and migrants presaged the sudden death of political dialogue in the German Social Forum preparatory meetings.

My first case, the Italian national preparatory meetings of the ESF, documents how the return of stories of past conflict challenged political mediation in a setting that initially looked very fruitful for building dialogue among heterogeneous, divided groups. Created in a moment of political crisis, with massive protests against the G8 summit in Italy and the war in Afghanistan, the Italian preparatory assemblies for the first ESF encouraged pluralist and peaceful grassroots participation (della Porta and Mosca 2007). Among them were radical anarchist and autonomous groups such as the *Centri Sociali* (Social Centers), *Disobbedienti* (Disobedients), and environmentalist and left-Catholic groups, as well as small independent trade unions like COBAS[2] or the more "moderate" Attac network, and groups associated with sections of the parties and unions of the Old Left.[3]

A young anarchist activist from the Florentine radical group *Centro Sociale CPA Firenze Sud,* previously skeptical toward cooperating with unionists, described the feeling that the ESF in his home town, Florence, was a "moment in which everything [was] possible," a level of cooperation that had never happened before:

It was incredible. All [the] streets were full of people, I believed ... for the first time in my life [that] everything is possible.[4]

Like this activist in his late twenties, many young, radical Italian activists experienced the ESF as a revolutionary "moment of madness" constituting an egalitarian community among very different, antagonistic groups (Zolberg 1972: 184). Before Florence, Italian leftist political parties, unions, and social movements had been fighting each other for years (Caruso 2005). This peaceful moment in Florence internationally strengthened the Social Forum movement as it countered the media image of violent protests (della Porta 2005b). Said Marco Berlinguer, professional activist of the transnational network Transform:

I think that we here in Italy are in a completely new process.... There is an emerging postnational subject, a new innovative process. A critique of the separatism of politics, or representative democracy and delegation.[5]

What remains silent in most of the memories of participants whom I interviewed, however, is that the perceived inclusionary setting for political dialogue in the ESF in Florence in 2002 was based on the hard work of mediation in the Italian national preparatory assembly that preceded that event (della Porta and Mosca 2007). As in Berlinguer's case, my interviewees who worked as professional activists for "moderate" national leftist party associations and unions or transnational think tanks such as Berlinguer felt personally *part* of social movements. Some professional activists also worked as mediators to facilitate dialogue in the Italian national preparatory assemblies.

Those professional activists actively *wanted* "old" conflicts to be resolved and aimed for cooperation with anarchist and feminist groups whom their organizations had fought against in the 1960s and 1970s. However, those earlier conflicts returned. A young participant in the national preparatory meetings and member of the radical group *Giovani/e Comunisti/e* noted how easily prior "bad stories" of conflicts between an older generation of activist groups fostered new conflicts in present Social Forum meetings:

I entered the Social Forum process in 2002, when a lot of things were going on. Less at the national level, it was local first of all. Later the very hard scissions and cleavages that have existed since '68, they first reappeared in the Social Forum process, they reproduced themselves.... I would even say they deepened. For us younger ones this is difficult to understand, but the '68 generation knows these problems from the ideological fights in the '70s, and then also the even bigger problems in the '80s.... Then the *Disobbedienti* left.[6]

In this quote, a Social Forum participant from the "radical" leftist youth network *Giovani/e Comunisti/e* reflects on how past "cleavages ... reappeared" and prevented successful cooperation in Italian Social Forum meetings. The interviewee's unfinished narrative indicates that the timing of the return of those "old" conflicts foreshadowed the very moment in which radical youth groups and the anarchist *Disobbedienti* network disengaged from the national preparatory group meetings altogether. The interviewee's narrative documents how younger participants can get caught up in the dynamic stories of memories of conflict: the interviewee (describing himself as "younger") says he "cannot understand" the reason for the conflict and yet, nevertheless, participates in it. Still, the interviewee did not say exactly how the cross-generational transmission of previous conflicts occurred in meetings, the dynamics of which I demonstrate below in the discussion of the British case.

In contrast to Italy, the UK from the very beginning created a less open, less dialogical, and less cooperative national Social Forum preparatory process, which activists and analysts described as "poisoned" by past conflicts. Most social movement scholars and many activists, have understood the crisis of the British Social Forum as a result of "clashing" ideological differences and antagonistic group identities (see, e.g. Maeckelbergh 2009; Papadimitrou et al. 2007). However, by looking at conflicting memories and silencing, I argue that in comparison to Italy, the high intensity of conflict in the British case can be understood through the prefiguring practices of transmission by different groups and organizations within the British global justice movements. In comparison to the Italian case, radical anarchist social movement groups had few intermediate, personal contacts with institutional leftist political parties and unions. What is intriguing is that, without such personal contacts and without broad collective efforts made to mediate across ideological boundaries, "bad" memories about failed cooperation in the past transformed into a "narrative media." By the term narrative media I mean that activists from one side of the conflict were telling each other stories constructing the opposing side as "Other." This telling was a practice of remediation, in Assman's sense, where the fresh telling of "bad" stories from the past would constrain any future dialogical encounters across groups. Memories provided a powerful narrative media through which to remember the importance of previous conflict and reestablish long-passed political fights across different generations of activists.

Like in Italy, the political context in which the ESF process began in the UK should have been positive. To protest the pro-war policy of the British government, London's leftist mayor Ken Livingstone proposed hosting the ESF 2004 in London, which he did together with radical leftist political parties (the Socialist Worker's Party, SWP, and the group Socialist Action), unions, and NGOs (cf. Reyes 2006).

However, a harmful rumor seemed to prefigure future democratic crises and blocked future cooperation at the UK Social Forum from the very beginning: British anarchist groups involved in organizing local Social Forum groups were suspicious of the socialist London mayor and felt excluded from his idea of organizing a Social Forum in the UK. Rodrigo Nunes, an activist and analyst engaged in local British Social Forum groups, described why many autonomous and anarchist social movement activists saw the hosting of an ESF by the London mayor as alienating and exclusionary:

> The London bid for the European Social Forum was presented in Paris during the second edition as the result of an agreement between the Socialist Worker's Party (SWP) and the Greater London Authority (GLA). It was discussed and approved at a closed meeting.... The decision to present London as an alternative was never debated among British movements. (Nunes 2004: 1)

Why did British anarchist groups involved in local Social Forums perceive the London mayor's initiative as a secretive, exclusionary threat? The evidence from participant observation may help to answer this question. I was a participant observer in several of the small group meetings organized for brainstorming by autonomous and anarchist groups before the first national preparatory assembly in London was organized. In contrast to the Italian meetings I attended, memories of violent exclusion were explicitly told and celebrated at the those small group meetings from the beginning. In reaction to stories of violent exclusion expressed by older activists, young participants in the early meetings began to join in the atmosphere of despair, interpreting the London mayor's proposal to host the ESF in London in purely negative terms, as a conspiracy against themselves.[7] The subsequent meetings I attended had a spirit of anger that included long discussions among those groups who had met to unite against the major.[8] Those negative memories also, much earlier than in Italy, were disseminated through activists from previous generations using their e-mail lists to transmit stories of past conflict to newcomers. Even before the first European preparatory assembly was held in London, older, autonomous and anarchist local Social Forum participants circulated personal statements across e-mail lists predicting a troubled future. One such e-mail stated:

> The problem with consensus in the UK is not that it means endless decisions, but that it allows people like the SWP [Socialist Workers Party] for twenty-five years to appropriate the process in the UK, in the way that they stand in the center and take the process over and manipulate.[9]

At the same time, when I interviewed the so called "verticals," professional party activists working for the London mayor who were accused of "manipulating" others, those professional activists made no secret of their negative opinion of local social movement activists who called themselves the "horizontals":

> Personally, the groups that call themselves "horizontals" behaved like children—how could we have trusted them? In the meetings, they behaved in an arrogant [upper class] manner towards us organizers whom they call "verticals." London is riddled with left-wing sectarian groups. Actually, the meetings took place in a public building of the Mayor's office. They asked for money, but they did not represent anyone—why should unionists who spoke for many members give the money to them?[10]

Building self-defensive stories as responsible unionists, professional activists constructed their own role as that of "serious" coordinators. In narrative terms, the cryptic notion of "seriousness" justified the explicit exclusion of grassroots activists whom professionals marked as unprofessional, childish people. Both sides of the conflict constructed themselves as morally superior by using dichotomous images, each denigrating the other group.

But the interesting thing the data reveals is that at the origin of those condensed images of "othering" were memories of violent exclusion—memories implicitly transmitted through cryptic, self-defensive images of "horizontals" versus "serious" professional organizers. Conflicting memories concentrated as those images allowed oppositional groups to keep ideological conflict stable across different generations. Negative stories circulated in jokes during coffee breaks and in anecdotes on e-mail lists and blogs. As opposed to the Italian case, dichotomous images of "real" Social Forum people and "secretive" professionals came to contaminate mediators' ways of making sense of the meetings, making intermediary work between leftist political party organizers and anarchists understandably difficult. One of the mediators said:

> There was a cultural clash between what I would call the real Social Forum people and the professional "Old Left" organizations who brought the European Social Forum to London. It poisoned all the meetings and finally killed the forum. Also, these different movements usually do not cooperate. [The Old Left, that is,] the organizers around Ken Livingstone and the GLA, the Socialist Workers Party, Socialist Action, also the Campaign for Nuclear Disarmament which has long been infiltrated by the Communist Party. [They] acted in a little transparent, secretive, and closed way from the first meeting.[11]

As in the quote from the interview with one of the mediators, the plot about the "secretive" initiative by the London mayor was the most frequent storyline recounted by interviewees from the UK. The violence reflected in the terminology of mediators, and the metaphors used ("clash," "poisoned," "killed") in my view are very important. They appear to confirm the hypothesis that at the basis of the political conflict that "poisoned" the British Social Forum were deeply remembered experiences of violent exclusion. These experiences, I argue, transmitted in narrative crypts (Schwab 2011), came to "entangle" all participants. As a result of this, even the mediators I interviewed came to conceptualize conflict in the genre of highly dichotomist crypts that distinguished the "real" Social Forum people from professional activists who tried to "kill" the building of the joint ESF.

These impressions of participants reveal the prefigurative power of memories; memories of violent exclusions prevented the remediation of past conflict among the groups involved in the present British Social Forum assemblies. Members accused of previous violence constructed self-defensive narratives to justify ongoing exclusionary decision-making practices while traumatized protesters felt excluded by official organizers whom they constructed as adversaries in narratives that they told each other and others in e-mail lists and online blogs before the first meeting had even occurred.

Historical divides were less obvious and explicit during the launching of the German national preparatory assemblies in June 2004. In this case, it was an immediate event that triggered the conflicting power of memories of violent symbolic exclusion in past German social movements and caused democratic crisis in the present. Unlike British "horizontals," local Social Forum activists in Germany had originally cooperated with professional leftist leaders from unions and political parties, until they collectively decided to walk out of joint meetings following what they saw as a violent and unexpected form of silencing and exclusion of grassroots activists, when a particular collective decision had to be taken in the spring of 2004.

Unlike in the Italian case, German organizers of the national preparatory assemblies lacked previous personal networks or a history of interpersonal conflict (Rucht et al. 2005). Inspired by the ESF in Florence, they, for several years, succeeded in cooperating without major organizational conflict (Doerr, forthcoming). My participant observation of the German Social Forum assemblies at the national level shows that organizational crisis emerged abruptly in mid 2004, when violent memories of exclusion in past movements were recalled. In the period from 2003 to mid 2004, a diverse number of both radical and moderate groups had been involved.[12] In June 2004, though, the more radical part of grassroots activists left the joint meetings after a few professional activists from Attac Germany and the German Left Party had informally agreed on the organization of a "Social Forum in Germany" event without asking the assembly. Those who had exclusively decided on the city of Erfurt as the location for their first German Social Forum summit (excluding other cities that grassroots activists had preferred) used a defensive narrative to justify this unilateral decision:

> Conditions for organizing a Social Forum in Germany were difficult, and then when [Wolfgang] got the Erfurt Mayor into our boat without necessarily asking all other groups in the assembly this was immediately interpreted as factionalism. Then comes this citizens' initiative from Southern Germany that claims the restitution of their travel costs to the preparatory meetings. By whom? By which salary? By the unions? I just critically asked this and immediately they were silent.[13]

Interviewees, as in the example quoted, defended the unilateral decision of professional activists to host the German Social Forum in a small the Eastern European town of Erfurt. In the above quote, a professional activist, remembering that particular decision, saw limited financial means as a source of conflict that had escalated in the meeting he described. Indeed, according to the interviewee quoted, professional activists solved such conflicts pragmatically, for example by silencing a group of grassroots activists from the "citizen initiative" through referring to financial conditions ("immediately they were silent"). But as a participant observer I noted that these grassroots activists in fact did not insist on unionists' financial support, as the interviewee had suggested. Following the meeting, what grassroots activists recalled explicitly, and could not forget, instead was the alienating character of exclusive decision-making practiced by Left Party organizers and unionists who had made a decision about the location of the Social Forum without including any other group. These exclusions seemed to repeat Left Party organizations' behavior toward anarchist activists and other ideological groups from the past. Frustrated grassroots participants wrote "open letters" over e-mail lists confronting professional activists for their unilateral decision-making among insiders:

> Dear Wolfgang,[14] you three, Harald Baum, Erwin Lang and yourself ... have self-mandatedly [taken the decision to host the Social Forum in Erfurt], giving the impression that you were legitimized by the coordination circle of the Social Forum process in Germany. Through this you have maneuvered yourself into a leadership position, abusing an authority that had been built collectively by all participants in the preparatory assemblies of the Social Forum in Germany beforehand. ... You have been pretending to make the assembly decide a Social Forum that you had already decided. ... Harald has already outed himself as a Marxist and I have the impression that your ideological home is similar to his.[15]

This "open letter" demonstrates the construction of a story of "bad cooperation" in a setting previously characterized by interviewees' enthusiasm for the new, transnational process that started with the ESF in Florence (see also Andretta and Reiter 2009). The writer of the letter argues that the group of radical grassroots activists only decided to leave the German Social Forum process collectively when professional activists started "abusing an authority that had been built collectively by all the participants ... beforehand." Note, importantly, that the violent experience of abuse made for the defensive construction of a narrative about different ideologies—attacking leaders' behavior as in line with "Marxism"—an image that revealed a much older memory of conflict in the 1960s and 1970s in the German context (Rucht et al. 2007).

After the event recounted in the letter, German interviewees would frequently refer to informal national Social Forum leaders as Marxists, an image that "made sense" of present practices of silencing in line with familiar narratives about historical conflicts in the Left. My participant observation confirms that leaders, by contrast, continued to silence the letter itself in the official public discourse of later meetings, while constructing a new e-mail list to communicate unproblematically with new incoming grassroots participants. But newcomers in 2004 and 2005, after initial engagement, again frequently left national preparatory meetings, which they perceived to be fairly top-down oriented: "[T]here is no open space for networking, no inspiration, it is just boring, dead, split."[16] Silencing oppositional voices had prefigured the "death" of the German Social Forum as a lively, participatory democracy.

In theoretical terms, note that the comparatively dramatic exit of more than half of the non-professional participants of the German Social Forum preparatory group occurred at an unexpected moment: namely *after* a relatively long initial phase of sustained participation in national meetings in the years from 2003 to 2004. Analysts have explained this exit as due to the dominance of the Attac network, the Left party, and the unions (Rucht et al. 2007), but my analysis shows its relationship to silencing. The moment of silencing of emerging narratives of political dissent and the silencing of traditionally marginalized voices are both factors in the timing and the spontaneous, collective character of disengagement in the German case.

Indeed, tracing back the origin of self-defensive narratives of exclusion, as used in the German case, I found that professional Social Forum "insiders," among them Attac leaders, unionists, and party members, had been first used to "silence" members of traditionally disadvantaged groups such as migrant women and working class participants. Evidence for this is documented in the first of the German preparatory meetings I studied, in which major conflicts had not yet escalated. However, traditionally disadvantaged groups such as migrant women, and/or socially disadvantaged participants among them, experienced their stories being ignored. One of them said:

> As a migrant, I have, like many others, a big problem with London as the place where the next European Social Forum shall take place. The probability that my visa request will be rejected is about fifty percent, because I cannot prove to the English authorities that I have a stable employment and salary in Germany. ... In the preparatory meeting today, again, [my demand to speak about visa opportunities] has been pushed back from public debate with the justification that we don't have time for this right now. ... They do not like to bother with it. They believe that these are the problems of foreigners [German: *Ausländerprobleme*].[17]

The German Attac facilitator who was accused of having failed to listen to migrants reconstructed his own memory of the plenary discussion concerning claims made by migrants in a joke that he told me after the meeting. During this interview, he explained his pragmatic decision not to debate the immigrants' questions:

> Maybe the English foreign minister will make an exception. Now we don't need public discussions about this. Maybe people could secretly travel in other people's jacket pockets.[18]

Complementing migrants' and facilitators' perceptions of being excluded from full participation, my participant observation shows that German facilitators, acting as hosts of meetings, often interrupted statements made by migrants—their actions flatly contradicting their own stated wish to include these groups.

Conclusion and Implications

Sociologists of storytelling disagree on exactly how people's stories preserve and transmit lines of conflict across time and on whether a democratic discourse requires a shared narrative of collective memory or does not (Polletta et al. 2011). My focus on storytelling in the transgenerational arena of the ESF allowed me to demonstrate the prevailing power of conflicting memories as triggers for present democratic crises in settings of political dialogue of social movements. Despite all attempts to deliberate, dialogue, or mediate, silenced memories provide a powerful "narrative media" to effectively recall past conflict and successfully uphold boundaries of identity and ideology across different generations. In a transnational, comparative perspective, this ethnography of storytelling in the ESF confirms that implicitly transmitted memories of exclusion from the past explain the variations and intensity of democratic crises in the present, across the countries and cases studied.

While social movement studies have documented the conflicting impact of different ideologies and identities, we know less about the timing of democratic crises. It has been difficult to understand exactly when a group's perceived differences turned into essentialist narratives of difference and contributed to the death of lively participatory democracies. The research focus here on silenced memories helps to shed light on the origins, timing, and intensity of democratic crises that beset the ESF in ways that studies focusing on the social basis of political conflict (in relation to differences of identity, ideology, and asymmetric resources of groups), have missed. The moments in which silenced memories reappeared in public discourse prefigured the early "democratic death" of the British Social Forum, the sudden exit of German grassroots activists, and the late-stage departure of young Italian participants. Across these different cases, examining the operations of collective memory shows that public remembering that denies violent exclusions in the past can ritually remobilize existing symbolic boundaries and foster conflicts that entangle all participants. Whenever social movement participants perceived a "poisoned" atmosphere during democratic interactions in national Social Forums, they sensed the arrival of ghost-like memories, the memories of silenced conflicts from the past decades' movements, which prefigured a traumatic return of the past in the present (Eyerman 2004: 160).

If institutional insiders, acting as facilitators and organizers of these national-level meetings, officially silenced memories of symbolic exclusion, these stories were nonetheless informally transmitted across time and place, forming *narrative crypts* (Schwab 2011). Against this public silencing by institutional insiders, groups such as immigrant women and members of resource-poor groups remembered past conflict and exclusion and transmitted those memories. The public reappearance of those silenced stories predicted a potential future disintegration of democracy. The return of these memories acted as a highly effective trigger for political crisis, as narrative crypts symbolically reenact dichotomist images of good and bad, friend and foe—eventually constraining the political language even of conflict mediators and making future cooperation extremely difficult. This suggests the need for comparative studies on the ways in which stories, inside or at the margin of transnational political discourse, store and change collective memory across time: how the past becomes the present and potentially blocks future democratic cooperation.

Notes

I want to thank the anonymous reviewers of this chapter and the participants in the New School for Social Research Interdisciplinary Memory Conference for their great comments, and I am grateful to Rachel Einwohner, Francesca Polletta, and Vera Zolberg for their inspiration and fine theoretical suggestions.

1. "'Cryptonymy' refers to operations in language that emerge as manifestations of a psychic crypt, often in the form of fragmentations, distortions, gaps, or ellipses. Abraham and Torok write about the crypt as an effect of failed mourning: it is a burial place inside the self for a love object that is lost but kept inside the self like a living dead" (Schwab 2010: 103).
2. COBAS are trade unions organized as radically democratic grassroots groups in opposition to the "established" confederation of unions like CGIL, CISL, and UIL (see della Porta et al. 2002: 58).
3. For example, the party *Rifondazione Comunista,* the cultural organization ARCI, and the union FIOM.
4. Background communication with an activist from *Ricercatori Precari* (Precarious Researchers), Florence, November 2006.
5. Interview with Marco Berlinguer, Transform Institute, Assembly for the Charter of Principles for another Europe meeting, Florence, Nov. 13, 2005.
6. Activist from *Giovani/e Communisti/e.* Interview conducted in Florence, November 2005.
7. My fieldnotes, small group meeting, ESF Paris, November 2003.
8. My fieldnotes, small group meeting, London, December 2003.
9. E-mail of an activist from Wales circulated among local Social Forum participants before the first British-European preparatory assembly in London, December 2003.
10. Interview with a member of the official preparatory group of the London ESF.
11. Interview with an activist from Indymedia, London, June 2007.
12. Participants were activists from local Social Forums, autonomous spaces, migrant and solidarity networks, religious groups, and unemployment initiatives, together with the organizers and hosts of these meetings: professional activists from Attac associated with Old Left parties, Trotskyite groups, and unions.
13. Interview within the European preparatory assembly to the ESF, Istanbul, September 2005.
14. Names changed.
15. E-mail correspondence, download date: July 1, 2005.
16. Interview with an activist from Euro Mayday, Erfurt, July 2005.
17. My translation. Interview with a participant from a migrant women's network after the preparatory assembly in Frankfurt, Feb. 21–22, 2004.
18. My translation. Interview with the facilitator (Attac) after the meeting of the preparatory assembly in Frankfurt, Feb. 21–22, 2004.

References

Abraham, N., and M. Torok. 1994. *The Shell and the Kernel: Renewals of Psychoanalysis.* Edited and translated by Nicholas T. Rand. Chicago: University of Chicago Press.
Alexander, J. C. 2006. *The Civic Sphere.* Oxford: Oxford University Press.
Andretta, M., and H. Reiter. 2009. "Parties, Unions and Movements: The European Left and the ESF." In *Another Europe: Conceptions and Practices of Democracy in the European Social Forums,* edited by Donatella della Porta. New York: Routledge.
Assmann, A. 2005. "Impact and Resonance—A Culturalist Approach to the Emotional Deep Structure of Memory." Paper, http://www.liv.ac.uk/soclas/conferences/Theorizing/Kurzfassungok2.pdf (accessed Jan. 3, 2011).

Assmann, A., and S. Conrad. 2010. "Introduction." In *Memory in a Global Age: Discourses, Practices, and Trajectories,* edited by Aleida Assmann and Sebastian Conrad, 1–16.

Boéri, J. 2006. "The Role of Babels in the ESF in London 2004," in *Conference Papers of the Eleventh International Conference on "Alternative Futures and Popular Protest,"* edited by C. Barker and M. Tyldesley, 22–30. Manchester University, April 19–21, 2006.

Caruso, F. 2005. *Maledetta Globalizazzione. Frammenti di vita e di disobbedienza sociale.* Roma: Carocci.

Daase, C. 2010. "Witnessing in a Global Arena." In *Memory in a Global Age: Discourses, Practices, and Trajectories,* edited by Assman and Conrad, 19–31.

della Porta, D. 2005a. "Making The Polis: Social Forums and Democracy in the Global Justice Movement." *Mobilization* 10.1: 73–94.

———. 2005b. "Multiple Belongings, Tolerant Identities, and the Construction of 'Another Politics': Between the European Social Forum and the Local Social Fora." In *Transnational Protest and Global Activism,* edited by Donatella della Porta and Sidney G. Tarrow, 175–202. Lanham, MD: Rowman and Littlefield.

della Porta, D., ed. 2009. "An Introduction." In *Another Europe: Conceptions and Practices of Democracy in the European Social Forums.* New York: Routledge.

della Porta, D., and L. Mosca. 2007. "In movimento: 'Contamination' in action and the Italian Global Justice Movement." *Global Networks* 7.1: 1–27.

Doerr, N. 2010. "Exploring Cosmopolitan and Critical Europeanist Discourse Practices in the European Social Forums." In: *The Transnational Condition. Protest Dynamics in an Entangled Europe.* Ed. S. Teune. New York, Berghahn: 165–182.

———. Forthcoming. "Democracy in Translation: How Activists Practice Deliberation in the European Social Forum Process." *European Political Science Review.*

Eder, K. 2009. "Communicative Action and the Narrative Structure of Social Life: The Social Embeddedness of Discourse and Market—A Theoretical Essay." In *Critical Turns in Critical Theory: New Directions in Social and Political Thought,* edited by S. O'Tuama, 63–79. London: Tauris & Co. Ltd.

Eyerman, R. 2004. "Culture and the Transmission of Memory." *Acta Sociologica* 47.2: 159–69.

Fraser, N. 2007. "Transnationalizing the Public Sphere—On the Legitimacy and Efficiency of Public Opinion in a Post-Westphalian World." *Theory, Culture and Society* 24.4: 7–30.

Gilman, S. L., and K. Remmler. 1994. *Reemerging Jewish Culture: Life and Literature Since 1989.* New York: New York University Press.

Halbwachs, M. 1992 [1925]. *On Collective Memory.* Edited by Lewis Coser. Chicago: University of Chicago Press.

Hirsch, M. 1997. *Family Frames: Photography, Narrative and Postmemory.* Cambridge: Harvard University Press.

Maeckelbergh, M. 2009. *The Will of the Many: How the Alterglobalisation Movement is Changing the Face of Democracy.* London: Pluto.

Nunes, R. 2004. "Territory and Deterritory: Inside and Outside the ESF 2004 New Movement Subjectivities." In *Euromovements Newsletter 1,* edited by Oscar Reyes, Hilary Wainwright, Mayo Fuster i Morell, and Marco Berlinguer (December). Accessed Oct. 1, 2008, http://www.euromovements.info/newsletter/.

Olick, J. K. 1999. "Collective Memory: The Two Cultures." *Sociological Theory* 17.3: 333–48.

182   Nicole Doerr

Olick, J. K., and D. Levy. 1997. "Collective Memory and Cultural Constraint: Holocaust Myth and Rationality in German Politics." *American Sociological Review* 62.6: 920–36.

Olick, J. K., V. Vinitzky-Seroussi, and D. Levy. 2011. Introduction to *The Collective Memory Reader,* 3–63. Oxford/New York: Oxford University Press.

Papadimitrou, T., Saunders, C., and C. Rootes. 2007. "Democracy and the London European Social Forum." Paper presented at the ECPR Workshop, Helsinki, May 2007.

Polletta, F. 2002. *Freedom Is an Endless Meeting: Democracy in American Social Movements.* Chicago: University of Chicago Press.

———. 2005. "How Participatory Democracy Became White: Culture and Organizational Choice." *Mobilization* 10.2: 271–88.

———. 2006. *It Was Like a Fever: Storytelling in Protest and Politics.* Chicago: Chicago University Press.

———. 2008. "Culture and Social Movements." *Annals of the American Academy of Political and Social Science,* 619. 1: 78–96.

Polletta, F., et al. 2011. "The Sociology of Storytelling." *Annual Review of Sociology* 37.1: 109–30.

Reyes, Oscar. 2006. "Exception or Rule? The Case of the London ESF 2004." In subsection "Social Forums: Radical Beacon or Strategic Infrastructure?" by Marlies Glasius and Jill Timms, in *Global Civil Society 2005/6,* edited by Marlies Glasius, Mary Kaldor, and Helmut Anheier, 243–44. London: Sage.

Rucht D., S. Teune, and M. Yang. 2007. "Moving Together: Global Justice Movements in Germany." In *The Global Justice Movement—Cross-national and Transnational Perspectives,* edited by Donatella della Porta, 157–83. New York: Paradigm.

Schudson, M. 1992. *Watergate in American Memory: How We Remember, Forget, and Reconstruct the Past.* New York: Basic Books.

Schwab, G. 2011. "Writing Against Memory and Forgetting." In *Haunting Legacies: Violent Histories and Transgenerational Trauma.* New York: Columbia University Press.

Smith, J. M., et al. 2007. *Global Democracy and the World Social Forums.* Boulder, CO: Paradigm.

Straughn, J. B. 2009. "Culture, Memory, and Structural Change: Explaining Support for 'Socialism' in a Post-socialist Society." *Theory and Society* 38:485–525.

Tymoczko, M. 2000. "Translation and Political Engagement: Activism, Social Change and the Role of Translation in Geopolitical Shifts." *The Translator* 6.1: 23–47.

Wagner-Pacifici, R. 2011. "Memories in the Making—The Shape of Things that Went." *Qualitative Sociology* 19.3: 301–21.

Wodak, R. 1996. *Disorders of Discourse.* London: Longman.

Wrainwright, H. 2004. "European Social Forum: Debating the Challenges for Its Future." *Red Pepper* (December). Accessed Jan. 1, 2011, http://www.redpepper.org.uk/european-social-forum-debating-the.

Zolberg, A. R. 1972. "Moments of Madness." *Politics and Society* 2: 183–207.

Zolberg, V. L. 1998. "Contested Remembrance: The Hiroshima Exhibit Controversy." *Special Issue on Interpreting Historical Change at the End of the Twentieth Century. Theory and Society* 27.4: 565–90.

Chapter 9

Memories of Jews and the Holocaust in Post-Communist Eastern Europe

The Case of Poland

Joanna B. Michlic

Introduction

This chapter considers the representations of Jews and the Holocaust in post-communist Poland from 2002—the year when the public debate about the Jedwabne massacre of July 10, 1941 culminated in the publication of the forensic report of the Institute of National Memory—until 2011. The debate about Jedwabne was the most profound and the longest of any historical issue in Poland since the political transformation of 1989. The almost constant preoccupation with all things Jewish- and Holocaust-related in the realm of national discourse about "who we are" and "who we wish to be" makes Polish society stand out among the post-communist countries. This situation has prompted some individuals in Poland involved in memory work to claim that the country is a unique state in Europe with regard to the "recovery" and commemoration of the Jewish past. As Janusz Makuch has argued: "Poland has been one of the few countries in Europe—perhaps the only one—to confront its own past systematically" (Makuch 2010: 131).

   Similarly to Makuch, other dedicated activists of the Polish-Jewish dialogue, as well as Polish diplomats and official authorities, regularly utter corresponding statements at the openings of international conferences and symposia in the country and abroad, dedicated to Polish-

Jewish and Polish-Israeli matters. Some foreign journalists, pundits, and descendants of Polish Jewry also offer an enthusiastically optimistic interpretation of the current memory projects focusing on Jews and the Holocaust in Poland. This position centers on the most positive changes in the public memory of Jews and the Holocaust that have taken place in the country over the last decade or so. However, it does not take into account the eruptions of conflicting memories of Jews and the Holocaust, nor does it pinpoint that some of this memory work is in practice problematic. Notwithstanding many significant positive developments, we cannot ignore the simultaneous presence of conflicting memories of Jews and the Holocaust. Only when we analyze these conflicting memories side by side do we gain a deeper insight into the complexities of the memory projects in Poland.

Poland presents a particularly highly developed case of the transformation of the memory of Jews and the Holocaust in post-communist Europe. It can serve as a paradigm in comparative studies of the scope, dynamics, complexities, and challenges of this memory transformation. But such studies have to take into account two aspects: first, the historical differences in how the Holocaust played out in each of the nation-states and variations in postwar memories of and relations with Jews; and second, the transnational features of some contemporary remaking of the memory of Jews and the Holocaust and the impact of the West on this remaking process.[1] Some themes and strategies for dealing with the memory of the Holocaust and Jews in Poland resemble those of other post-communist states, but in the latter these aspects appear to emerge on a smaller scale and to reach a less developed stage or, in the case of Ukraine or Belarus, to be in a nascent form.[2]

The memory of Jews and the Holocaust in post-communist Poland has persistently occupied a central stage in public debate since what the historian Padraic Kenney calls the peaceful "carnival of the revolutions" of 1989 (Kenney 2002).[3] At present, the more than twenty-year-old boom of the theater of Jewish memory does not show signs of declining. From the onset, intense and strong emotions have characterized the process of uncovering the Jewish past in and for Polish history. Other key features of this theater of memory are the elasticity and multiplicity of the representations of Jews and the Holocaust, the fusion of official and private memories absent during the communist era, and the variety of participants in memory projects, including Polish Jewish Holocaust survivors and their descendants living in Poland, Israel, and the West. The memory boom does not however mean that the archeology of the Polish Jewish past has been completed and that a broad public consensus has been reached on how to remember the Jews and the Holocaust.

No doubt, different assumptions and agendas have underpinned the recovery of the memory of Jews in Poland and one can differentiate three key dimensions in this landscape of memory. I call them "remembering to remember," "remembering to benefit," and "remembering to forget."[4] "Remembering to remember" is a process that underscores, on both the cognitive and the moral level, the void left after the genocide of Polish Jewry, and Polish-Jewish relations in all its aspects, including all the wrongs done to the Jewish minority before, during, and after the Holocaust. The intention of the advocates of "remembering to remember" is to mourn and to commemorate the loss of ten percent of Poland's prewar citizens and to come to terms with the dark past in relations to the Jewish minority by making this past part of Polish history, present historical consciousness, and public memory. Moreover, they frequently insist not only on integrating the history of Polish Jews and other ethnic and national minorities into Polish history, but also on treating Polish Jews and members of other minorities as members of the Polish nation in a civic sense. On a cultural level, their major goal is to create both a "community of identification" with and an empathic memory for the Jews who were historically perceived as the key internal "Threatening Other"[5] on political, cultural, social, and economic levels. Thus, they are engaged in building a forward-looking and inclusive Polish society based on a civic concept of national belonging, and a respect for multiculturalism and for humanitarian values. They perceive themselves as a community engaged in performing the necessary, solemn spectacle of the recovery of uncomfortable memories.

In "remembering to benefit" the key intention behind the recalling and commemoration of the Jews and the Holocaust is to achieve tangible goals on the individual, regional, and national level. Here the focus is not so much on the past, but rather on the utilization of the past in order to obtain concrete benefits, such as an elevated status and respectability and legitimacy in the international arena. The advocates of this mode of remembering are also future-minded and underscore that the Polish Jews have had a long presence in the country, and that today the descendants of the Polish Jews living abroad are welcome to be part of and to invest in the new post-communist Poland. They insist that Israeli Jews and Diaspora Jews should view Poland with a fresh eye, and regard this particular moment in history as a zero point in forging new and mutually beneficial Polish-Jewish and Polish-Israeli relationships. Though they acknowledge the dark past in the history of their nation, for them that past is a completely closed chapter, on which one should not dwell, but instead look to the future. In the name of this bright future, they claim it is better to concentrate on those chapters in the history of the nation's relations with the Jews that cast a good light, rather than on the dark history of anti-Semitism and the Holocaust. Thus, they perceive themselves as a community engaged in building a safe screen from the dark past.

In the mode of "remembering to forget," the memory of Jews and the Holocaust is understood as an awkward problem that does not fit in well with the conservative, Catholic, and ethno-nationalist model of Poland the advocates of this position affirm. Here, the recent wave of intense commemorations of the Holocaust and un-abating interest in the Polish Jewish past is greeted with tense feelings and is disdainfully referred to as "*moda na Żydów*" (fashion for Jews).[6] The advocates of "remembering to forget" view the painful dark past of Polish relations with its Jews, which is being gradually and systematically uncovered in the country and abroad, as an unjust insult on Polish history and memory and as a threat to national identity. Therefore they often lash back at the advocates of "remembering to remember." They see themselves as a community creating the "just" silence around the unacceptable painful past. In "remembering to forget" the archeology of the dark and uncomfortable past provokes an upsurge of old anti-Jewish prejudices and stereotypes that are being carefully modified and repackaged and expressed either overtly or covertly.

Each of these three approaches to memory is dynamic and manifest in subtly different versions, depending on the key actors engaged with the past. Moreover, among specific actors—particular institutions and organizations—a great variety of approaches can be observed. For example, within the Polish Catholic Church, which in the past, played a major role in shaping attitudes toward the Jews, one can observe an advocacy and support for "remembering to remember," especially among the members of the Club of Catholic Intelligentsia, individual priests such as Rev. Adam Boniecki, Rev. Wojciech Lemański, and the late Archbishop Józef Mirosław Życiński (1948–2011), and the so-called liberal Catholic journals and related milieus, such as the monthlies *Znak, Więź,* and *Przegląd Powszechny,* and the weekly *Tygodnik Powszechny.* In contrast, the so-called Rydzyk's Church with its daily *Nasz Dziennik* represents the core of the "remembering to forget" position. In addition, some versions of "remembering to remember" overlap with some variants of "remembering to benefit" and these can be difficult to differentiate. Thus, given the mosaic of approaches to the past and their representatives, the contemporary memory landscapes of Jews and the Holocaust does not add up to a single story. This essay will use vignettes of five key scenes as a way to explore the different ways in which the three dimensions of remembering emerge.

Scene 1: Jews in Vogue

Poland today is exuberant with the theater of Jewish memories and cultural and social activities aimed at celebrating Jewish heritage and commemorating its loss. As one Jewish survivor visiting from New York put it jokingly, Poland is now a place "where Jews are being carried in arms" (*Żydzi noszeni są na rękach*). One illustration of this process is the boom in Jewish festivals throughout the state that crystallized in the late 1980s. Such festivals have been taking place in large cities such as Łódź (Festival of Four Cultures, Yiddish Culture Festival),[7] Poznań (Tzadik Poznań Festival),[8] Wrocław (Simcha Festival),[9] and Białystok (Zachor Festival).[10] They are also organized in smaller towns such as Chmielnik and Szydłów,[11] Leżajsk (Festival of Jewish Culture "Kwitełech"),[12] Szczekociny (Yahad-Together Szczekociny Festival of Jewish Culture),[13] and Włodawa (Festival of Three Cultures).[14] Members of local political and cultural elites take upon themselves the role of enthusiastic and dynamic organizers and supporters of these events which in some localities have become an annual affair, celebrating the multiethnic past and commemorating its loss and the disappearance of the Jewish community during the Holocaust from local landscapes. The organizers of these events invite former Jewish inhabitants and their families from the West and Israel as honored guests and stress the positive contribution of Jews to the cultural and economic development of the area. For example, the official announcement of the "Rymanów Encounter" Society in 2008 reads: "August 13, 2008 is the sixty-sixth anniversary of the Rymanów ghetto liquidation. On this day, sixty-six years ago, one of the oldest and most creative Jewish communities in Poland ended its existence. On August 12 and 13 August 2008, the 'Rymanów Encounter' Society wishes to commemorate Rymanów Jews by symbolic and unconventional activities. ... Former inhabitants of Rymanów as well as their Israeli, American, and European families are going to be invited."[15] "Remembering to benefit" is frequently the driving force behind such events, but the modes of "remembering to remember" and "remembering to forget" are also visible.

Of course, not all the large and small towns in Poland where Jewish life thrived before World War II have now unanimously embarked on the project of celebrating their Jewish past either out of seeking tangible benefits or because of genuine nostalgia for the lost Jewish past. This is also not to say that among those that have done so, all present the same high-quality artistic and educational programs aimed at eradicating the old, stereotypical images of the Jews and disseminating profound reflections about the Holocaust and its consequences for the region as prescribed in the "remembering to remember" mode. Because of their popular, mass-culture nature, these festivals are rife with kitschy, commercial, and poor quality artistic events.[16] In that sense they do not differ from any other popular mass-culture festivals organized in the country. But because of that, at times they can reinforce the old stereotype of the Jews as an exotic, alien ethnic group that dwelled in the Polish nation in the pre-1939 period. This kind of portrayal presents the Jewish population only in this narrow ethnic sense, instead of challenging the old stereotypes and presenting a more nuanced and sophisticated portrayal of Polish Jews past and present.

However, what is even more troubling is that some of these small towns possess dark histories that directly and profoundly clash with the idea of commemorating and honoring the Jewish inhabitants murdered during the Holocaust. For example, Chmielnik, in Kielce County, Świętokrzyskie Voivodeship in central Poland, has recently become a battlefield between celebrations and commemorations of the Jewish past on the one hand, and the local Polish heroes who had fought in the underground units of the "Home Army" (*Armia Krajowa*) during World War II on the other.[17] Some of these local heroes, whose offspring are often the driving force behind commemorating their parents' "heroic wartime past," were killers and denouncers of Jews during the Holocaust. Can one commemorate the Jewish past and the local murderers of Jews in the same town? Is this possible? Is it moral? For the locals, these are profound and challenging questions that prompt emotional, heated discussions and inevitably lead to disagreements among the members of local elites and the community at large, dividing them into those who condemn the wartime crimes against Jews, those who view the Jews as an obstacle to honoring the wartime patriotic deeds of "good Poles," and those who do not care much about the wartime history of their town. In such cases, we observe direct, intense clashes between the "remembering to remember" and the "remembering to forget" modes.

The dramatic recent change in making dead and living Jews into a "hot item" in mainstream political and cultural spheres and the public visibility of the "remembering to remember" mode have even raised feelings of envy or resentment among individuals belonging to other small present-day minorities in Poland. In his personal interview for *Gazeta Wyborcza*, the main liberal newspaper, Mamadou Diouf, a Polish-based journalist born in Senegal, complains that these days, anti-Semitic utterances have been disappearing from the public because of the imposition of political correctness, whereas racist remarks are still common.[18] However, ethnic Polish critics, including a respected poet of the Solidarity movement of the 1980s, Jarosław Marian Rymkiewicz, take a different stance toward the political transformation of attitudes toward Jews. That stance is deeply rooted in pre-1939 anti-Semitic imagery. Rymkiewicz covertly suggests that the state-sponsored interest in Jews is one of the clear signs that Poles, meaning "true" Poles, no longer govern the country.[19] Some supporters of the main right-wing conservative party Law and Justice (*PiS*), headed by Jarosław Kaczyński, express similar sentiments during their demonstrations against the liberal government led by Prime Minister Donald Tusk. Neo-fascist, racist, and extreme ethno-nationalist groups and organizations articulate these sentiments in the most radical fashion, using slogans such as "Here is Poland, not Israel," "We do not apologize for Jedwabne," "Jews were easily perishable [during the Holocaust]," and "Poland only for the white people."

The positive reevaluation of the role of Polish Jews in national politics, culture, and economy is a post-communist phenomenon. Prior to the political and economic transformation of the country that began in 1989, only a small minority of liberal-leaning public intellectuals, writers, and politicians advocated a positive evaluation of Polish Jews and their contributions to the development of the Polish nation-state throughout the centuries. This new re-conceptualization is rooted in two different approaches that correspond with the two dimensions of memory, "remembering to benefit" and "remembering to remember," respectively. Not only do they interact with each other, but in some instances they become closely interwoven.

Firstly, the pragmatic desires of Polish politicians to rebuild the state economy and advance economically and culturally is the driving force behind the new recasting of Jews that serves as a proof of endorsement of Western-style capitalist culture. Current political elites have realized that praising the lost multi-ethnic past and commemorating the Holocaust are key means of gaining respectability and visible international status in the West, as well as effective and convincing ways of showing that the country today is free of its past anti-Semitic and xenophobic traditions, ready to forge a new chapter in the history of its ties with Israel, the Jewish Diaspora, and Jews at home. Perhaps no one has articulated this position as eloquently and skillfully as Radosław Sikorski, Polish Foreign Minister, in his interview of February 2011 with Adar Primor, a journalist of the Israeli daily *Haaretz*. Asked about the reasons for the renewal of Jewish culture in Poland today, Sikorski framed this renewal as free Poland's "return to its natural self,"[20] i.e., the return to the tradition of tolerance of which Poles are very proud.

Secondly, the new re-conceptualization of Polish Jews comes out of a genuine nostalgia for the multiethnic past expressed by enthusiastic individuals, mainly those who are regarded or regard themselves as the "virtual Jews" (Gruber 2002, 2009: 63–79) or "the self-proclaimed carriers of the lost East-European Jewish civilization,"[21] such as Janusz Makuch, director of the highly successful annual international Jewish Festival in Cracow who proclaimed in May 2007:

> People have to realize the dimensions of the enormous evil that was done here and understand that it is important to cleanse themselves of it. The festival creates a confessional space that should help people realize what happened here and what we have lost. We have to ask ourselves the question why we lost it, what our guilt is, what our Polish complicity is in the fact that this Jewish world is not only gone, but will never return.[22]

Scene 2: Jews as "Good Luck Charms"

The positive re-evaluation of formerly negative stereotypes of Jews is one of the most striking features of the novel re-conceptualization of Poland's Jewish past. For example, the negative stereotype of the Jew as a shrewd moneymaker has been transformed into the positive stereotype of the Jew as a prosperous and effective businessman, and as such is in vogue as something Poles should imitate in order to become successful in life. For that reason, tiny plastic figurines presenting "exotic" traditional Polish Jews belonging to the pre-1939 world, each holding a Polish grosz for good luck, as well as mass-produced paintings and drawings of elderly Orthodox Jewish male figures are both popular items. They are presented as gifts at private family celebrations and, in certain circles, are also "a must item" to be displayed by private business owners.[23]

This trend has even given rise to a new group of Polish artists specializing in painting "the Jew for good luck."[24] Some of these artists of younger generations display a lack of knowledge pertaining to the past, while others, belonging to older generations, are aware of the past negative connotations of the word Jew, but understand that this does not seem relevant to the current demands of the market. For them, the production of "good luck Jewish charms" is the right response to fulfill the desire of a new growing clientele and an opportunity to make a living. Their kitschy works become expressions of the new belief that having Jews around even in a symbolic sense could bring material wealth and success in life. This is articulated in an old, traditional saying: "a Jew at home, money in pocket" (*Żyd w sieni, pieniądz w kieszeni*) which some authors of "good luck Jewish charms" use in their artistic works as a leitmotif. Here, the mixture of kitsch and the utilization of reversed old anti-Jewish stereotypes reinforces the latter rather than erases them. Of course, this positive spin on old, strongly anti-Semitic stereotypes of Jews is not a uniquely Polish development. It takes places in other countries of post-communist Eastern Europe such as Romania, where one also observes various clashes among the "remembering to remember," "remembering to benefit," and "remembering to forget" modes (Oisteanu 2009). However, this is not to say that the old, pre-1939, anti-Semitic stereotype of the shrewd and stingy Jew has disappeared entirely from national cultures in the region. Some of the best examples of its persistence in Poland are visible in contemporary Polish language, for example: the phrase, *"przecież nie kupiłam/kupiłem u Żyda,"* (after all, I did not buy this from a Jew), which implies that the goods were purchased at the right price and the buyer was not cheated; and the increasingly common verb *"pożydzić"* (judaize), meaning that one has been denied financial support or help from a potential sponsor.

Scene 3: Grassroots Commemorative Projects

As laid out earlier, since the mid 2000s, Poland has witnessed a proliferation of festivals of Jewish culture and of spontaneous, grassroots initiatives organized by local priests, Polish literature and history teachers, and other local enthusiasts to commemorate and remember vanished local Jewish communities in cities, towns, and villages all over Poland. Various new social organizations and individuals have become engaged in maintaining abandoned Jewish cemeteries and placing commemorative plaques in areas known as Jewish before 1939. The number of such initiatives that belong to the "remembering to remember" dimension of the landscape of memory is difficult to assess, but it is definitely on the rise.[25] School children are sometimes involved through actions such as cleaning neglected local Jewish cemeteries with the authorization of the Jewish community. Given the fact that the number of Jewish cemeteries in Poland is estimated at fourteen hundred and many of them are located outside of the areas of the eight Jewish communities restored in post-communist Poland, this is a highly desirable material culture preservation project. Without such efforts, coordinated with the representatives of the Polish Jewish community, many Jewish cemeteries and other sites of Jewish heritage would eventually face oblivion. High school students are also engaged in collecting information about vanished Jewish communities and writing essays about the multicultural world their grandparents were the last generation to personally experience.[26]

The relationships and intersections between these individual memorialization projects and the broader public memory of the Holocaust is a subject that merits an entire study on its own. Though at present we do not have data to evaluate the extent to which these projects have in-

fluenced the historical consciousness and memory of the young participants, the fact of participation itself represents a significant change and a
rupture from the communist past.

In 2009, an unusual grassroots initiative called "Atlantyd" was organized by Captain Artur Cyrylik, a policeman from Hajnówka in northeastern Poland.[27] The initiative was aimed at saving traces of the multicultural
past, including Jewish material culture. Thanks to his efforts, prisoners
cleaned and restored five Jewish cemeteries in Jedwabne, Łomża, Na-
rew, Narewka, and Zambrowo, in the region where the worst instances
of anti-Jewish violence had taken place in the summer of 1941. Most
recently, *Fundacja Ochrony Dziedzictwa Żydowskiego* (The Foundation
for the Preservation of Jewish Heritage in Poland), which was set up in
2002, decided to imitate this local program and transform it into a national project.[28] The prison authorities hope the participation of prisoners
in this initiative will improve the image of Polish prisons and teach the
prisoners respect for other cultures and religions.

Scene 4: The New Recasting of the Christian Polish Rescuers

Another recent development is the boom of interest in Christian Polish
rescuers. The recently intensified attention to rescuers in contemporary
Poland is influenced by two contradictory cultural trends. On the one
hand, there is the desire to participate in the new Europe through education for democratic citizenship and new investigations of the past embedded in critical history writings. On the other hand, there are older patterns
of thinking about and manipulating the memory of rescuers for particular political, social, and moral aims. Here, "remembering to remember"
and "remembering to forget" profoundly clash with each other.

In pre-1989 Poland, the subject of rescuers was a marginal topic in public memories and commemorations of wartime heroism, which was also
skewed in historiography. In the Polish pre-1989 historiography concerning rescuers, the three dominant tendencies were: first, to underscore the
large number of rescuers; second, to downplay or ignore the low societal
approval of rescue activities; and third, not to differentiate among the various categories of rescuers, protectors, and helpers and their motivations.

Throughout the entire communist period the subject of rescuers was
usually brought up not because of its intrinsic intellectual and moral
merits, but predominantly to defend the good name of Poles and to silence any commentaries showing Poles in a bad light. Around this, by
the 1960s and 1970s, both communist elites in the country and anti-communist elites abroad reached a peculiar agreement.[29] This way of writing

about rescuers has persisted in the post-communist period and is part of the so-called *polityka historyczna* (historical policy) enforced in late 2005 by the then right-wing conservative government of the twin brothers Lech and Jarosław Kaczyński. Though the adherents of *polityka historyczna* are preoccupied with more than the Jedwabne debate,[30] it was that debate and public attention to the dark aspects of Polish history that raised fears among conservative politicians, triggering the implementation of *polityka historyczna*. Jarosław Kaczyński articulated perhaps the most exaggerated version of these fears: "We are faced with a situation where in the next few decades or less World War II will be understood as two great crimes: the Holocaust, in which Poles had allegedly taken part, and the expulsion of the Germans [from Poland in 1945], in general, the outcome of Polish actions."[31]

Historians and journalists practicing *polityka historyczna*[32] often cite the number of Christian Polish rescuers of Jews honored to date by the Yad Vashem Memorial Institute in Jerusalem, numbering approximately 6,350, as a tool to "normalize" the dark past. By employing this data, they claim that Polish anti-Semitism and nationalism did not have much of a damaging influence on Polish-Jewish relations, in order to restore the image of Poles as solely heroes and martyrs.[33] They tend to focus on a description of the histories of individual rescuers. What their writings lack is a more nuanced historical context and a discussion of Polish society's hostility toward both the Jewish fugitives and their Christian rescuers.[34]

Nevertheless, by the middle of the 2000s, in spite of the continuous manipulation of the subject by champions of *polityka historyczna* and right-wing nationalistic historians in the country and the Polish Diaspora, young Poles began to show a genuine interest in new scholarship on rescuers. This interest has not been motivated by the notion of saving the good name of Poland at the expense of historical truth, but by a desire to understand the complexities of national history, including its uncomfortable and painful aspects. A growing number of works challenge the pre-1989 hegemonic historical interpretation of rescuers as a monolithic, altruistic group, and typical representatives of Polish behavior toward Jews during World War II. These works, as a rule, shift the emphasis of historical inquiry to the varied crimes of ordinary Poles against Jews during and after the Holocaust.[35] For example, the fourth volume of *Zagłada Żydów. Studia i materiały,* an academic journal of the Polish Center for Holocaust Research based in Warsaw,[36] chiefly examines paid rescuers, some who later denounced those they rescued and some who then murdered their Jewish charges. Other works also discuss the history of paid rescuers and the uneasy relationship between Jewish survivors and paid rescuers,[37] as well as the complexities of wartime life for rescuers and survivors in specific localities.[38] Many of these works, no doubt inspired by Jan T. Gross's writings, underscore what I call the "vast grey zone" of rescue activities.

In the second half of the 2000s, with the emergence of new critical history writing about Polish-Jewish relations, Poland also developed new rituals of honoring Polish rescuers of Jews. One of the first such commemoration projects was initiated by the short-lived grassroots Polish-American Jewish Alliance for Youth Action (PAJA), established by two Americans, Dennis Misler and Zofia Zager. PAJA presented each of the living "Polish Righteous" a special "Tree of Gratitude and Honor" award and aimed to establish them as heroes in Poland. Currently the Galicia Museum in Cracow continues PAJA's work with rescuers and survivors.[39] Simultaneously, there were genuine calls for honoring rescuers by naming local schools after them to firmly establish them as Polish wartime heroes in the eyes of Polish youth. Initially, this idea met with negative reactions and rejection from local political elites and communities.[40]

Generating new collections of oral histories of rescuers and survivors is another development of the second half of the 2000s that contributes to the reinterpretation of the history of Polish-Jewish relations and Polish behavior towards Jews during the Holocaust. The Polish-English-German language publication *Światła w ciemności. Sprawiedliwi wśrod narodów świata* is one such oral history initiative.[41] A group of young enthusiasts from the Lublin-based cultural center Brama Grodzka-Teatr NN are the authors of this collection of sixty-one interviews conducted in the 2000s with Polish rescuers, their children, and other eyewitnesses from the Lublin province and other southeast areas. Like many other initiatives of Brama Grodzka, this work is dedicated to the memory of the Holocaust.

Unlike Brama Grodzka, which is a local grassroots project, the online project *Polacy Sprawiedliwi-Przywracanie pamięci,* established in 2007 by the Museum of Polish Jews Project in Warsaw, is a state-sponsored initiative to memorialize rescuers as Polish heroes and to gather their oral histories. So far, the organizers of the project have conducted three hundred interviews with rescuers who, in the majority, have already been awarded the Israeli Yad Vashem Award of the Righteous Among The Nations.[42] The project's leaders have also launched a number of Warsaw-based educational initiatives for building a civic democratic society, *Żolibórz-ogród Sprawiedliwych wśród Narodów Świata.* The first in a series was a workshop that introduced the participants to the history of rescuers in Żoliborz, a pre-1939 socialist (PPS) neighborhood of Warsaw, where a high number of rescue operations took place.[43]

The late Irena Sendlerowa (1910–2008) represents the best-known case of the current process of uncovering rescuers. Sendlerowa (wartime nickname "Jolanta") has virtually overnight become the most famous Polish rescuer of Jews in both Poland and abroad.[44] Her name is evoked in almost every public discussion of the subject and she has been transformed into a major feature film heroine.[45] In 2007, the Polish Association of Child Holocaust Survivors (*Stowarzyszenia Dzieci Holocaustu*) and the American Foundation "Life in a Jar" established an award in her name *"Za naprawianie świata,"* which is annually bestowed upon educators and public figures involved in building a civil society free of prejudice in post-communist Poland.[46] Yet, until the mid 2000s, she was a little known figure in public life, and was in fact first "discovered" outside of Poland by American schoolgirls from Kansas who wrote a play about her and her wartime deeds.[47] But, in 2007, one year prior to her death at the age of 98, representatives of the Polish state made efforts to nominate her for a Nobel Peace Prize, a diplomatic move addressed at audiences abroad to show that Poland today is free of ethnic and racial prejudice and that it pays tribute to those who rescued Polish Jews. As a part of this campaign, on March 14 of the same year the Polish Senate honored her actions and the actions of the wartime Council to Assist the Jews—*Żegota*—for which Sendlerowa clandestinely worked.

Poland's "discovery" of Sendlerowa is also part of building new diplomatic relations with Israel. The broad positive public outcome of such commemorations in the country lies in the reaffirmation of rescuers' wartime deeds as an honorable and heroic aspect of Polish wartime history. In right-wing and nationalistic public debate and writing, however, rescuers are used instrumentally as a counterbalance to the narratives of the dark aspects of Polish-Jewish relations during the Holocaust. The case in point is the family of Józef and Wiktoria Ulm from the village of Markowa in the Rzeszów province. While Irena Sendlerowa, a member of the left-wing Polish socialist milieu, survived the war in spite of denunciations, on March 24, 1944, the Germans brutally murdered Józef and Wiktoria Ulm, all their children, and the Jewish fugitives they were hiding.[48] The right-wing politicians, historians and journalists refer to the Ulm family as the chief example of rescuers who helped Jews for purely humanitarian reasons and ultimately sacrificed their lives for them. What they do not discuss is the situation of these rescuers in their community in Markowa and their actions in the context of the very mixed attitudes and behavior toward Jews in the Rzeszów province as a whole.

The most recent attempt to counterbalance the "dark history" by underscoring and manipulating the Ulm family's wartime biography—the undoubtedly positive history—is visible in the first reactions of politicians of Law and Justice (*PiS*)[49] and journalists from the right-wing Catholic newspaper *Nasz Dziennik* to the new controversial book by Jan Tomasz Gross, *Golden Harvest* (*Złote żniwa*), written in collaboration with Irena Grudzińska-Gross. The monograph discusses the brutal history of the seizure of Jewish assets by ordinary Poles during and after the Holocaust. The liberal Catholic publisher *Znak,* based in Cracow, published the book in Polish in March 2011. As in the case of Gross's previous works, *Neighbors* and *Fear* (Gross 2001, 2006), the right-wing historian Marek Jan Chodakiewicz produced a counter-work, *Heart of Gold or a Golden Harvest?,* in which he entirely rejected Gross's arguments. Thus, Chodakiewicz and other right-wing pundits and journalists attempt to erase the dark past by insisting only on the existence of the "good past"; their works belong to the "remembering to forget" approach to the memory of Jews and the Holocaust.[50]

Scene 5: Remembering the Dark Past

In 2009 the eminent Polish historian Jerzy Jedlicki named the difficulty of disseminating the accounts of the uncomfortable aspects of Polish-Jewish relations during the Holocaust to broader segments of Polish society: *powerlessness (bezradność)*. At the same time, he considered the process of self-critical assessments of the Polish national past crucial to Polish cultural renewal.[51] Such a renewal process was activated by the Jedwabne debate in 2000–2002, triggered by the publication of Jan Tomasz Gross's book *Neighbors* in 2001.[52] Gross's position in *Neighbors* resembles the optimistic progressive position of American sociologist Robert N. Bellah, who argues that a national community is continually engaged in retelling the constitutive narratives of its collective history. "If the community is completely honest," Bellah writes, "it will remember stories not only of suffering received but also of suffering inflicted—dangerous memories, for they call the community to alter ancient evil."[53] Thus, *Neighbors* set out a definite counter-memory to all narratives in the accepted canon of remembering the Holocaust, Polish-Jewish relations, and Polish society during World War II.

Today, in the post-Jedwabne debate period, the Jedwabne massacre of Jews by their Polish neighbors on July 10, 1941 does not simply function as a single painful historical fact, but has become a symbol of all dark aspects of Polish-Jewish relations during the Holocaust and its aftermath, and even of the entire Polish-Jewish relations during the Holocaust, as noted by the sociologist Antoni Sułek.[54] Jedwabne stands at the core of the "remembering to remember" mode as a crucial historical event that

Poles have to be constantly reminded of in order to understand that they were not just victims and heroes, but also perpetrators of crimes against others. In contrast, among the advocates of the "remembering to forget" mode, Jedwabne has become a symbol of Poland's unjustified humiliation and dishonor. Therefore their favorite slogan during demonstrations, public debates, and in journalistic writing is "We do not apologize for Jedwabne" (*Nie przepraszamy za Jedwabne*).[55]

Jedwabne not only inspires historians and scholars to investigate other uncomfortable aspects of Polish-Jewish relations, but also inspires visual artists, writers, poets, playwrights, and filmmakers who adhere to the "remembering to remember" mode. For them, coming to terms with the uncomfortable past is part of making up a new post-communist collective biography in order to create a progressive and inclusive society. These individuals, dissatisfied with the slow integration of and indifference toward the accounts of difficult aspects of the Polish-Jewish past, openly take upon themselves the role of "Polish conscience," a tradition that has its roots in the position initiated by the late literary critic Jan Błoński's essay "The Poor Poles Look at the Ghetto" (1987). In this groundbreaking article, Błoński raised difficult questions about the "insufficient concern" of Poles about the fate of Jews during the Holocaust, arguing that in part it was the result of widespread anti-Jewish feelings in the prewar period. He suggested that the Poles had difficulties with reexamining their wartime relations with the Jews because they saw *themselves* as the primary victims of the German occupation and were unable to acknowledge that they, too, were capable of wrongdoing.

In 1987 Błoński was a solitary voice, whereas the last decade has seen the emergence of a new literary and artistic school addressing vexing problems about national identity and responsibility for the wrongs done to others in the past. Marek Baczewski's *Nie używaj tego ognia* (*Do Not Use That Light*) (2008), Małgorzata Sikorska-Miszczuk's *Burmistrz* (*Mayor*) (2009), Artur Pałyga's *Żyd* (*A Jew*) (2008), and Paweł Demirski's and Michał Zadara's *Tykocin* (2009)[56] are good examples of recent plays inspired by the new moral resolve to uncover the skeletons in the national closet and engage the public with painful questions about "who we, the Poles, are," "who we want to be," "how we behaved toward the Jews" and "the implications of this behavior." Some of these artists are only known in small milieus, while others have succeeded in triggering short-lived public debates and generating national interest in the media.

Tadeusz Słobodzianek, an accomplished playwright, received Poland's highest literary award, the Nike Prize, in 2010 for his play *Nasza klasa* (*Our Class*), which was directly inspired by the revelations about the Jedwabne massacre and the emotionally heated public debate about the event. Some critics in Poland compared the play to a necessary medicine that Poles should be prescribed to cure themselves of the anti-Jewish prejudices inherited from their forefathers. In *Our Class,* Słobodzianek, born in 1955, paints a picture of the prewar, seemingly peaceful bi-ethnic community of young Catholic Poles and Jews of Jedwabne and its devastating wartime and postwar fate. At the center of his exploration is the aftermath of the crime: the effect of the murders of the Jewish classmates on the lives of both the perpetrators and the survivors. He explores the topics of guilt, responsibility, justice, and traumatic memories that become like ghosts that do not want to go away. In one of his interviews, Słobodzianek reveals why he wrote the play. His main questions are about the impact of the traumatic past on the chief protagonists and about what these protagonists have done with this traumatic past, what coping strategies they have used to keep that past at a safe distance. His concerns are with freedom, fate, and conscience. He declares that "he does not believe in clean conscience" and "in an ideology that gives us a weapon to humiliate and exclude others," but in "pain, suffering and laborious building of self-knowledge."[57] *Our Class* has already been staged in London (world premier, September 2009), Warsaw (October 2010), Toronto, Philadelphia (October–November 2011), and Boston (February 2012). Correspondingly, the filmmaker Władysław Pasikowski, the director of the cult feature film *Psy* about the secret communist police, felt compelled out of shame and shock caused by his reading of Gross's *Neighbors* to make the feature film *Pokłosie*. The film explores the aftermath of the massacre of the Jedwabne Jews and the memories of the event. For Pasikowski, who started to shoot the film on the seventieth anniversary of the Jedwabne massacre in July 2011, it is high time Polish cinema began to tackle dark parts of Polish history such as Jedwabne. Pasikowski, who also wrote the film script, delivers a film in which the audience faces the human and moral dimension of the crime, and he views the Jedwabne massacre as a crime committed by Poles against other Poles—the Polish Jews.[58] *Pokłosie* aired in some Polish cinemas in the autumn of 2012 and caused a short-lasting, emotional debate in the media, similar in nature to the one about the Jedwabne pogrom. Several journalists and commentators who represent the position "remembering to forget" have crudely and insolently accused Pasikowski of making an anti-Polish film.

Similarly Rafał Betlejewski, the controversial young performance and visual artist (sometimes accused of self-serving agendas), declared on his website titled "I miss you Jew" (*Tęsknię za tobą Żydzie!*)[59] that "for Poles the synonym of the word *Genocide of Jews* should be the word *loss*" (*Dla Polaków synonimem słowa Zagłada powinno byc słowo Utrata*).[60] Betlejewski interprets his most controversial, unconventional, and cathartic performance, namely the burning of a barn in the village Zawada, near Tomaszów Mazowiecki in central Poland on the sixty-ninth anniversary of the Jedwabne massacre, as a visual representation of the Poles' role in the Holocaust. According to the artist, this symbolic burning, which was aired on the major channels of Polish television networks, should shock and cleanse and, thus, eradicate the vestiges of anti-Semitism in Polish society today.[61]

The works by artists such as Słobodzianek, Pasikowski, Betlejewski, and many others can be interpreted as one form of manifesting disagreement with the lack of a broad national reassessment of Polish national history in the face of the dark past in relations to Jews during the Holocaust. Today Jews constitute a numerically insignificant ethnic and cultural minority in contemporary Poland. Nevertheless attitudes toward the Jewish past and "the dead Polish Jews" are still considered a marker of the strength of Polish democracy among progressive Polish public intellectuals, even when the discussion from time to time shifts to the rights of the Polish gay and lesbian community, which only recently assumed a more prominent public role. This evaluation of the strength of Polish democracy on the grounds of the attitudes toward Jews and other minorities has its intellectual and ideological roots in the interwar period.

Conclusion: Splits Over the Dark Past

Strong emotions and conflicting assertions characterize the process of uncovering the Polish past in relation to Jews in and for Polish history and social/collective memory, from the beginning of the pioneering public debates of the late 1980s and 1990s through the present. As the second half of the 2000s reveals, the archeology of the painful past has not yet been completed. Nor has a broad public consensus been reached on the position of the uncomfortable past of Polish-Jewish relations in Polish history, collective memory, and identity. In political and popular culture and in historical studies pertaining to the evaluation of the dark past, different approaches proliferate and splits are contentious. A good example of such a split was the public reaction to an article, "Hitlers europäische Helfer beim Judenmord," ("Hitler's European Holocaust Helpers"), published on May 18, 2009 in the German weekly *Der Spiegel*, which astutely discussed various official and nonofficial collaborators and voluntary perpetrators in the murder of six million Jews in Nazi occupied Europe.[62] This well-researched article outraged some mainstream political and journalistic circles in Poland. Right-wing conservative circles and individuals, including the former Prime Minister Jarosław

Kaczyński, the chief journalists of major center-right newspaper *Rzecz-pospolita,* right-wing Catholic *Nasz Dziennik,* and officials of the *Instytut Pamięci Narodowej* (Institute of National Remembrance, IPN), all accused *Der Spiegel* of foisting guilt for the Nazi crimes off onto others, and announced that Germans had no right to refer to Hitler's European helpers.[63] Conversely, liberal politicians and journalists, including former Polish Minister of Foreign Affairs Adam Daniel Rotfeld, himself a child Holocaust survivor, and Marek Beylin of *Gazeta Wyborcza,* did not find anything in the article contemptible; nor did they feel it led to a relativization of German guilt.[64]

Another major split was observable in the reactions to Jan T. Gross's *Fear,* a sequel to *Neighbors,* published first in English in the summer of 2006 and then in Polish on January 11, 2008 (Gross 2006). *Fear* analyzes a well-known massacre of Polish Jews in the early post-Holocaust period, the pogrom in Kielce on July 4, 1946, and discusses the etiology of the early postwar anti-Jewish violence. The book became a subject of serious critical discussion by scholars like the American-Israeli historian David Engel, as well as by Polish historians such as Paweł Machcewicz and Bożena Szaynok, who do not belong to the ethnonationalist school of history writing. The champions of *polityka historyczna* in the country, however, reacted to *Fear* with extreme hostility and unequivocally rejected it.[65]

The IPN's promotion of the Polish translation of Marek Jan Chodakiewicz's *After the Holocaust: Polish-Jewish Conflict in the Wake of World War II* (*Po zagładzie. Stosunki polsko-żydowskie 1944–1947*) is illustrative of this profound dismissal.[66] Chodakiewicz's work was promoted on the Internet and in the press simultaneously with the launch of the Polish edition of *Fear* in January 2008. On January 11, 2008 in Warsaw, IPN organized the first official launch of Chodakiewicz's monograph. In addition, the Polish Studies and European Studies Program at Columbia University invited and sponsored Chodakiewicz's lecture "Poland in America's Crooked Mirror: The Case of *Fear,*" which took place on February 18 that year.

The promoters of *Po zagładzie* conceived of it as a counterwork to *Fear,* one that would block its positive reception and unmask its alleged anti-Polish character. This strategy reveals the extent to which the IPN under the chairmanship of the late Janusz Kurtyka (1960–2010) tended to politicize history as a discipline. This politicization of history may prove the biggest threat to the future of scholarly history writing in Poland and specifically to the integration of the dark history of Polish-Jewish relations and the Holocaust into Polish history and memory, without historical bias. It must be stressed, however, that the IPN as an institution has shifted its position regarding the subject of Polish-Jewish history under the new chairmanship of Łukasz Kamiński, who took office in the summer of 2011: they are now part of IPN's investigations without the top-down pressure of framing them according to the agenda of *polityka historyczna*.

These splits illustrate how, despite the boom of memory projects focusing on Polish-Jewish relations, including new fact-based and sophisticated educational programs about the Holocaust,[67] as well as impressive historical research conducted in the country and abroad, Poles still have difficulty integrating the dark past into the narrative of twentieth-century Polish history, historical consciousness, and public memory. During the communist period, scholars in Poland did not investigate the dark past and historical data on the subject was not publically known. In the present, this is no longer true; instead, many Poles seem to be looking at this past but refusing to properly see it. Goethe's saying, "everyone hears only what he understands," captures how different groups and individuals, including professional historians, approach inconvenient dark historical truths. This is, of course, by no means an exclusive problem of Polish society.

This Goethe saying might be viewed as one plausible interpretation of the presence of conflicting and disparate evaluations of inconvenient dark historical truths. Here the key issue is how much of the dark truth is "too much truth" for Polish history, collective memory, and identity, how much of it could be channeled into the collective historical awareness and national mythology, and how much of it is "indigestible," frightful, alien, and disturbing not only to the old, but also to the young generations.[68] Another key issue is the problem of dissemination of the dark truth in an effective and productive manner that will not trigger strong self-defense mechanisms. Does such a manner exist? How can it be practiced and successfully implemented? What are the limits of it? Could it be dependent on the scope of the transformation of national traditions and mythologies in general? In light of the current opposition to the full integration of the dark past of Polish-Jewish relations, we must consider the danger that the splits over history could become a fixed landmark of the process of memorialization of Jews and the Holocaust in the future.

It might prove difficult for Polish society as a whole to come to terms with the dark past fully because of the deep shameful nature of this past and the emotive power of fundamental Polish national myths about World War II. As exemplified in a number of polls conducted throughout the 2000s, Polish society still sees World War II as a central event, embodying national heroism, pride, and victimhood. According to the first poll conducted a few months before Poland joined the European Union in early May 2004, only three percent of those who were interviewed felt ashamed about negative attitudes toward Jews in World War II.[69] None of the interviewees mentioned the name Jedwabne in their own statements, and the researchers concluded that memory of the massacre has been embraced only by the Polish intelligentsia for whom Jedwabne represents a moral and historical problem. The second poll, conducted on the eve of the seventieth anniversary of the outbreak of World War II, confirmed the results gathered five years earlier.[70] According to this poll, seventy-three percent of those interviewed were convinced that Poles had many reasons to be proud of their conduct during the war, including rescue activities extended to Jews, whereas only seventeen percent stated that there were wartime events that Poles should feel ashamed of. Though Jedwabne was recalled by many of those interviewed, a cognitive confusion is widespread about who were the real perpetrators of the massacre; many attributed the crime to the Germans and not to the local Poles. The first major antihero in Polish history that survey respondents cited was the infamous communist leader Bolesław Bierut of the early postwar communist era. They perceived the wartime period as free of antiheroes and filled with heroes instead. Poles still consistently perceive the war as the embodiment of Polish collective martyrdom and heroism.

The recent report by Antoni Sułek, in which the author discusses two polls about the Jedwabne massacre conducted respectively in 2002 and 2011, also confirms the results of the abovementioned polls. Sułek, who was the author of both questionnaires, concludes that Jedwabne as a historical event has not entered long-term social memory, and that respondents continuously show a great deal of confusion with regard to defining the perpetrators of the crime (Sułek 2011: 43–44). It is basically very difficult for the Poles to accept that the history of their nation is full not only of heroes and victims, but also of perpetrators of crimes against others. Sułek argues that one of the main reasons for the persistence of such beliefs lies in the lack of public commemoration of other massacres of Jews, such as those that occurred in the summer of 1941 in northeastern Poland. He also contends that another reason lies in the weaknesses of the Polish educational system: history textbooks for high schools in which Jedwabne is given proper attention are rather rare. Yet, in his conclusions, Sułek optimistically points out that another poll, conducted by the prestigious *Centralny Ośrodek Badań Społecznych* (CBOS) in 2010, demonstrates that five percent of respondents named attitudes of Poles toward Jews during World War II as a shameful event in national history, and five percent of respondents declared that they felt ashamed because of anti-Semitism. In this poll, the total number of respondents who felt ashamed of any events in Polish history numbered thirty-one percent of all the interviewees. This shows that a change of historical awareness in national history and national mythology is possible, even if the transformation is rather slow. However, a recent poll studying intolerance, prejudice, and discrimination in Europe, published in Germany in 2011, offers different and rather troubling insights. According to this poll, 49.9 percent of Polish (and 69.2 percent of Hungarian) respondents believe that Jews in their countries have too much power. The results also showed that 72.2 percent of Polish respondents believe that Jews try to take advantage of having been victims during the Nazi era, in comparison to 68.1 percent of Hungarian and 52.2 percent of Portuguese respondents. But, at the same time, 51.2 percent of Polish, 57.3 percent of Hungarian, and 51.9 percent of Portuguese respondents agreed that Jews contribute to enrichment for their culture (Zick, Küpper, and Hövermann 2011: 57–58).

Given the various factors and circumstances discussed in this chapter, in the immediate future the three modes of remembering Jews and the Holocaust will likely continue to exist: "remembering to remember," "remembering to benefit," and "remembering to forget." This landscape of memory will continue, consisting of multiple, conflicting recollections and interpretations—many of them fascinating and intellectually and morally uplifting, others, confusing, hypocritical, intellectually dull, morally despicable, and opportunistic. This should not be surprising given the protracted, difficult history of Polish-Jewish relations and the current re-evaluations of Jews and the Holocaust by social actors representing various political, social, and cultural agendas. Looking closely at this landscape, perceptive students of memory could easily critique those evaluations that claim that the dark past in Polish-Jewish relations has been overcome completely and that the memory of Jews and the Holocaust in Poland is an uncomplicated, progressive project, without twists and murky areas. Conceptualizing the landscape of memory through these three modes of remembering provides a framework to better understand the important issue of how the past impacts the present and how the present impacts the past.

Notes

An earlier version of this chapter appeared as part of the Jerusalem Center for Public Affairs' Post-Holocaust and Anti-Semitism online publication series (jcpa.org/publication/phas).

 1. See Werner Bergmann, "Anti-Semitic Attitudes in Europe: A Comparative Perspective," *Journal of Social Issues* 64, no.2 (2008): 343–62. Bergmann's quantitative comparative analysis is based on surveys commissioned by the American Jewish

Committee (AJC) and Anti-Defamation League (ADL) during the last two decades in several European countries.

2. For the study of a wide range of commonalities and differences in the reception of the Holocaust in all of post-communist Europe, see John-Paul Himka and Joanna B. Michlic, eds., *Bringing the Dark to Light: The Reception of the Holocaust in Postcommunist Europe* (Lincoln, NE: NUP, 2013). Hereafter Himka and Michlic, eds., *Bringing the Dark to Light: The Reception of the Holocaust in Postcommunist Europe.*

3. On subsequent rightwing ideological interpretations of peaceful revolutions in Central Europe as "stolen" or "unfinished," see István Rév, *Retroactive Justice: Prehistory of Post-Communism* (Stanford, CA: Stanford University Press, 2005): 304–36.

4. Barbie Zelizer was perhaps the first scholar to use the term "remembering to forget" in her study *Remembering to Forget: Holocaust Memory Through the Camera's Eye* (Chicago: University of Chicago Press, 1998).

5. For a synthetic socio-historical study of the concept of the Jew as the "Threatening Other," see Joanna B. Michlic, *Poland's Threatening Other. The Image of the Jew from 1880 to the Present* (Lincoln and London: University of Nebraska Press, 2008).

6. See, for example, the website Żydzi- Nonsensopedia, polska encyclopedia humoru, http://nosensopedia.wikia.com/wiki/ percentC5 percentBBydzi (accessed October 10, 2010).

7. http://www.festiwal.jewishlodz.org.pl/index1.html (accessed June 9, 2009).

8. http://www.jewish.org.pl/index.php?option=com_content&task=view&id=1554&Itemid=58 (accessed June 9, 2009).

9. http://www.simcha.art.pl/simcha.htm (accessed June 9, 2009).

10. http://www.wrotapodlasia.pl/pl/wiadomosci (accessed June 9, 2009).

11. http://www.jewish.org.pl/index.php?option=com_content&task=view&id=1537&Itemid=58 (accessed June 9, 2009).

12. http://aord.republika.pl/kwit.htm (accessed June 9, 2009).

13. http://www.szczekociny.pl/upload/szczekociny_poster_A3b_small.pdf (accessed June 9, 2009).

14. http://www.jewish.org.pl/index.php?option=com_content&task=view&id=1699&Itemid=58 (accessed June 9, 2009).

15. www.znak.org.pl/files/RymanowAng.doc (accessed December 18, 2009).

16. Some members of the position "remembering to remember" have lately become critical of the nature and dynamics of popular festivals of Jewish culture. See, for example, Bogdan Białek, "Szary człowiek i Żydzi," *Tygodnik Powszechny,* July 4, 2011, http://tygodnik.onet.pl/1,65424,druk.html (accessed December 12, 2011).

17. On the battle of commemorations in Chmielnik, see Zuzanna Radzik, "Bohater i Żydzi," *Tygodnik Powszechny,* June 28, 2011, http://tygodnik.onet.pl/165187,druk.htlm (accessed December 12, 2011).

18. Mamadou Diouf in an interview with Piotr Smoleński, "Mentalność Murzynka Bambo," *Gazeta Wyborcza,* January 25, 2011, http://wyborcza.pl/2029020,75515,9000748.html?ssms_code= (accessed January 26, 2011).

19. Bogdan Wróblewski, "Poeta zaprasza na process," *Gazeta Wyborcza,* March 13, 2011, http://wyborcza.pl/2029020,75248,9276209.html?sms_code= (accessed March 15, 2011).

20. Radosław Sikorski in an interview with Adar Primor, "Polish Foreign Minister to Haaretz: Nazi Germany carried out the Holocaust against our will," *Haaretz,* February 27, 2011, http://www.haaretz.com/misc/article-print-page/polish-fm-to-haaretz (accessed February 28, 2011).

21. On specific unconventional ways of encountering and interpreting Jewish identity by non-Jewish Poles as an integral part of their own identity, see Erica Lehrer's "Bearing False Witness: Vicarious Jewish Identity and the Politics of Affinity," in Dorota Glowacka and Joanna Zylinska, eds., *Imaginary Neighbors Mediating Polish-Jewish Relations After the Holocaust* (Lincoln: University of Nebraska Press, 2007), 84–109.

22. Janusz Makuch in an interview with Magdalena Waligórska, May 3, 2007, "Fiddler as a Fig Leaf: The Politicisation of Klezmer in Poland," *Osteuropa: Impulses for Europe* (2008): 232.

23. "Zabobony w biznesie: Portret Żyda na szczęście?" by Mateusz Wesierski on the website of the Polish online banking paper Bankier.pl, http://www.bankier.pl/wiadomosc/ Zabobony-w-biznesie-Portr, and the discussion triggered by this article (accessed October 11, 2010).

24. See, for example, the website of Barbara Rabiega, "Portret Żyda na szczęście," http:// portret-zyd-na-szczescie-barbara-rabiega.blog.onet.pl (accessed October 11, 2010).

25. "Common Ground: Polish Volunteers Caring for Jewish Cemeteries," http://www .youtube.com/watch?v=qTgaxUBSp0g&feature=related (accessed December 18, 2009) and Zuzanna Radzik, "Miasteczka odżywają," *Więź*, no. 4 (2005): 31–42.

26. See the collage of interviews and historical information on the wooden synagogue in the Praga neighborhood in Warsaw that was destroyed by Germans in 1939, prepared by pupils of Gymnasium no. 9 in Warsaw, *Karta*, no. 43 (2004): 52–55, and the website of the Centrum Żydowskie w Oświęcimiu, particularly the page dedicated to the information about high school pupils from local schools who receive an annual award for writing on the subject "Jews in my Imagination" (accessed December 18, 2009).

27. For a report on the involvement of prisoners in cleaning Jewish cemeteries, see Rafał Kowalski, "Więźniowie posprzątają żydowskie cmentarze," *Gazeta Wyborcza*, August 10, 2009, http://wyborcza.pl/1,76842,6914938,Wiezniowie_posprzataja_zydowskie_ cmentarze.html (accessed December 18, 2009).

28. See the Foundation's website, http://fodz.pl/?d=1&l=pl (accessed August 10, 2009).

29. On similar attitudes toward anti-Semitism in Poland and Polish Diaspora during the communist era, see Joanna B. Michlic, "Antisemitism in Contemporary Poland: Does It Matter? And for Whom Does It Matter?" in *Rethinking Poles and Jews. Troubled Past, Brighter Future,* ed. Robert Cherry and Annamaria Orla-Bukowska, 155–56 (Lanham, MD: Rowman and Littlefield Publishers, 2007).

30. The adherents of *polityka historyczna* tend to minimize the achievements of the leaders of the original Solidarity like Lech Wałęsa, accusing them of alleged collaboration with communist regimes prior to 1989. For a critical study of *polityka historyczna* and its impact on the Polish state and Polish historical culture, see Joanna Tokarska-Bakir, "Nędza polityki historycznej," and Aleksander Smolar, "Władza i geografia pamięci," in *Pamięć jako przedmiot władzy,* ed. Piotr Kosiewski, 27–30, 49–74 (Warsaw: Fundacja im. Stefana Batorego, 2008); Paweł Machcewicz, "Debata o stosunku III RP do przeszłości. Dwa mity ideologów polityki historycznej IV RP," *Gazeta Wyborcza*, August 29, 2008, http://wyborcza.pl/2029020,75515,5637705.html?sms_code (accessed September 5, 2008).

31. Jarosław Kaczyński's statement in *Gazeta Wyborcza*, February 9–10, 2008, cited in Smolar, "Władza i geografia pamięci," 53–54.

32. On the full impact of *polityka historyczna* on the memory of the Holocaust in Poland between 2006 and 2010, see Joanna B. Michlic and Małgorzata Melchior, "The Memory of the Holocaust in Post-1989 Poland: Renewal—Its Accomplishments and

Its Powerlessness," in *Bringing the Dark to Light: The Reception of the Holocaust in Post-communist Europe,* ed. Himka and Michlic.

33. For the old pre-1989 tendencies present in contemporary debate and historical writing, see, for example, the website www.ŻyciezaŻycie.pl (accessed June 8, 2008) dedicated to the educational film project *Życie za Życie,* about ten cases of Christian Polish rescuers. See especially the preface to the film by Jan Żaryn, an IPN historian. (These materials are no longer on the website.) See also Anna Poray-Wybranowska, "Naród bohaterów," *Nasz Dziennik,* October 9, 2004; Dariusz Baliszewski, "Czy jesteśmy nacjonalistami?" *Wprost,* April 2, 2006, http://www.wprost.pl/ar/88353/Czy-jestesmy-nacjonalistami/ (accessed December 18, 2009); and Marcin Urynowicz, "Liczenie z pamięci," *Tygodnik Powszechny,* October 30, 2007, http://tygodnik2003-2007.onet .pl/1547,1448231,0,547780,dzial.html (accessed December 18, 2009), for the claim that in Poland there were 400,000 Christian Polish rescuers of Jews. He draws on Gunnar S. Paulsson's numerical estimates of Jews who survived in wartime Warsaw. See the critical response questioning Urynowicz's assumptions and methodology by Jacek Leociak and Dariusz Libionka, "Żonglerka liczbami," *Tygodnik Powszechny,* November 27, 2007, http://tygodnik2003-2007.onet.pl/1547,1454440,0,554745,dzial.html (accessed June 8, 2008).

34. Some contemporary memoirs of Christian Poles throw light onto the complex historical context. See, for example, Tadeusz Markiel, "Zagłada domu Trinczerów," *Znak* 4 (2008): 119–46 with a postscript by Dariusz Libionka, "Zagłada Domu Trinczerów— refleksje historyka."

35. For the latest examples of this history genre, see Jan Grabowski, Judenjagd. Polowanie na Żydów 1942–1945. Studium dziejów pewnego powiatu and Barbara Engelking Jest Taki Piękny Słoneczny Dzien … Losy Żydów szukających ratunku na wsi polskiej 1942–1945. Both works were published in February 2011 by the Polish Center for Holocaust Research based in Warsaw.

36. *Zagłada Żydów. Studia i materiały,* vol. 4, published in 2008, includes major articles by Dariusz Libonka, Jan Grabowski, Grzegorz Berendt, Barbara Engelking, and Joanna Tokarska-Bakir.

37. See, for example, Jan Grabowski, "Rescue for Money: Paid Helpers in Poland, 1939–1945," *Search and Research. Lectures and Papers,* no. 13 (Jerusalem: Yad Vashem, 2008), hereafter Grabowski, "Rescue for Money: Paid Helpers in Poland, 1939–1945." See also Witold Mędykowski, "Sprawiedliwi, niesprawiedliwi? O złożoności stosunków pomiędzy ratującymi a ocalonymi w okresie Zagłady," in *Z dziejów polsko-żydowskich w XX wieku,* ed. Edyta Czop and Elżbieta Rączy, 27–37 (Rzeszów: IPN and Uniwersytet Rzeszowski, 2009).

38. See, for example, Andrzej Żbikowski, ed. *Polacy i Żydzi pod okupacją niemiecką 1939–1945. Studia i materiały* (Warsaw: IPN, 2006), chapters 9 and 10 by Elżbieta Rączy and Anna Pyżewska, respectively; and Elżbieta Rączy, *Pomoc Polaków dla ludności żydowskiej na Rzeszowczyznie, 1939–1945* (Rzeszów: IPN, 2008); Jacek Leociak, *Ratowanie. Opowieści Polaków i Żydów* (Kraków: Wydawnictwo Literackie, 2010); and Małgorzata Melchior, *Zagłada i tożsamość: Polscy Żydzi ocaleni "na aryjskich papierach"* (Warsaw: Wydawnictwo IFiS PAN, 2004).

39. The PAJA's educational packet "Those Who Acted … " (Kraków: Polish-American Jewish Alliance for Youth Action, 2003).

40. Paweł P. Reszka, "Szkoła im. Sprawiedliwych wśrod narodów świata," *Gazeta Wyborcza,* February 20, 2006; and voices on the forum of *Gazeta Wyborcza,* http://forum .gazeta.pl/forum/w,62,37195375.html (accessed December 18, 2009).

41. *Światła w ciemności. Sprawiedliwi wśrod narodów świata* (Lublin: Brama Grodzka–
Teatr NN, 2008). The book is available online: http://teatrnn.pl/sprawiedliwi/node/9/
Biblioteka.
42. The interviews are made available online on the website www.sprawiedliwi.org.pl.
43. "Pospaceruj po Żoliborzu śladami tych, którzy ratowali Żydów," http://warsawa
.gazeta.pl/warszawa/1,95190,8334348, Pospaceruj (accessed September 22, 2010).
44. Anna Mieszkowska, *Matka dzieci holokaustu. Historia Ireny Sendlerowej* (Warsaw:
Wyd. Literackie Muza, 2004) (Hebrew edition 2009 and English edition 2011), and
the documentary film by Mary Skinner, *Irena Sendle: In the Name of Their Mothers,*
which aired in the United States on PBS in 2011.
45. *Dzieci Ireny Sendlerowej* by John Kent Harrison, 2009. The film is based on Anna
Mieszkowska, *Matka dzieci holokaustu. Historia Ireny Sendlerowej.*
46. See report "Za naprawianie świata," April 28, 2008, http://www.forum-znak.org.pl/
print.php?t=wydarzenia&id=7212&l=pl (accessed September 5, 2010).
47. For an encounter of elderly Sendlerowa with the American schoolgirls in Warsaw,
see the documentary film, *Lista Sendlerowej* by Michał J. Dudziewicz. See the DVD
"Irena Sendlerowa," Narodowe Centrum Kultury, Multimedialne Wydawnictwo Edu-
kacyjne, 2009.
48. On the Ulm family, but without a nuanced historical context, see Mateusz Szpytma
and Jarosław Szarek, *Sprawiedliwi wśród narodów świata. Przejmująca historia polskiej rodziny, która poświęciła swoje życie ratując Żydów,* 2d expanded ed. (Kraków:
Dom Wydawniczy Rafael, 2004), and Mateusz Szpytma, *The Risk of Survival: The
Rescue of the Jews by the Poles and the Tragic Consequences for the Ulma Family
from Markowa* (Warsaw-Kraków: IPN, 2009).
49. The report "PiS chce oddać hołd Polakom ukrywającym Żydów," *Wprost,* March
7, 2011, http://www.wprost.pl/ar/234625/PiS-chce-oddac-hold-Polak (accessed on
March 7, 2011).
50. See Małgorzata Rutkowska, "Prymitywna antypolska propaganda Grossa" and accompanied testimonies of rescuers "Godni synowie naszej Ojczyzny," *Nasz Dziennik,*
January 5–6, 2011, 20–21.
51. Jerzy Jedlicki, "Polacy wobec Żydów. Bezradność," *Gazeta Wyborcza,* June 26, 2009,
http://wyborcza.pl/2029020,97863,6762343.html (accessed July 3, 2009).
52. For an analysis of the Jedwabne debate and an extensive selection in English of various voices that participated in the debate, see Antony Polonsky and Joanna B. Michlic,
eds., *The Neighbors Respond: The Controversy over the Jedwabne Massacre in Poland* (Princeton, NJ, and Oxford: Princeton University Press, 2004).
53. Robert N. Bellah, Richard Madsen, William M. Sullivan, Ann Swidler, and Steven M.
Tipton, *Habits of the Heart: Individualism and Commitment in American Life* (Berkeley, Los Angeles, London: University of California Press, 1996). By comparison, on
attitudes toward regret and shame in American and German culture, see the insightful
article by Barry Schwartz and Horst-Alfred Heinrich, "Shadings of Regret: America
and Germany," in *Framing Public Memory,* ed. Kendall R. Phillips, 115–44 (Tuscaloosa: University of Alabama Press, 2004).
54. Antoni Sułek, "Pamięć Polaków o Zbrodni w Jedwabnem," *Nauka,* no. 3 (2011): 39–
49. Hereafter Sułek, "Pamięć Polaków o zbrodni w Jedwabnem."
55. The slogan *"Nie przepraszamy za Jedwabne"* is used in various discussions and debates not necessarily directly related to the Jedwabne massacre. For an example, see
the statement of the Polish TVP (Polish Television) journalist Jan Pospieszalski in
which he refuses to apologize for allegedly accusing the late historian and states-

man Bronislaw Geremek of becoming a communist agent in 1981 and thus betraying the first Solidarity movement. See the report "Prezes przeprasza, Pospieszalski nie," *Gazeta Wyborcza,* December 14, 2011, http://wyborcza.pl/2029020,75478,10815460 .html?sms_code= (accessed December 14, 2011).

56. On the tradition of addressing vexing problems and coming to terms with the difficult past in Polish drama, see the interesting article by Krystyna Duniec and Joanna Krakowska "Nie opłakali ich?" *Didaskalia. Gazeta Teatralna,* no. 103 (October 2011), http://www.didaskalia.pl/105_spis.htm.

57. An interview with Tadeusz Słobodzianek with Juliusz Kurkiewicz, Chcę komplikować odpowiedzi, *Gazeta Wyborcza,* July 6, 2010, 13. For an interesting, rare critical review of Słobodzianek's play as a work rooted in misguided assumptions about Polish-Jewish relations, see the article by Henryk Grynberg, a child Holocaust survivor from Poland, in *Dwutygodnik,* no. 93 (2012), http://www.dwutygodnik.com/artykul/4058-nasza-klasa-w-waszyngtonie.html. Grynberg observes that Słobodzianek bases his play on the idea of symmetry between Poles and Jews, which is historically wrong.

58. See the report "W cieniu zbrodni," *Rzeczpospolita,* July 20, 2011, A15.

59. For a lively critical discussion of Betlejewski's project see, Paula Sawicka, "Odczarować słowo Żyd" *Gazeta Wyborcza Warszawa,* March 25, 2010, 2; Jerzy Bralczyk and Agnieszka Kowalska "Odczarujmy słowo 'Żyd'" *Gazeta Wyborcza Warszawa,* March 23, 2010, 2; Dorota Jarecka "Kicz to sztuka szczęścia. Prowokacja czy ściema" *Gazeta Wyborcza,* May 29–30, 2010, 21. On the project, see http://www.tesknie.com/ (accessed October 10, 2010).

60. See www.tesknie.com (accessed October 12, 2010).

61. See Betlejewski's various interviews and reports on the cathartic barn-burning on his website www.tesknie.com (accessed October 12, 2010).

62. Georg Bönisch, Jan Friedmann, Cordula Mayer, Michael Sontheimer, and Klaus Wiegrefe, "Hitlers europäische Helfer beim Judenmord," *Der Spiegel,* no. 21 (May 18, 2009): 82–92. An English version, "Hitler's European Holocaust Helpers," is available online at http://www.spiegel.de/international/europe/0,1518,625824,00.html (accessed December 8, 2009).

63. *Der Spiegel* reported on the negative Polish reactions in Jan Puhl, "A Wave of Outrage: Polish Reactions to *Spiegel* Cover Story," http://www.spiegel.de/international/europe/0,1518,626171,00.html (accessed July 4, 2009).

64. Adam Daniel Rotfeld, "Rotfeld o publikacji w 'Spieglu,'" *Gazeta Wyborcza,* May 22, 2009, http://wborcza.pl/2029020,75515,6635503.html (accessed May 25, 2009), and Marek Beylin, "Zatupać 'Spiegla,'" *Gazeta Wyborcza,* May 22, 2009, http://wyborcza .pl/2029020,76842,6640733.html (accessed May 25, 2009). Beylin's short text serves as an introduction to the Polish translation of the *Der Spiegel* article. See "Der Spiegel: zbrodniarze i pomocnicy," (pełen tekst), *Gazeta Wyborcza,* May 22, 2009, http:// wyborcza.pl/1,97849,6640582,Der_Spiegel__zbrodniarze_i_pomocnicy__pelen_tek st_.html (accessed May 25, 2009).

65. For an analysis of the historical discussion about *Fear,* see Joanna B. Michlic, "'The Past That Will Not Go Away': The Polish Historical Debate about Jan T. Gross's *Fear: Anti-Semitism in Poland after Auschwitz* (2006, 2008) and the Study of Early Postwar Anti-Semitism," paper presented at the international conference "Between Coexistence and Divorce: 25 Years of Research on the History and Culture of Polish Jewry and Polish-Jewish Relations," the Hebrew University of Jerusalem, March 17–19, 2009.

66. Marek J. Chodakiewicz's monograph *After the Holocaust* was published in Polish translation as *Po zagładzie. Stosunki polsko-żydowskie 1944–1947* by IPN in early

2008. See also Paweł Lisicki, "Żydzi, Polacy i przeszłość," *Rzeczpospolita,* January 11, 2008, A2 [Polish]; Janusz Kurtyka, "Gross to wampir historiografii," *Gazeta
Wyborcza,* January 10, 2008 [Polish]; interview with Kurtyka in *Rzeczpospolita,* January 18, 2008: A16 [Polish]; Piotr Gontarczyk, "Daleko od prawdy," *Rzeczpospolita,*
January 12, 2008: A12–A15 [Polish]; Jan Żaryn, "Pogarda dla kontekstu," *Rzeczpospolita,* January 19, 2008: A28–A29 [Polish].
67. See, e.g., Robert Szuchta and Piotr Trojański, *Holocaust. Program nauczania o historii
i zagładzie Żydów na lekcjach przedmiotów humanistycznych w szkołach ponadpodstawowych* (Warsaw: Wydawnictwo Szkolne PWN, 2000) [Polish]; Robert Szuchta
and Piotr Trojański, *Holocaust: zrozumieć dlaczego* (Warsaw: Dom Wydawniczy Bellona, 2003) [Polish].
68. On the problems of the refusal to accept dark truths and lack of empathy toward
Jewish victims and survivors of the Holocaust among Polish youth, see Michał Bilewicz, "Społeczna pamięć Holokaustu i Auschwitz wśród licealistów: wokół projektu
badawczego: 'Trudnego Pytania,'" in *Auschwitz i Holokaust. Dylematy i wyzwania
polskiej edukacji,* ed. Piotr Trojański, 31–33. (Oświęcim: Państwowe Muzeum Auschwitz-Birkenau, 2008).
69. See the report on the poll, "Duma i wstyd Polaków—sondaż," *Gazeta Wyborcza,*
September 17, 2004, http://serwisy.gazeta.pl/kraj/2029020,34317,2289803.html (accessed September 22, 2004).
70. See Wojciech Szacki, "Poplątana pamięć o II wojnie," *Gazeta Wyborcza,* August 18,
2009, http://wyborcza.pl/2029020,75248,6936373html?sms_code (accessed August
22, 2009), and Wojciech Szacki, "Sondaż. Nasza duma i wstyd," *Gazeta Wyborcza,*
August 19, 2009, http://wyborcza.pl/2029020,75248,6940133html?sms_code (accessed August 22, 2009).

References

Bellah, Robert N., Richard Madsen, William M. Sullivan, Ann Swidler, and Steven M. Tip-
ton. 1996. *Habits of the Heart: Individualism and Commitment in American Life.*
Berkeley, Los Angeles, London: University of California Press.
Bergmann, Werner. 2008. "Anti-Semitic Attitudes in Europe: A Comparative Perspective."
Journal of Social Issues 64. 2: 343–62.
Beylin, Marek. 2009. "Zatupać 'Spiegla.'" *Gazeta Wyborcza,* May 22, 2009.
Białek, Bogdan. 2011. "Szary człowiek i Żydzi." *Tygodnik Powszechny,* July 4, 2011.
Bilewicz, Michał. 2008. "Społeczna pamięć Holokaustu i Auschwitz wśród licealistów:
wokół projektu badawczego: 'Trudnego Pytania.'" In *Auschwitz i Holokaust. Dy-
lematy i wyzwania polskiej edukacji,* edited by Piotr Trojański, 31–33. Oświęcim,
Państwowe Muzeum Auschwitz-Birkenau.
Bönisch, Georg, Jan Friedmann, Cordula Mayer, Michael Sontheimer, and Klaus Wiegrefe.
2009. "Hitlers europäische Helfer beim Judenmord." *Der Spiegel,* no. 21 (May
18): 82–92.
Bralczyk, Jerzy, and Agnieszka Kowalska. 2010. "Odczarujmy słowo 'Żyd.'" *Gazeta
Wyborcza Warszawa,* March 23: 2.
"Chcę komplikować odpowiedzi." *Gazeta Wyborcza,* July 6: 13.
Chodakiewicz, Marek J. 2008. *After the Holocaust.* In Polish translation: *Po zagładzie.
Stosunki polsko-żydowskie 1944–1947.* Warsaw: IPN.

"Der Spiegel: zbrodniarze i pomocnicy." *Gazeta Wyborcza,* May 22, 2009.

Dudziewicz, Michał J. 2002. *Lista Sendlerowej.* DVD/TV. Directed by Michał J. Dudziewicz. Poland: Studio Filmowe Camera 94/Telewizja Polska—Agencja Filmowa (dla Programu 2).

"Duma i wstyd Polaków—sondaż." *Gazeta Wyborcza* September 17, 2004.

Duniec, Krystyna, and Joanna Krakowska. 2011. "Nie opłakali ich?" Didaskalia. *Gazeta Teatralna,* no. 103 (October).

Engelking, Barbara. 2011. *Jest Taki Piękny Słoneczny Dzien ... Losy Żydów szukających ratunku na wsi polskiej 1942–1945.* Warsaw: Polish Center for Holocaust Research.

"Fiddler as a Fig Leaf: The Politicisation of Klezmer in Poland." *Osteuropa: Impulses for Europe,* May 3, 2007.

"Godni synowie naszej Ojczyzny." 2011. *Nasz Dziennik.* January 5–6: 20–21.

Gontarczyk, Piotr. 2008. "Daleko od prawdy." *Rzeczpospolita,* January 12: A12–A15.

Grabowski, Jan. 2008. "Rescue for Money. Paid Helpers in Poland, 1939–1945." *Search and Research. Lectures and Papers,* no. 13. Jerusalem, Yad Vashem.

———. 2011. *Judenjagd. Polowanie na Żydów 1942–1945. Studium dziejów pewnego powiatu.* Warsaw, Poland: Polish Center for Holocaust Research.

Gross, Jan T. 2001. *Neighbors: The Destruction of the Jewish Community in Jedwabne, Poland.* Princeton, NJ: Princeton University Press.

———. 2006. *Fear: Anti-Semitism in Poland after Auschwitz: An Essay in Historical Interpretation.* New York: Random House. (In translation: *Strach. Antysemityzm w Polsce tuż po wojnie. Historia moralnej zapaści.* Kraków, Wydawnictwo Znak, 2008.)

Gruber, Ruth E. 2002. *Virtually Jewish: Reinventing Jewish Culture in Europe.* Berkeley and Los Angeles: University of California Press.

———. 2009. "Beyond Virtually Jewish: Balancing the Real, the Surreal and Real Imaginary Places." In *Reclaiming Memory: Urban Regeneration in the Historic Jewish Quarters of Central European Cities,* edited by Monika Murzyn-Kupisz and Jacek Purchla, 63–79. Cracow, Poland: International Cultural Centre.

Harrison, John Kent, Lawrence John Spagnola, Anna Paquin, Goran Visnjic, Marcia Gay Harden, Jerzy Zielinski, Jan A. P. Kaczmarek, and Anna Mieszkowska. 2009–2010. *Dzieci Ireny Sendlerowej.* DVD/TV. Directed by John Kent Harrison. Warsaw, Poland: TiM Film Studio.

Himka, John-Paul, and Joanna B. Michlic, eds. 2013. *Bringing the Dark to Light: The Reception of the Holocaust in Postcommunist Europe.* Lincoln, NE: NUP.

Jarecka, Dorota. 2010. "Kicz to sztuka szczęścia. Prowokacja czy ściema." *Gazeta Wyborcza,* May 29–30.

Jedlicki, Jerzy. 2009. "Polacy wobec Żydów. Bezradność." *Gazeta Wyborcza,* June 26.

Kenney, Padraic. 2002. *A Carnival of Revolution: Central Europe, 1989.* Princeton, NJ: Princeton University Press.

Kowalski, Rafał. 2009. "Więźniowie posprzątają żydowskie cmentarze." *Gazeta Wyborcza,* August 10.

Kurtyka, Janusz. 2008. "Gross to wampir historiografii." *Gazeta Wyborcza,* January 10.

Lehrer, Erica. 2007. "Bearing False Witness: Vicarious Jewish Identity and the Politics of Affinity." In *Imaginary Neighbors: Mediating Polish-Jewish Relations After the Holocaust,* edited by Dorota Glowacka and Joanna Zylinska, 84–109. Lincoln, NE: University of Nebraska Press.

Leociak, Jacek. 2010. *Ratowanie. Opowieści Polaków i Żydów.* Cracow: Wydawnictwo Literackie.

Leociak, Jacek, and Dariusz Libionka. 2007. "Żonglerka liczbami." *Tygodnik Powszechny,* November 27.
Lisicki, Paweł. 2008. "Żydzi, Polacy i przeszłość." *Rzeczpospolita,* January 11, A2.
Machcewicz, Paweł. 2008. "Debata o stosunku III RP do przeszłości. Dwa mity ideologów polityki historycznej IV RP." *Gazeta Wyborcza,* August 29.
Makuch, Janusz. 2010. "The Jewish Cultural Festival, Kraków." In *Poland: A Jewish Matter,* edited by Kate Craddy, Mike Levy and Jakub Nowakowski. Warsaw, Poland: Adam Mickiewicz Institute (Proceedings of a symposium exploring Jewish life in Poland, part of the "Polska! Year" cultural program series).
Markiel, Tadeusz. 2008. "Zagłada domu Trinczerów." *Znak* 4: 119–46 (with postscript by Dariusz Libionka "Zagłada Domu Trinczerów—refleksje historyka")
Mędykowski, Witold. 2009. "Sprawiedliwi, niesprawiedliwi? O złożoności stosunków pomiędzy ratującymi a ocalonymi w okresie Zagłady." In *Z dziejów polsko-żydowskich w XX wieku,* edited by Edyta Czop and Elżbieta Rączy. Rzeszów, IPN and Uniwersytet Rzeszowski.
Melchior, Małgorzata. 2004. *Zagłada i tożsamość: Polscy Żydzi ocaleni "na aryjskich papierach."* Warsaw: Wydawnictwo IFiS PAN.
Michlic, Joanna B. 2007. "Antisemitism in Contemporary Poland. Does it Matter? And For Whom Does It Matter?" In *Rethinking Poles and Jews. Troubled Past, Brighter Future,* edited by Robert Cherry and Annamaria Orla-Bukowska. Lanham, MD: Rowman and Littlefield Publishers, Inc.
———. 2008. *Poland's Threatening Other: The Image of the Jew from 1880 to the Present.* Lincoln, NE and London: University of Nebraska Press.
———. 2009. "'The Past That Will Not Go Away': The Polish Historical Debate about Jan T. Gross's Fear: Anti-Semitism in Poland after Auschwitz (2006, 2008) and the Study of Early Postwar Anti-Semitism." Paper presented at the international conference "Between Coexistence and Divorce: 25 Years of Research on the History and Culture of Polish Jewry and Polish-Jewish Relations," Hebrew University of Jerusalem, March 17–19.
Mieszkowska, Anna. 2004. *Matka dzieci holokaustu. Historia Ireny Sendlerowej.* Warsaw: Wyd. Literackie Muza.
Oisteanu, Andrei. 2009. *Inventing the Jew: Antisemitic Stereotypes in Romanian and Other Central-East European Cultures.* Foreword by Moshe Idel. Lincoln, NE: Nebraska University Press.
"Polish Foreign Minister to Haaretz: Nazi Germany Carried out the Holocaust against Our Will." 2011. *Haaretz,* February 27.
Polonsky, Antony, and Joanna B. Michlic, eds. 2004. *The Neighbors Respond: The Controversy over the Jedwabne Massacre in Poland.* Princeton, NJ and Oxford: Princeton University Press.
"Prezes przeprasza, Pospieszalski nie." 2011. *Gazeta Wyborcza,* December 14.
Rączy, Elżbieta. 2008. *Pomoc Polaków dla ludności żydowskiej na Rzeszowczyznie, 1939–1945.* Rzeszów, IPN.
Radzik, Zuzanna. 2005. "Miasteczka odżywają." *Więź* no. 4: 31–42.
———. 2011. "Bohater i Żydzi." *Tygodnik Powszechny,* June 28.
Reszka, Paweł P. 2006. "Szkoła im. Sprawiedliwych wśród narodów świata." *Gazeta Wyborcza,* February 20.
Rév, István. 2005. *Retroactive Justice: Prehistory of Post-Communism.* Stanford, CA: Stanford University Press.
Rotfeld, Adam Daniel. 2009. "Rotfeld o publikacji w 'Spieglu.'" *Gazeta Wyborcza,* May 22.

Rutkowska, Małgorzata. 2011. "Prymitywna antypolska propaganda Grossa." *Nasz Dziennik,* January 5–6: 20–21.

Rzeczpospolita. 2008. January 18, A16.

Sawicka, Paula. 2010. "Odczarować słowo Żyd." *Gazeta Wyborcza Warszawa,* March 25, 2.

Schwartz, Barry, and Horst-Alfred Heinrich. 2004. "Shadings of Regret: America and Germany." In *Framing Public Memory,* edited by Kendall R. Phillips, 113–44. Tuscaloosa, AL: University of Alabama Press.

Skinner, Mary, Slawomir Grundberg, Piotr Piwowarczyk, Jan Becker, Mary Skinner, and Piotr Piwowarczyk. 2011. *Irena Sendler: In the Name of Their Mothers.* DVD/TV. Directed by Mary Skinner. United States edition. 2B Productions/PBS Distribution.

Smolar, Aleksander. 2008. "Władza i geografia pamięci." In *Pamięć jako przedmiot władzy,* edited by Piotr Kosiewski, 49–74. Warsaw, Poland: Fundacja im. Stefana Batorego.

Sułek, Antoni. 2011. "Pamięć Polaków o Zbrodni w Jedwabnem." *Nauka,* no. 3: 39–49.

Światła w ciemności. Sprawiedliwi wśrod narodów świata. Lublin, Brama Grodzka –Teatr NN. 2008. Available online: http://teatrnn.pl/sprawiedliwi/node/9/Biblioteka.

Szacki, Wojciech. 2009. "Poplątana pamięć o II wojnie." *Gazeta Wyborcza,* August 18.

———. 2009. "Sondaż. Nasza duma i wstyd." *Gazeta Wyborcza,* August 19.

Szpytma, Mateusz. 2009. *The Risk of Survival: The Rescue of the Jews by the Poles and the Tragic Consequences for the Ulma Family From Markowa.* Warsaw-Kraków: IPN.

Szpytma, Mateusz, and Jarosław Szarek. 2004. *Sprawiedliwi wśród narodów świata. Przejmująca historia polskiej rodziny, która poświęciła swoje życie ratując Żydów.* 2d expanded ed. Kraków, Poland: Dom Wydawniczy Rafael.

Szuchta, Robert, and Piotr Trojański. 2000. *Holocaust. Program nauczania o historii i zagładzie Żydów na lekcjach przedmiotów humanistycznych w szkołach ponadpodstawowych.* Warsaw: Wydawnictwo Szkolne PWN.

———. 2003. *Holocaust: zrozumieć dlaczego.* Warsaw: Dom Wydawniczy Bellona.

Tokarska-Bakir, Joanna. 2008. "Nędza polityki historycznej." In *Pamięć jako przedmiot władzy,* edited by Piotr Kosiewski. Warsaw, Poland: Fundacja im. Stefana Batorego.

"W cieniu zbrodni." 2011. *Rzeczpospolita,* July 20, A15.

"Warsaw." 2004. *Karta,* no. 43.

Wróblewski, Bogdan. 2011. "Poeta zaprasza na process." *Gazeta Wyborcza,* March 13.

Zagłada Żydów. Studia i materiały. 2008. Vol. 4.

Zalizer, Barbie. 1998. *Remembering to Forget: Holocaust Memory Through the Camera's Eye.* Chicago: University of Chicago Press.

Żaryn. 2008. "Pogarda dla kontekstu," *Rzeczpospolita,* January 19: A28–A29.

Żbikowski, Andrzej, ed. 2006. "Polacy i Żydzi pod okupacją niemiecką 1939–1945." *Studia i materiały,* Warsaw, IPN.

Zick, Andreas, Beate Küpper, and Andreas Hövermann. 2011. *Intolerance, Prejudice and Discrimination. A European Report,* 57–58. Berlin: Nora Langenbacher Friedrich-Ebert-Stiftung.

Chapter 10

1989 as Collective Memory "Refolution"

East-Central Europe Confronts Memorial Silence

Susan C. Pearce

Our late modern era is saturated with collective spectacles of memory, as well as confrontations with memorial silences. Ethnic groups, generations, and entire nations project their collective memories onto screens that are often framed by the concerns of the present. An explosion of attention to social memory (Olick et al. 2011) has become both a public and scholarly concern. Erika Doss speaks of a "memorial mania" as a present-day obsession, accompanied by "an urgent, excessive desire to claim—or secure—those issues in visibly public culture" (Doss 2008: 7). Americans, for example, have seen one museum and memorial after another move into the public spaces of Washington D.C., often accompanied by monument and exhibit "wars" as interpretation and representation preferences clashed (see Zolberg 1998).

What is feeding this global phenomenon? Scholars have identified several dynamics that are both common across the globe and regionally specific. These dynamics offer stages or screens for collectively held memorial projects: a recently closed century of mass bloodshed aided by technology never before available; national border changes of both the divisive and uniting kind; dramatic political upheavals and regime transitions; and a changing culture of claims by previously excluded and marginalized groups for their place at the societal and memorial table (Kammen 1995: 248). Paul Williams (2007) and others have documented the growth of memorial sites of collective trauma across the world; Jeffrey Olick (2003a) has described what he terms a "politics of regret," or public apologies and recompense for the past that seem to have proliferated.

Enter the former Eastern Bloc. This chapter takes a moment to tele-scope in on one region that is, in many ways, pivotal to this global memory boom: Central and Eastern Europe. In 1989, in a virtual domino dis-play of overnight revolutions across seven months, the state-communist regimes of Poland, (East) Germany, Hungary, the Czech Republic, Slova-kia, Bulgaria, and Romania collapsed. From the first semi-free elections in Poland on June 4 to the execution of the Romanian dictator Nicolae Ceauçescu and his wife Elena on December 25, the so-called Eastern Bloc was no more. The scholar Timothy Garton Ash has termed these historic events "refolutions" (a reform-revolution fusion) (1990), since the notion of nonviolent revolutions was basically unprecedented, and given the gradual process of a transfer of power in countries such as Po-land. Once the entire Soviet Union collapsed in 1991, fully closing the Cold-War era, a new global shift of power began to emerge, accompanied by a sudden opening of previously closed societies. While headline news covered the political and economic openings, this story is also about a multi-faceted reconstruction in the realms of culture.

Let us take, for example, the cultural arena of collective memory. We might extend Garton Ash's term to the arena of collective memory and assert that this set of events across 1989 resulted in a "refolution" in the region's collective memory as well, although with a great deal of un-evenness. One reason for considering the former Eastern Bloc as a key epicenter of the global memory boom is that several of the transnational strands of memory work mentioned earlier are present: trials to expose and bring perpetrators to justice; the uncovering of previously unknown or silenced histories; the presence of "counter-memory," or minority claims to heritage marking; the intentional reconstruction of myths of national origin; and the opportunity to correct or reconstruct historical narratives that political regimes had distorted. A growing civil society and democratically elected state actors had the opportunity to revise of-ficial, state-narrated memory, the power to persecute (Krapfl 2001) and to prosecute, and the right to remember.

The centrality of this impetus on the remembrance front in Central and Eastern Europe to the global memory boom cannot be overstated. In 1995, in fact, Michael Kammen suggested that among nine factors con-tributing to the memory boom were the end of the Cold War and intense debates over the history of the Holocaust (Kammen 1995). Jeffrey Olick has outlined the role that the fall of the Berlin Wall in 1989 played in Germany's attempts to "normalize the past" (1998: 552). The silences of the recent past, the screens of history on which these countries projected their current concerns, and the spectacles of new monuments and anniversary events began to characterize the memory arenas of the post-1989 Central and Eastern European region.

What follows is an overview of the various memory terrains that have roots in 1989, which take different forms and have contrasting agendas and often vary across countries, with an emphasis on the most recent commemorations of the 1989 events. Methodologically, I combine a survey of cross-disciplinary empirical research literature on these phenomena with my own interview and participant-observation research as a sociologist. I resided and worked in Gdańsk and Warsaw, Poland between 1996 and 2001. In addition, I conducted formal research on the memories of the *Solidarność* (Solidarity) movement in Poland during 2006, following the twenty-fifth anniversary commemorations of the movement, which involved event and museum attendance and interviews with several dozen Poles, spanning activists and non-activists, as well as those too young to remember the movement. I conducted a participant observation of the events organized to commemorate the twentieth anniversary commemorations of 1989 across Poland, Germany, Hungary, the Czech Republic, Slovakia, Bulgaria, and Romania during four months in the fall of 2009.[1] I interviewed approximately fifty individuals during this research visit, from current and former activists to event participants. In this chapter, I outline the varied terrains of memory work that the refolutions made possible, and then move into a description of the unfinished business of remembering the 1989 refolutions themselves.

Conceptualizing Memory Work

I use the term "memory work" to designate those intentional acts of coming to terms with a past, of constructing or reconstructing, in contrast to less-questioned inherited legacies or the less-conscious reproduction of collective memories through everyday practices.[2] The latter, which we could call "memory routines," closely resemble what Pierre Bourdieu delineated as a *doxa,* or the background noise of societal truths that are taken for granted (Bourdieu 1984). "Memory work," however, comes into play in this particular region and era in large part because a *doxa* has been disrupted. Without delving into a discussion about whether the pre-

1989 state-imposed *doxa* was truly unquestioned, it certainly operated through force or threat of force across these societies. In other words, any independent action to create, defy, or reconstruct memory outside of official channels was impossible and risked punishment, including prosecution (Czepczyński 2008: 84).

After 1989, it is a different story. Given that we are considering the results of a regional social movement that brought about these regime changes, or presumed changes, we are speaking, sociologically, of the efforts of human agency—both at the level of political/economic change and at the level of collective memory. For the most part, this involves active and intentional deliberation: organizing, lobbying, researching, traveling, fundraising, producing, voting, and voluntarily attending. It does not resemble the daily reproduction of a social *doxa*.

"Memory work" is a neutral term with great potential breadth, incorporating intentions and emotions on the continuum from trauma to celebration, from the exclusive to the inclusive, from new recovery to reminders of the familiar, from defiance to conciliation. It happens at the individual and the group levels. In fact, the breadth of this process is present across the corners of the post-1989 Central and Eastern European region. A strong and continuing strand of public memory activities both within and across these societies involves human-rights-oriented social justice concerns, which was a prominent theme of the social movements that brought down these regimes. Through his research on the *Solidarność* and other movements of the era, French sociologist Alain Touraine came to the conclusion that the "actor" had returned both in societies and in sociological theory: while social structures hold potent sway over human life, the resistant and creative work of individual agents continued to wield their own dynamic potency (Touraine 1988). This agency is clear in the realm of post-1989 memory work, as citizens became memory entrepreneurs on behalf of victims and silenced histories. We will also see examples of post-1989 memory agency that work in the opposite direction—toward *closing down* rights. As will be illustrated, the historical setting of this extremely active memory work within immediate post-1989 Central and Eastern Europe intersects with, and can help inform, scholarship on collective memory more generally.

I am using the metaphors of "silence, screen, and spectacle," echoing the themes of this volume, to give voice to the empirical materials on collective memory from this region. In doing so, I emphasize the themes that presented themselves in this research: in particular, the unfinished business of revolution—and its partner, the unfinished business of memory.

Silences

> *"I wanted my freedom while I was still young and beautiful."*
> —Bulgarian scholar, 2009

Spoken by a Bulgarian about her impatience over having to wait until after 1989 for her dream, this quote illustrates the futuristic orientation of the revolutions—and any revolution. Although social movements and contentious politics incorporate shared historical meanings into their action—from significant anniversary dates and places to commemoration of fallen heroes—the vision of an alternative future that fuels the activist commitment and sacrifice vies for activist responsibility toward their shared past. This premise allows us to understand that much of the initial memory work stemming from 1989 was motivated by an urge to topple the symbolic landscape markers that represented the regime that had been figuratively beheaded. In other words, *particular* symbols of the recent past were painful reminders or barriers whose continual presence was unneeded. Clearly, among the first casualties was the notoriously symbolic Berlin Wall.

This memory-beheading represented one moment of a multilayered phenomenon of silencing in recent history, though for different purposes. Looking back almost a century prior, the moment—or moments—of ushering in modernity were intentionally amnesiatic, reflected in the dismissal of tradition (and thus, collective memory) by social theorists such as Marx and Durkheim who wrote key scripts of modern social progress. Layering silence further, the state-communist regimes that attempted to further a particular modernist vision became expert at using public memory control as a tool of power. As the world long knew, photos were airbrushed, documents suppressed or destroyed, textbooks altered, and propaganda and museum texts produced with particular interpretive slants.

Therefore, one of the region's post-1989 agendas was to confront the silences of (manipulated) collective memory; through a range of efforts, this was taken on as an object of discontent. The clearing of landscapes became a high priority to the extent that, in my years of residence in Poland, friends joked about one given that they would encounter on any excursion: the ubiquitously posted sign announcing *"remont"* (remodel). One dynamic behind this "cleansing" of cityscapes was the new empowerment of local governments as the post-1989 societies decentralized political power—thus the local interest in rehabilitating local symbolic and practical structures. Most landscape erasures of Stalinist-era housing or Soviet war memorials, in fact, go uncontested (Czepczyński 2008). Citizens across the region saw street names change overnight; gone were the names of the heroes of the former regime. In their place were signs that consisted of 1989 heroes and even dates, such as that of the Romanian 1989 revolution. In Warsaw, one can stand at the corner where two streets, and their requisite signs, cross: *"Solidarność"* (Solidarity) and *"Jana Pawła II"* (Pope John Paul II).

Polish geographer Mariusz Czepczyński has reviewed the radical changes in post-socialist urban landscapes across the region since 1989, applying the descriptor of "oblivion" to these efforts of erasure, which he describes as creating "landscapes of silence" (Czepczyński 2008). Soon, many former museums that glorified the communist party had vanished, their previous locations nearly forgotten. In 2007, for example, Berlin's Palace of the Republic, a building that symbolized the former GDR, was demolished—signaling the unfinished, ongoing business of memory work up to the present day (Czepczyński 2008: 124–25).[3] Czepczyński reminds us:

> Museums of revolutionary or/and [sic] workers' movements were probably the most popular type of ideological shrines. Every major city in Bulgaria, Romania and East Germany had to have one. There were also museums personally dedicated to Lenin, like in Warsaw, Kraków or small village of Poronin in Poland, to Marx and Engels in Bucharest, or Rosa Luxemburg … in Leipzig. (Czepczyński 2008: 128)

There is a second side to the "unfinished business" of these silencing activities, since some remnants of the former landscapes remain (Czepczyński 2008: 125; Jordan 2006). Socialist-realist carvings remain etched into buildings across the region, which would involve great expense to remove. I visited one remaining memorial remnant in 2009: the "Alesha" Monument to the Soviet soldier in Plovdiv, Bulgaria, an imposing structure that is said to be the world's largest granite monument. This monument has not been torn down because it remains popular among locals as a symbol of the city. The more common trend is that buildings and public spaces that served the practical or symbolic ends of the pre-1989 regimes have been repurposed for private or public ends.

Although such (unfinished) amnesiatic activities may appear at counter-purposes to collective memorial goals, they are making their own statements about the meanings and non-meanings of memory. Exemplifying the multiple layers of silence that are in play here, post-1989 citizens were tackling the silences of those pre-1989 social worlds at the same time that they attempted to silence the memory "noise" of those regimes as inaccurate, irrelevant, or simply tired. In so doing, they plowed the way for other intensive work on recovering the past.

Screen

As Central and Eastern Europeans were burying their past woes, trau-
mas, and fears with those toppled monuments, recovery and preservation
were simultaneously underway. Since storytelling about the past plays
an integral role in the cultural tapestry and identity formation of any
society, a societal reconstruction is in many ways a storytelling process:
the break in a political/ideological/economic regime interrupts the public
narratives of the previous system, starts a new narrative, and represents
a story in and of itself. Silence began to be replaced by recovered or reconstructed memories. As George Schöpflin has suggested, the region's
historical culture played a strong role in this process:

> No Central European would ever make this mistake, that of neglecting the past. Small
> nations, small in population not in prestige or renown or achievement, cannot afford the
> kind of complacency that large ones make their own. (Schöpflin 2000: 76)

What were the new screens on which these countries projected their
reconstructed memories? In *Cities after the Fall of Communism,* John
Czaplicka, Nida Gelazis, and Blair A. Ruble explain that the dismantling,
or *demontage,* that characterized so many cities after 1989 was often followed by a "re-*embourgeoisment*" of the historic city centers. Public decisions over the destruction or preservation of historic structures evoked
discussions of the respective cities' (restored) ethnic identities and the
retrieval of a "radiant past" (reappropriating the communist language of
a "radiant future"). These cities position themselves as either re-placing
themselves on a European map (a "European turn") or re-rooting themselves in their pre-Soviet local identities (a "local turn") (Czaplicka et al.
2009). Czepczyński (2008) also documented how new landscapes across
the region now attempt to represent what the region terms the "New Europe," referring to post-socialist Central Europe.

A number of ethnographic studies document how local, municipal
communities in the new decentralized political settings have the power
and opportunity to represent their own pasts in their landscapes, reaching
back to recover forgotten pasts, some of which fit squarely into the new
projects of integrating into a pan-European, cosmopolitan future (Ewa
Ochman (2009) documented this in the Silesia region of Poland; Thum
(2009) and Musekamp (2009) have written about these processes in two
other Polish cities). Thus, several "screens" of the present day operate
in the choice of which pasts to represent. One could add to this that an
impetus behind the memory recovery was in fact to newly remember
the meaning of the nation that had partially disappeared through the former ideological and political colonization. As dissident leader and first

post-1989 president Václáv Havel announced to the Czechs and Slovaks upon his inauguration on New Year's Day in 1990: "Your country has returned to you" (Kenney 2006: 100). Thus, a resurgence of allegiances to national identities across the region reached a fever pitch—manifesting both high forms of the inclusive and humane imagined communities that can be discerned in Schöpflin's description, and the Janus-faced opposite, the violent, cruel, and exclusive forms.

If these countries were burying and attempting to forget the traumatic nature of living under a regime that arrested free thinkers and dissidents, controlled travel, and constricted people's life options, the access to newly available information brought these publics face to face with traumatic pieces of "Truth." Individuals could excavate their own histories. The region is discovering that there were internal resistance movements against the communist regimes that were erased through repression and murder. Recently exhumed graves in Romania, for example, are now exposing Romanians to unpublicized histories of their compatriots' dissidence. In line with Benedict Anderson's (1983) suggestion that nations imagine themselves as communities that incorporate past and future members, a virtual adoption was taking place to mnemonically usher these martyrs into their places in the newly constituted nation (see Vukov 2007).

For the individuals involved, such histories are personally, emotionally, and politically significant. Early on, Germany set up museums to archive the secret Stasi (secret police) files. By 2005, more than 1.6 million individuals had requested and received access to their Stasi files from the former German Democratic Republic ("Requests to See…" 2009). New access to this information even made its way into popular culture, as could be seen in the poignant and well-received German film, *The Lives of Others* (2006), which chronicled the claustrophobic lives of those in the theater world, who were under minute-by-minute surveillance, illustrating the palpable anxiety of never knowing who in one's lifeworld was watching.

Still, among the elements of unfinished business in the reconstruction of memory is that many artifacts are still in the process of being uncovered and may never be available. In the immediate aftermath of the 1989 upheavals, secret police in the region destroyed records or quickly and quietly shuttled files away to private residences. A Bulgarian journalist described to me the intensity of this practice in his country. Since 1989 portended to represent a regime change grounded in claims related to social justice and human rights, the deeply controversial question of prosecuting past offenders of those rights has been on national agendas. Integral to such a task has been the fact that the (free) press is a key institution for reproducing and interrogating a society's memory; the establishment of independent journalism, therefore, restores the journalistic narrator in the storytelling experience. As I have elaborated elsewhere (Pearce 2011), the seven countries of the region have varied in their approaches to the process that Central and Eastern Europe terms "lustration" (from a Latin term for "purification"), or bringing to light the actions of past officials. Even more contentious is the question of whether and how those officials should be brought before courts and publics as a matter of transitional justice.

Although Poland's first post-1989 Prime Minister Tadeusz Mazowiecki had stated that the country should draw a thick dark line between past and present in order to move forward, the country only ten years later set up a well-endowed organization, the Institute of National Memory, to investigate the backgrounds of the former system's leadership. With 1,400 full-time staff positions in this institute, opportunities abound for young academics, many of whom have difficulties securing work in the limited number of positions in the universities, where those in power are viewed as holdovers from the former system. Michal Kopeček (2008), a scholar in the Czech Republic, suggests that these revisionist employees often harbor personal agendas that could affect the outcomes of their research. How beneficial is lustration for these societies? Early research suggests that lustration potentially serves a similar purpose as war tribunals, to symbolically break with the past and symbolize the birth of a new era with transformed norms (Letki 2002). Nevertheless, public opinion on the process ranges across the spectrum, since the deeper the investigations go, the more likely it is that huge swaths of society will be caught in the net of the potentially guilty: Did one collaborate out of coercion, for example, or to keep one's profession or family safe? Did the secret police fabricate a record to meet a quota? How does one know that a code name was attached to a particular individual? The Bulgarian man who reported the many files that were whisked away insisted, "If all the files are not available, then no one should be prosecuted."

Increasingly, the region has been displaying two juxtaposed screens: the recounting of the history of World War II and the recounting of the communist era. Yet, often these screens are connected through overlapping themes. Among the examples of this is the *House of Terror* in Budapest, which pairs the Nazi and communist eras in a parallel exhibit, damning both for common crimes against humanity. Its exhibit on persecution of religion, for example, combines the communist and Nazi histories to suppress religious freedom.[4] Again, the purpose is to "other" both of these histories in a "Never Again" mnemonic representation. By the time of the twentieth anniversary of the 1989 revolutions, vocal leaders within the countries of the former Eastern Bloc raised the pitch for a call for national and continental expiation of the Communist era as a criminal regime, analogous to Nazism. These calls continued into 2012.

Significantly, within post-9/11 global political culture, it is terrorism that has emerged as the new despised-and-feared "ism." It is telling, therefore, that this is the present-day rhetoric that the region is choosing to adopt in its exposure of its dark past, folding the fascist and communist eras into a historical continuum of terror, elevating the level of their crimes into the more recognizable public discourse of today.

As politics swirled around the indicting and criminalizing style of coming face-to-face with the underbelly of the now deposed and delegitimized system, a trend within popular, particularly commercial, culture that oddly countered these processes has appeared in the region: a nostalgia for remnants of the former system. Today, a visit to Monument Park in Budapest, Hungary, offers not only a glimpse at the former socialist-realist statuary that once dominated and communicated an ominous power over public spaces (Verdery 1999), but also the opportunity to purchase a CD of recordings of the former party songs, a coffee mug with Lenin's face, and t-shirts playfully satirizing the era. Communist kitsch can be acquired in other countries of the region as well: hammer-and-sickle caps are sold in Prague kiosks, and symbols of the former Eastern Germany (and Berlin) are prolific across Berlin, such as the quirky silhouette of a short stout man in a hat that East Berliners remember as representing their "walk" sign for road crossings. Germans have created the term *Ostalgie,* to designate this nostalgia for the (former) East Germany. While walking in Sopot, Poland in 2009, I spotted a retro-style van that had parked on a heavily trafficked pedestrian promenade unannounced and begun to sell soda pops that were popular during communist times; the inventory sold out immediately. Such expressions should not be over-interpreted as a move to return to the past. This latter example was sponsored by the museum of the history of the Solidarity movement.

At the risk of claiming that these seemingly contradictory trends to criminalize and to elevate through popular memento are somehow parallel, I suggest that they share a commonality: commercializing the products of the former system is also drawing a thick line between past and present. The purchase of the memento results in othering that lost world, temporarily sampling it, but through a secondary representation, not fully situated in its previous social environment. Its commercial value is, in fact, fully tied to its scarcity.

In addition to the efforts to parallel communism with Nazism/fascism, other memory work devoted to new opportunities to excavate, re-represent, and make amends for the Second World War are in process. A major museum to German Jews and a massive landscape memorial to the Holocaust, "Memorial to the Murdered Jews of Europe," both located in Berlin, are evidences of the fact that the post-1989 era represents an unprecedented moment of new societal and regional reckoning with this history. The "Museum of the History of Polish Jews" is near completion in Warsaw following the recent opening of another major Warsaw museum to commemorate the Poles who resisted the Nazis during the Warsaw Uprising.

The screens that these new efforts represent have more than one source. Benoît Challand (2009) has indicated the way in which European leadership has focused on collective commemoration of the Holocaust as representing a nucleus of mnemonic unifications. In other words, a collective confession of the human-rights wrongs of the Holocaust is being seen as a common identity marker across Europe that is almost akin to a collective founding moment of community origin. Thus, the newly imagined (returned) European community is linking collective identity, memory, and programs of social justice, as the former Eastern Bloc is reconfiguring its own parallel agendas. Since all seven of these former Eastern Bloc countries are now members of the European Union, the desire to "return to Europe" at the same time that these countries "return to self" is a key screen for formulating memory of the war. A second screen that these seven countries share, to which the West was largely immune, was the insistence that the story that the communist party told about the war carried its own agenda. The Warsaw Uprising museum, for example, indicts the Soviet forces for abandoning Poles as Warsaw was under attack by the Axis powers. Across other countries in the region, new interpretations of the war revised the story from the one promoted under the communist era as a glorification of heroes who fought fascism or an emphasis on the Soviet army as a liberator to a narrative with fuller, more nuanced detail (Vukov 2007). The new commemorative war "screens" are doubled as narratives of these countries as victimizers and victimized.

At the moment when Jewish survivors or descendants can finally make pilgrimages to their former Eastern European homes, a level of touristic opportunity has also arisen. As an example of this Holocaust tourism, a "Schindler's List" tour in Kraków, Poland, cycles visitors through the sites made famous by the popular Hollywood film of the same name; small carts can be rented to carry the visitor on pre-recorded tours to the various stations of Jewish and Holocaust histories in Kraków. How do these tourist-packaged memory screens affect the personal and collective memories of the Holocaust? Among the many commentaries on this topic is that of Ruth Gruber who wonders about a "virtual Jewish world" reproduced in areas where there are few, if any, actual Jews (2002). Further, Tim Cole in *Selling the Holocaust: From Auschwitz to Schindler: How History is Bought, Packaged, and Sold* (1999) asserts that these sites often become simply stops among many on tourists' itineraries, creating a "feel good" personal experience for them after paying homage.

Through these examples, it is clear that both the desire to return to Europe on the part of Eastern Europeans and a need to draw a line that strictly distinguishes past from present (and future) are instrumental screens in determining how/why/whether to publicly perform memories of these dark histories. We have seen how these screens of remembering both the socialist and the World War II eras reveal two poles of a continuum: a nostalgic commodification with strains of humor and whimsy and a re-traumatization in facing new or repeated confrontation with painful histories. Both poles, however, function to put brackets around the past, othering it into a social realm of a distant set of social norms, peopled by the deposed and irrelevant, even as recognizable faces retain some levels of political and economic power.

Spectacle: Remembering 1989

Although it was the historic events of 1989 that ushered in the *collective memory refolution* described here, those events are still so recent in collective imaginations that they are sometimes considered as belonging to the present epoch rather than one that has passed. Until recently, in fact, Canadian-based historian James Krapfl ran into repeated resistance to his proposition that the events of 1989—and his research on that year—belonged in the academic discipline of history.[5] Only three of the seven countries (Czech Republic, Hungary, and Slovakia) have declared a national holiday on the date of their 1989 revolution to commemorate the event. This does not in and of itself demonstrate that 1989 does not carry the mantle of historical significance for a country. In two cases, there were proposals for national holidays, but they were in competition with other significant histories. In Germany, this was the November 9 remembrance of the Nazi attack on Jews in 1938 known as *Kristallnacht* (Olick 2003a), and in Romania, there was a stalemate over which December date to commemorate, leaving them to choose to commemorate a different historical event altogether, the first of December, which is when Transylvania unified with Romania in 1918 (Bucur 2009).

To some extent, the histories of 1989 have met silence in the public spheres through societal neglect to commemorate the most recent past and to attend to the meanings and preservations of—and guilt-driven confrontations with—these other, more traumatic histories we have just discussed (see Pearce 2009). Some remnants of the near past are still quite raw and thus speak for themselves without calling for physical interpretive markings. These remnants range from the remaining segments of the Berlin Wall to the bullet-pocked walls in Timisoara, Romania to the 1989 heritage that political parties currently in power in some countries claim as political capital. Returning to our juxtaposition of spectacle and silence, there has been an odd reversal: it is the former spectacle of 1989 that has faded from view, as the previously silenced histories that it unleashed took on a new societal clamor (see Olick 2003b).

In the fall of 2009, as I wandered across the region in search of signs of memory work on the histories of the 1989 revolutions, somewhat contrary to my expectations, I found spectacles. It appeared that the year 2009 did emerge as an important moment for region-wide reflection on the meanings of 1989—even if there were also unsettled and conflicted approaches to the history. I attended events that hosted audiences numbering tens of thousands and more. I found countless art displays, concerts, museum exhibits, ceremonies, religious services, publications, new monuments, and protests. The Czech Republic alone hosted several hundred exhibits scattered across the country's cities and towns. Broadly speaking, the twentieth anniversary commemorations ranged on a spectrum from the communal to the contentious, with some strong contrasts: from celebrations and fireworks in Berlin to somber (national) self-reflections in Bucharest. Hungary had fewer exhibits and events than its neighbors; its officially sponsored commemoration on October 23 was small, by invitation only. These manifestations of memory work appeared across public and private spaces, organized by public figures and individual citizens. There were no public events in Bulgaria. The relatively nondramatic regime change in this country on November 10, 1989, coupled with many citizens' questions about whether there has been a refolution, and much less a revolution, contributed to the low fanfare on the 2009 anniversary.

In contrast to previous years, for at least six of the seven countries enough historical distance from the year 1989 seems to have passed for the region's citizens to begin to actively mold a narrative that inscribes 1989 in their cultural memory. This may come as no surprise to collective memory scholars, who have noticed that it takes about twenty years—the approximate cycling through of a generation—to begin to organize collective commemorations of a historic event. A generational effect did appear to be in process, as those who were too young to remember the epochal events entered the collective memory arena as participants or independent memory entrepreneurs. I sat next to a young adult son of a former Solidarity movement activist in a theatrical event based on the events of the strikes and located in a former Gdańsk shipyard building.

He came out of curiosity and in homage to his father's efforts. And I sat down with young student activists in Prague and Brno in the Czech Republic to hear about their street processionals and theatrical satires organized for the anniversary. Their hope was to engage the Czech public in more direct involvement with their democracy, to wrest decision-making control from the hands of current professional politicians with whom they were disappointed. These were examples among others of memory work that emerged from individual citizens' own volition and creativity, not steered from above.

How did these spectacles also serve as screens on which memories of 1989 were projected, and refracted through the issues of the present? One common thread that repeated itself across these countries, including Bulgaria, was that of unfinished business: of the memory of 1989, and more centrally, the unfinished business of revolution. Momentum appears to be building—however slowly—to ensure that the events of 1989 take a prominent place in national collective memory in these countries. Cities in at least four countries unveiled new monuments and plaques to the history of 1989 during 2009. A rusty wall of heavy iron chains representing the former Iron Curtain, for example, now stands in Budapest, declaring "And finally, we tore it down!" As I wrote to a museum curator in advance of my autumn visit to Germany, she explained that I was a little late, as "we have been celebrating all year!" I was, however, able to arrive in time for the country's primary celebration in Berlin on November 9—a spectacle consisting of the toppling of a row of 1,000 hand-painted 8-foot-tall dominos and a ceremony with major heads of state on the *dais*, speeches, and musical performances. In some cities, 2009 set some new commemoration events in motion that have continued in 2010 and 2011: Prague and Leipzig are two examples of places where this has happened. Leipzig has already planned its annual commemorations through 2014, for the twenty-fifth anniversary. In both of these places, the core of the commemorative experience is a public processional that traces the actual path of the 1989 activists and culminates in a public square. In 2009, each of these processionals drew major crowds: an estimated 100,000 marched in Leipzig, and around 45,000 in Prague. The enthusiasm of those who attended, many of whom had been a part of the original protests and many of whom were too young to have done so, communicated a desire to return to this turning point in their recent histories. On October 9, for example, many Leipzig attendees continued to process even after completing the officially organized route, placing candles in significant places such as at the Stasi Museum and St. Nicholas Church. In Prague, the procession ended with joyous jingling of keys to recall the practice of the peaceful protests during the Velvet Revolution.

Figure 10.1. Monument to the Iron Curtain in Budapest. (Photo by Susan C. Pearce.)

As I will describe, however, there was plenty of cynicism and divisiveness over the direction of the changes since 1989. Officially organized Prague street exhibits of photographs and interviews with former activists included blatantly honest critiques of the country's post-1989 leadership. In Berlin, one man who appeared to be in his seventies approached me as I photographed that city's exhibits, and with tears in his eyes told of his loneliness and disappointments, his isolated one-room flat, and his friends' suicides. Gesturing toward a nearby fashion shop named "New York," he exclaimed, "*This* is what we got?" Having lived in the region in addition to attending these events, I can attest that consensus over the meaning of 1989 will never be a remote possibility either within or between the spaces that these countries occupy. There is one *possible* exception, however, which was evident across these countries, perhaps even in Romania: that the year 1989 was a riveting moment of collective effervescence and hope, whatever one's political persuasion or station in life. In fact, one of the most omnipresent images in the public exhibits was the photograph of a 1989 ecstatic crowd—leaping, crying, laughing, dancing, and kissing—in public squares as far as the eye could see.

In 2009, efforts to return to that moment bore some similarities across several sites. In Leipzig, Berlin, Bucharest, and Budapest, outdoor events included projected films on building walls and screens of the original events that were being marked. The Leipzig films, with loudly broadcast sounds of activist chants, offered a particular dose of realism to the occasion as the crowds processed along the former protest route. While interviewing a young woman who had attended the 2009 events I used the term "reenactment." I was quickly corrected. "That was *not* a reenactment," she insisted. "I remember that night. I was 11. As my parents left for the protest, they told my brother and me, 'if we don't come back, you are going to live with your grandparents.'" I stood corrected.

The performance of the unfinished business of memory was particularly salient in the homages to the movements' victims in several places. In Prague, crowds pushed their way into the covered walkway of a building with a small plaque to the events of November 17, 1989, the date of the "Velvet Revolution" student march, which ended in repression by state riot police. (Czechs also commemorate a second national memory on this date: the 1939 martyrdom of university student Jan Opletal as an anti-Nazi demonstrator. In fact, the 1989 march was organized in his memory, on International Students' Day, named for him.) A floor of blazing votive candles lined the entire, otherwise chilly, evening space. At Wenceslas Square, Czechs also lit candles before the images of students Jan Palach and Jan Zajíc, who self-immolated following the 1968 Soviet invasion of Czechoslovakia. Romania, perhaps most predictably, performed more of a victim narrative than a celebratory narrative. Many questions remain unanswered regarding the bloodshed of 1989 in that country, including who really orchestrated the crackdown and eventual executions. Newly produced documentary films for the 2009 commemorations featured Romanians who recounted details of the son or mother who was shot in front of them, helping the viewer to relive that year "up close and personal." Individuals lined up to write, pensively, in a signature book erected as part of a memorial exhibit at the site of student protests. Both in the city of Timişoara, where the revolution began, and in Bucharest, where it ended, the commemorations consisted of solemn wreath-laying and candle-lighting—a far cry from the fireworks of Berlin and Prague. Notably, Berlin also had its contemplative space to honor victims. During the day on November 9, visitors lit candles at a remaining segment of the Berlin Wall on the street, Bernauer Strasse, the site of a memorial-in-process, which had its third installment nearly two years later, in August 2011, for the fiftieth anniversary of the building of the Wall.[6]

Throughout these events and exhibits, there was a clear theme of the unfinished business of the revolution. This came across in several ways. One was the disappointment with the aftermath of the changes. No country seemed exempt from this sentiment. In Bulgaria, where there were no commemorative events in 2009, a woman explained to me, "It's the same people in power." Because of this and other reasons, she believed, their society did not have a revolution. "But in Poland," she insisted, "*they* really had a revolution." This exemplifies what Krapfl (forthcoming) has termed "revolution envy," which he has documented across the region—even in Poland, where citizens credit the 1989 victory to the negotiation of leaders in a closed Roundtable session, rather than an overturning of power through grassroots efforts. What were the feelings in 2009 Poland, which was being touted as one of the strongest economies in Europe at the time, amidst a deep global recession? There was unquestionably pride in the country's dissident history, and the June 4 anniversary of the first semi-free elections saw champagne toasts and whimsical mustache-growing to mimic the style of Lech Wałęsa, supplementing the officially organized ceremony in Kraków, not open to the public. Further, there was an interesting theme on revolution envy, emanating *from* Poland: concern that the 2009 attention to Berlin Wall commemorations would leave the important contributions of Poles in the shadows. This manifested itself through contestations over an EU-produced commemorative video that glossed over the Solidarity Movement's accomplishments, teams of young people with large Polish banners at the Berlin events, and huge billboards in Berlin declaring, "It all began with a Roundtable." On another level, however, the country remained torn over the issue of coming together as a whole to celebrate jointly, given sharp divisions between the political parties in power and tensions between cosmopolitan and traditional values.

Among the more dramatic presentations of unfinished business were those in Budapest, Hungary. I did not see evidence that, like Germany, Hungarians had been "celebrating all year." This country's anniversary date, October 23, is the same date as the 1956 (suppressed) revolution. Three years prior to the 2009 anniversary, Hungary attempted to celebrate the fiftieth anniversary of this revolution. Those attempts were quickly squashed, however, as the right-wing nationalist organization, the Hungarian Guardists, violently protested the revelation in 2006 that the government leaders—representing the socialist party—had lied to the country over the state of the economy. Would-be celebrants headed for safety as buildings were attacked and cars burned. On October 23, 2009, out of fear of a repeat performance, selected officials and guests attended a small, closed ceremony in front of the Parliament building, and processed to lay wreaths at the nearby monument to Imre Nagy, leader of the 1956 uprising. The Hungarian Guardists, dressed in militant black, made a nearby appearance and organized a much larger staged event, centered around their nationalistic and blatantly anti-Semitic agendas.

Based on some form of "cosmopolitan" logic, the event celebrated the group's collaborations with nationalist parties across Europe, some of whom were invited guests. Continuing the theme of unfinished business into 2012, the once upstart youth political party Fidesz, currently in power, rolled back certain civil-society rights, such as freedom of the press, prompting the European Union to question pointedly the country's directions toward instituting democracy.

This is one example among others of the use of the screen of the 2009 commemorations as a platform for activism directed toward issues of the present. One repeated theme, particularly in ceremonies in Berlin and Kraków, where political elites from several nationalities were featured, was the unfinished business of revolution across the globe. In Berlin, the Polish dissident leader and first post-communist president, Lech Wałęsa, was given the honor of pushing the first of the 1,000 8-foot foam dominos along the route of the former Wall. As the dominos tumbled, however, they stopped at one uniquely stable, concrete domino. This domino had been sent from the Goethe Institute in China and was covered in invented Chinese characters that spelled out a German poem. At this point in the ceremony, the program focused on the countries still under autocratic rule and repression of freedoms, including North Korea. This same theme had been evident in the 2005 official ceremonies in Warsaw and Gdańsk, Poland, to celebrate the twenty-fifth birthday of Solidarność. The events' promotional poster, "It all started in Gdańsk," featured the image of Wałęsa on a domino that topples other dominos representing cities throughout the former Eastern Bloc, and then lists cities of the former Soviet Republic, ending with an ellipsis to suggest future cities to come.

This theme of extra-regional struggles for freedom was audible in several civil-society-generated forms as well. For example, one of those dominos in Berlin had been sent by Mexican children. Paralleling the Berlin Wall with the Wall being built between Mexico and the United States, the images on the children's domino pointedly exposed the threatening power of the U.S. border patrol and the deaths of those Mexicans who unsuccessfully attempted to cross. This was an ironic representation of the unfinished business of democracy in the "West," given that then-Secretary of State Hillary Clinton was a featured speaker to congratulate the region on its progress. (President Obama addressed the crowd remotely from the United States via video.) New communications media were integral to the region's memory work, also unintentionally becoming a platform on which to address unfinished business. Using the social media technology Twitter, organizers of the German commemorations created a virtual Berlin Twitter Wall. Immediately, Chinese citizens be-

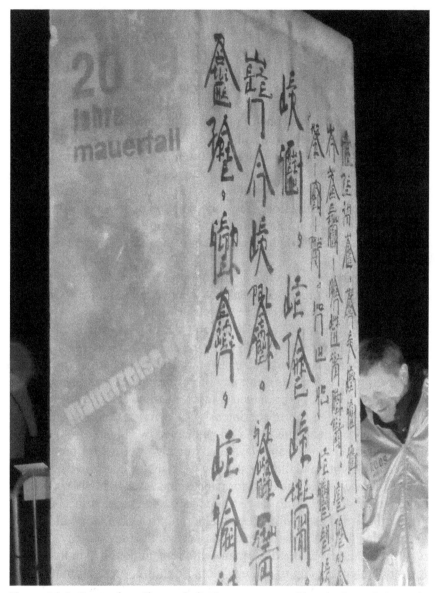

Figure 10.2. Domino from China at Berlin Commemorations. (Photo by Susan C. Pearce.)

gan using the site to inscribe their own virtual graffiti messages, such as "When is our Wall going to fall?" and "I want my Facebook!" Approximately 1,500 Chinese were able to voice their protests before the Chinese government "Great Firewalled" the site to their citizens.

Unfinished business on the memorial screens was audible and visible almost everywhere. At the infamous shipyards in Gdańsk, the present-day shipyard workers were building a fraction of the number of ships they built in the yard's heyday, employed by a foreign-owned private firm that rescued it from bankruptcy. Present-day Solidarność trade union members had protested the twenty-fifth anniversary commemoration as an elite occasion to which they were not invited, as they pressed for government involvement to save the shipyard. In August of 2009, the entrance to Gate Number 2 hosted photographs of protesting Solidarność activists that on first glance appeared to be the 1980s uprising; but these turned out to be current workers who were continuing to call for government intervention. In August 2009, they had occupied the grounds of the Gdańsk home of Prime Minister Donald Tusk. This movement appeared to be drawing little sympathy from the public. The son of a former Solidarność activist who sat next to me at the theater event in the shipyards said, "I don't think we should help them. It's not the same. They're a private company now."

Other public spectacles of commemorative events attracted the activist involvement of organized groups of young people. Leipzig, Germany offered one of the most visible examples of this: on October 9, the anniversary of their major protest, among the city's formally organized events was a "Democracy Market." Nonprofit and activist organizations staffed booths highlighting their causes, from church charities to environmental groups. There was a full day of performances on a public stage. A global justice group presented a mock auction of Germany's public institutions to poke fun of the intensity of privatization; the university system received the highest bids, accompanied by laughter from the student bidders. The following day, after Leipzig's successful processions with candle-lighting to fill four shallow wells that spelled out the number "1989," as well as musical performances and laser-light shows on city buildings, a group of anti-fascist demonstrators gathered in Leipzig to protest the previous evening's commemorations, which they called "The Great Leipzig Heist." Marching to the scene of the previous day's performances, protesters charged Germany with remaining mired in its past, as it restricted citizenship to exclude ethnic minorities and promoted pronatalist policies to populate the country with ethnic Germans.

A visible theme of unfinished business across a number of sites that I visited was that of homelessness. Gone is the socialist-era guarantee of a roof over one's head. Apartments were selling at market rates that in some places rivaled "Western" prices. I saw major advocacy campaigns by NGOs in both Gdańsk and Poland on behalf of the homeless; the Gdańsk campaign was a collaboration with University of Gdańsk professors from sociology and other departments. In Sofia, Bulgaria, one of the individuals that I interviewed pointed to two adults who were dumpster-

Figure 10.3. Mock Auction in Leipzig, Germany. (Photo by Susan C. Pearce.)

diving for food, and remarked, "we didn't have *that* before 1989." In both Sofia and Bucharest, Romania, I observed older women begging on city sidewalks in extreme cold, accompanied by rain and snow.

The involvement of youth in officially and unofficially organized commemorations and counter-commemorations intersected with a key theme repeated in the texts of many ceremonies: How do we pass on the lessons of this history to the next generation? From all appearances, in some corners, the youth were listening, and often producing their own new meanings.

Conclusion

> The history of revolutions—from the summer of 1776 in Philadelphia and the summer of 1789 in Paris to the autumn of 1956 in Budapest—which politically spells out the innermost story of the modern age, could be told in parable form as the tale of an age-old treasure which, under the most varied circumstances, appears abruptly, unexpectedly, and disappears again, under different mysterious conditions, as though it were a fata morgana. (Arendt [1961] 2006: 4)

If Hannah Arendt were alive today, might she add the spectacle of 1989 to her list of these lost treasures? By all accounts they were also unexpected, and by many accounts they have lost their early allure, generally replaced by disillusionment and feelings of betrayal. Attempts to approximate the effervescent feeling of that year were certainly evident in the 2009 commemorations. What this research uncovered was that the revolutions continue to be considered unfinished, and the formal spectacles of the anniversaries that were used to continue or complete them also suggested an unfinished nature to the memory work both unleashed by 1989 and *about* the 1989 events themselves. As historian James Krapfl has recently written, "there are insights to be gained from seeing the revolutions of 1989 not just as a moment, but as a process" (Krapfl forthcoming). Several scholars (Isaac 1999; Jedlicki 2005; Krapfl 2009; Pearce 2009) have documented the multiple meanings that 1989 holds not only across countries, but across individuals within those societies.

Just as the revolutions remain unfinished, so does memory work. Despite their differences in histories under communism (and since), these seven societies share a) the unsettled nature of memory work; b) the contested nature of memory work; c) productive, forward-moving memory work representing democratic processes and self-reckoning; and d) a package of histories that symbolically belong not only to this subcontinental region, but to the broader continent and even the globe. Will the historical legacy, as well as the collective memory, of the spectacle of 1989 go down in the history books as an enigma, as a solitary historical occurrence with epoch-changing consequences, or will its legacy be the first in a series? Does the globally owned collective memory of that spectacle become a cultural resource, a strategic model, for what will follow? Such questions were being asked across 2011 as journalists in particular began to call the Tunisian uprising a "jasmine revolution" to give it a place in the string of "color revolutions" across several post-Soviet countries since 1989. One journalist asked, "Is Tunis the Arab Gdańsk?" These references seemed to fade as the specific historical contingencies of the uprising in the Middle East became more apparent. The Arab Awakening protests, however, clearly recalled 1989 in a spirit of mimesis: where there were joyously packed public city squares, chanting and singing, they served as reminders that the events of 1989 were equally riveting international spectacles.

Research into the production of mnemonic places to remember World War II, the Soviet-controlled era, and the 1989 break provides a window into larger questions. At the formal level, what can studies of these moments and places of memory production tell us about the progress these countries are making in creating freer civil societies, supporting uncensored voices and independent associations? Can these societies now speak of a pluralistic public sphere? And at the level of content and substance, what do the newly produced mnemonic images and words communicate about the national/community values that are either being recovered or newly produced (or even borrowed)? Do these become instruments of catharsis and liberation, or are they transformed into new tools of power in the hands of a new (or partially new) elite?

Here is where we need a caveat to our use of the metaphor of "screen." There is a risk of overstating this truism that the past is always interpreted through the prism of the present. The newly produced performance does not necessarily veil the original meanings/intentions/feelings/experiences of the remembered event. Collective memory and a historiographer's meticulously researched record are not cleanly mutually exclusive (Schwartz et al. 2005). In an era of expanding public literacy, nonhistorians have access to historical particulars through newspaper accounts, accessibly written texts, formal education, and their own research initiatives. These countries are certainly working through these various screens, but are simultaneously embarking on new efforts of historical revisionism with every newly discovered document and uncovered burial.

We return to the metaphors of silence, screen, and spectacle, and their interactive relationships, which help convey the array of sound and sight of the memory work across these seven countries. The production of spectacle, the screen of complex historical conditions that bear on interpretation, the silencing of previous noise, and the replacement of previous silences with new content, are exemplifying the region's new and unfinished memory work. The year 2009 has ushered in a new phase in that work, particularly in regard to the commemoration of the 1989 events. The next generation is beginning to take up the mantle. This new phase appears to be one of lifting those silences and grappling with a script and physical manifestations that mark the perpetually unfolding meanings of the year 1989 for the present day.

Notes

1. In four countries (Germany, Hungary, Czech Republic, and Romania), I was present for the events scheduled for the anniversary. In Poland, I attended events for the 29th anniversary of *Solidarność* in August; I arrived in Slovakia just following its November 17 anniversary commemorations, though the center of these was in the Czech Republic.

2. In Irwin-Zarecka's account, memory work is "the work of giving order and meaning to the past" (1994: 145).

3. Czepczyński found differences across the region regarding the intensity with which landscapes were cleared, which he attributed to differences in present-day politics in these countries as well as historical and cultural experience. He states: "[I]n eastern

Germany the old icons of GDR are ignored, half-forgotten or considered as parts of their national identity, while in history-oriented Poland most of the remembrances of the former People's Republic recall oppression, misery or at least lost opportunities" (2008: 125). Czepczyński mentions Berlin's Palace of the Republic as a despised building whose demolition was publicly welcomed; Historian Hope Harrison, however, insists that the opposite was the case: the building carried strong, positive private memories for the East Germans; it had been the site of weddings and housed popular bowling alleys (Harrison, personal communication, August 2012).

4. This museum has been critiqued for giving less attention to the Holocaust than such a museum might be expected to do.

5. Personal communication, 2009.

6. The first installment was the November 2009 opening of a visitor's center; the second was the May 2010 ceremony marking the opening of the first part of the large outdoor memorial that included a part of the death strip, a memorial with pictures of victims (Harrison, personal communication, August 2012).

References

Anderson, Benedict. 1983. *Imagined Communities: Reflections on the Origin and Spread of Nationalism.* New York: Verso.

Arendt, Hannah. [1961] 2006. *Between Past and Present.* New York: Penguin Books.

Ash, Timothy Garton. 1990. *The Magic Lantern: The Revolution of '89 Witnessed in Warsaw, Budapest, Berlin, and Prague.* New York: Random House.

Bourdieu, Pierre. 1984. *Distinctions. A Social Critique of the Judgment of Taste.* Translated by Richard Nice. Cambridge, MA: Harvard University Press.

Bucur, Maria. 2009. *Heroes and Victims.* Bloomington and Indianapolis: Indiana University Press.

Challand, Benoît. 2009. "1989, Contested Memories and the Shifting Cognitive Maps of Europe." *European Journal of Social Theory* 12: 397–408

Cole, Tim. 1999. *Selling the Holocaust: From Auschwitz to Schindler: How History is Bought, Packaged, and Sold.* London, UK: Psychology Press.

Czaplicka, John J., Nida Gelazis, and Blair A. Ruble, eds., 2009. *Cities after the Fall of Communism: Reshaping Cultural Landscapes and European Identity.* Baltimore, MD: Johns Hopkins University Press.

Czepczyński, Mariusz. 2008. *Cultural Landscapes of Post-Socialist Cities.* Hampshire, UK and Burlington, VT: Ashgate.

Doss, Erika. 2008. "Memorial Mania: Fear, Anxiety, and Public Culture." *Museum* (March/April): 36–43, 72–75.

Gruber, Ruth. 2002. *Virtually Jewish: Reinventing Jewish Culture in Europe.* Berkeley: University of California Press.

Irwin-Zarecka, Iwona. 1994. *Frames of Remembrance.* New Brunswick, NJ and Oxford, UK: Transaction Publishers.

Jedlicki, Jerzy. 2005. "East-European Historical Bequest en Route to an Integrated Europe." In *Collective Memory and European Identity: The Effects of Integration and Enlargement,* edited by Klaus Eder and Willfried Spohn, 37–48. Surry, UK and Burlington, VT: Ashgate.

Jordan, Jennifer A. 2006. *Structures of Memory: Understanding Urban Change in Berlin and Beyond.* Stanford, CA: Stanford University Press.

Kammen, Michael. 1995. "Frames of Remembrance: The Dynamics of Collective Memory by Iwona Irwin-Zarecka." *History and Theory* 34: 245–61.

Kenney, Padraic. 2006. *The Burdens of Freedom: Eastern Europe since 1989.* London and New York: Zed Books.

Kopeček, Michal. 2008. "In Search of 'National Memory': The Politics of History, Nostalgia and the Historiography of Communism in the Czech Republic and East Central Europe." In *Past in the Making: Historical Revisionism in Central Europe after 1989,* edited by Michal Kopeček, 75–96. Budapest, Hungary: Central European University Press.

Krapfl, James. 2001. "The Sacred and the Velvet Revolution." *Kosmas: Czechoslovak and Central European Journal* 14: 51–63.

———. 2009. Personal correspondence.

———. Forthcoming. "Afterward: The Discursive Constitution of Revolution and Revolution Envy." In *The 1989 Revolutions in Central and Eastern Europe: From Communism to Post-Communism,* edited by Kevin McDermott and Matthew Stibbe. Manchester, UK: Manchester University Press.

Letki, Natalia. 2002. "Lustration and Democratisation in East-Central Europe." *Europe-Asia Studies* 54: 529–52.

Levy, Daniel, and Natan Sznaider. 2005. "The Politics of Commemoration: The Holocaust, Memory and Trauma." In *Handbook of Contemporary European Social Theory,* edited by Gerard Delanty, 289–97. London and New York: Routledge.

Ochman, Ewa. 2009. "Municipalities and the Search for the Local Past: Fragmented Memory of the Red Army in Upper Silesia." *East European Politics and Societies* 23: 392–420.

Olick, Jeffrey K. 1998. "What Does It Mean to Normalize the Past? Official Memory in German Politics since 1989." *Social Science History,* Vol. 22, No. 4, Special Issue: Memory and the Nation, pp. 547–571.

———. 2003a. "The Value of Regret? Lessons from and for Germany." In *Justice and the Politics of Memory: Religion and Public Life,* edited by Gabriel R. Ricci, 21–32. New Brunswick, NJ: Transaction Books.

Olick, Jeffrey K., ed. 2003b. *States of Memory: Continuities, Conflicts, and Transformations in National Retrospection.* Durham, NC: Duke University Press.

Olick, Jeffrey I., Vered Vinitzky-Seroussi, and Daniel Levy, eds. 2011. *The Collective Memory Reader.* Oxford: Oxford University Press.

Pearce, Susan C. 2009. "The Polish Solidarity Movement in Retrospect: In Search of a Mnemonic Mirror." *International Journal of Politics, Culture and Society* 22: 159–82.

Schöpflin, George. 2000. *Nations, Identity, Power.* New York: NYU Press.

Schwartz, Barry, Kazuya Fukuoka, and Sachiko Takita-Ishii. 2005. "Collective Memory: Why Culture Matters." In *The Blackwell Companion to the Sociology of Culture,* edited by Mark Jacobs and Nancy Weiss-Hanrahan, 253–71. Malden, MA: Blackwell Publishing.

Touraine, Alain. 1988. *Return of the Actor: Social Theory in Postindustrial Society.* Translated by Myrna Godzich. Minneapolis: University of Minnesota Press.

Verdery, Katherine. 1999. *The Political Lives of Dead Bodies.* New York: Columbia University Press.

Vukov, Nicolai. 2007. "The Commemorated and the Excluded: The Reshaped Pantheons in Eastern Europe, 1945–1956." In *Nation in Formation: Inclusion and Exclusion in Central and Eastern Europe: Papers from the 7th International Postgraduate Conference held at the School of Slavonic and East European Studies, UCL,* edited by Catherine Baker, Christopher J Gerry, Barbara Madaj, Liz Mellish and Jana Nahodilová, 3–23. London: School of Slavonic and East European Studies, UCL.

Williams, Paul. 2007. *Memorial Museums: The Global Rush to Commemorate Atrocities.* Oxford and New York: Berg.

Zolberg, Vera. 1998. "Contested Remembrance: The Hiroshima Exhibit Controversy." *Theory and Society* 27: 565–90.

Conclusion

Comments on Silence, Screen, and Spectacle

Lindsey A. Freeman, Benjamin Nienass, and Rachel Daniell

In previous eras, the study of social memory required a prowler of history with excellent hearing, and by this we mean a researcher with good listening skills, who would stealthily plunge into the historical record, get dusty in the archives, and if possible, listen to those witnesses still alive who were present at the "event." Make no mistake: these practices are still valuable. But today, for those interested in social memory a deeper skill set is necessary, as our abilities to record, store, recall, and shape social memories are enhanced, complicated, and challenged by new technologies. Today, we must move faster as the present sneaks away with ever-greater speed, piling up catastrophes for the nearsighted angel of history (Benjamin 1968). But, we must also move slower, acknowledging that the shape of the past sometimes takes time to develop. We need to take a moment to pause and to think, so that we may hold up an umbrella of critical thought to the spectacular assault of images and stories from the past, which rain down from all angles, threatening to drown out certain communities and voices.

Social memory is now filtered through more media and communications platforms than ever before. Each new technology brings new methods and ways of remembering, drawing attention to the past, and creating communities of awareness through virtual, digital, and embodied means and practices. Perhaps one of the most dramatic changes to social memory in recent years has been the increased ability to share and to archive the past, both individually and collectively, through digital technologies.

Jacques Derrida's *Archive Fever* (1996) anticipated the compulsion to "save," but did not imagine the extent to which we would be able to do so.

At what fever point does our archival temperature measure today? On the one hand, the mercury seems to have risen, with the panic of losing our witnesses to the atrocities of the first half of the twentieth century and with excitement over new archival forms. On the other hand, people seem to have cooled down, to be less bothered, less panicked, and more trusting with our seemingly infinite digital storage capacities—calmly filling another terabyte drive or near-limitless folder of cloud storage. Undeniably, current technologies offer new possibilities for our memories now and in the future. But, can we truly anticipate their future conditions of preservation and accessibility? Can we rely on the searchability of the past? Or do our new technologies also make it easier to erase inconvenient truths, opposing narratives, counter-memories, and those memories that, in the moment, might not seem important or necessary for future needs, simply by letting them fade into the endless proliferation of files?

While it is true that advancing memory technologies increase certain capabilities for remembering, we must also keep in mind that, much like moving from one living space to another, when we move technologies, some things are accidently lost, others are deliberately discarded because they will not "fit" in the new place, and still others are left behind because they seem (in the moment) outdated or insignificant. Foucault (1972) famously referred to the archive as "the law of what can be said"; as we move our archives into new digital realms, we sometimes forget our words.

At the same time, through new memory technologies fresh opportunities for coming together emerge; possibilities come to the fore for the commingling and/or "queering" of social communities of memory (Sosa, this volume; Butler 2005); new chances for "multidirectional memory" (Rothberg 2008) to shed light on the past are revealed; additional venues for "storytelling" present themselves (Doerr, this volume; Benjamin 2003); and new platforms for creating and consuming counter-spectacles and counter-memories that challenge dominant narratives become possible.

Communities of memory in this day and age stretch the globe and shatter old geographical and temporal barriers, making it possible for disparate communities in locations far from each other, such as Israel, Argentina, and Sierra Leone to remember together simultaneously and deliberately. Part of this is due to the increased ability of the everyday person to create and participate in what Debord (1994) termed the "spectacle." For Debord, spectacle was a fabulist tool wielded by the powerful—the state, the mass media, the captains of industry—that stupefied the masses. According to Debord (1998), over time the spectacle would be even more difficult to resist because a whole generation would have grown up under its guidance and would have known no other way of life. In the field of social remembrance, the rise of the spectacular has led to a "pure iconisation and aestheticisation of collective memory ... regulated solely by the repertoire of imagery" (Kaschuba 2010: 71). This, some have argued, could eventually also lead to the end of reflective and argumentative processes with regard to the past (Kaschuba 2010)—as we consume the spectacular, it consumes us in return.

In the present day, as technologies have advanced, counter-spectacular means are also much more available to the average person than they were in the time of Debord's writing—a progression he did not anticipate but hoped for. The spectacle was difficult to fight, according to Debord, because in order to do so, one had to employ spectacular means. Diana Taylor has argued that "digital technologies offer the updated Marxist promise for the twenty-first century: that we—individual users—now control the means of production, distribution, and access to information, communities, and online worlds" (2012). The Internet, social media, smart phones, and other technological advances have made it possible to record and dispense images and accounts of events with ease and speed. Undeniably, these new technologies have made it more possible to mobilize counter-memory and to allow for memories that might have been silenced or hidden in previous times to be seen, heard, and circulated.

Something has changed with regard to the transmission and accessibility of spectacles since Debord's original analysis. Some even claim that we live in an age that has left the spectacular more or less behind. According to this view, we have moved from representation to presence and from observation to participation, so that today's issue may "not [be] the distance brought about by spectacle but the engulfing, fleshy communions of non-spectacle" (Debray 1995: 139). Digital photography, live videos, and performance art are then best understood as a departure from the distance and deferment implied by the notion of spectacle and should be seen as examples of a new immediacy caused by the "indexical rupture" in our way of relating to the world around us (Debray 1995: 139). Whether one counts these potentially less distant mediums as sources of spectacle in their own right or as something altogether different, we must at least accept Debray's qualification that different spectacles have their own "way of conveying presence" (and past), and that consequently we are "not 'enslaved' in the same way to each of these" (1995: 140). In other words, each new form of media comes with different constraints and possibilities. With "the gradual displacement of aura from images of possessable objects to digitized flows of data," we may have indeed entered a time in which "pure flux itself [is] a commodity, [and] a spectacular and 'contemplative' relation to objects is undermined and supplanted by new kinds of investments" (Crary 1984: 287).

It remains to be seen what this new age will bring in terms of social memory practices: Will we remember differently? Will memory communities be based more on affinities than bloodlines and national and ethnic loyalties? Will different things be forgotten? Will we recover pasts long thought lost? Even in an age when so much can be catalogued and contained, the difficult questions of what is saved and what is jettisoned, what is remembered and what is forgotten, must still be asked. Despite the seemingly limitless possibilities for retaining the past, we still make choices. We know in our heart of hearts that total access to the past is the nostalgic's utopian dream. First, there are only so many minutes in the day, so many hours in one's life to store up the past. Second, even in the ever-expanding digital universe, where more people have cell phones than bank accounts, not everyone has access to new technologies. What will happen to their memories? How does the digital divide impact social remembering and in what ways might this shift along with future shifts in technology?

This volume has offered a critical look at the present state of social memory's production, transmission, and storage; we also offer a glimpse of what could be on the horizon for the future. What we explore is not a "true" representation of bygone events, but instead the ways in which the past is narrated, performed, screened, broadcasted, Facebooked, tweeted, and reflexively and spectacularly considered in new contexts. Ultimately, we look at how memories accrue meaning and how stories about the past are mobilized by various actors under contemporary conditions. As much as we may venture to represent the past as "what *really* happened," we know that we are doomed to fail. We know all too well that every socially shared account of the past that is held today is formed from competing memories, and that notions about the past arise from past struggles, present desires, and future expectations. We make memories now to use later (Taylor 2012).

As memory scholars, we used to talk about ruptures and voids as openings to new ways of thinking and remembering; now we can think of oversaturation and spectacle as new spaces and potential sites for counter-memory as well. The proliferation of ever more memories and counter-memories can not only lead to heightened noise levels, but also constitute new "lines of force which cause shivers of utopianism that we are obliged to explore" (Brian, Jaisson, and Mukherjee 2011). Counter-memory must be reiterated again and again because it plays a dual role as both reminder of a lost past and its questioning. Still, we must be aware that in itself memory is not a replacement for social and political action, but its interrogator and conduit. Finally, as this volume has shown, new distributions in the power to create, distribute, archive, and access memory also make new demands on the researcher—our prowler of history must now attend to these new spectacular forms and the ways they serve to silence, to screen, to recall, to forget, and perhaps to remember better together.

References

Benjamin, Walter. 1968. "Theses on the Philosophy of History." *Illuminations.* Translated by Harry Zohn, 253–64. New York: Schocken Books.
———. 2003. "The Storyteller." *Selected Writings: Volume 3, 1935–1938.* Cambridge, MA: Belknap Press.
Brian, É., Jaisson, M. and Mukherjee, S. R. (2011), "Introduction: Social Memory and Hypermodernity." *International Social Science Journal,* 62: 7–18.
Butler, Judith. 2005. *Giving an Account of Oneself.* New York: Fordham University Press.
Crary, Jonathan. 1984. "Eclipse of the Spectacle." In *Art After Modernism: Rethinking Representation,* edited by Brian Wallis, 283–296. New York: The New Museum of Contemporary Art.
Debray, Régis. 1995. "Remarks on the Spectacle." *New Left Review* I/214 (November–December): 134–42.
Debord, Guy. 1994. *The Society of the Spectacle.* New York: Zone Books.
———. 1998. *Comments on the Society of the Spectacle.* London and New York: Verso.
Derrida, Jacques. 1996. *Archive Fever.* Chicago: University of Chicago Press.
Foucault, Michel. 1972. *The Archaeology of Knowledge and the Discourse on Language.* New York: Pantheon Books.
Kaschuba, Wolfgang. 2010. "Iconic Remembering and Religious Icons: Fundamentalist Strategies in European Memory Politics?" In *A European Memory? Contested Histories and Politics of Remembrance,* edited by Malgorzata Pakier and Bo Strath, 64–75. New York: Berghahn Books.
Rothberg, Michael. 2008. *Multidirectional Memory: Remembering the Holocaust in an Age of Decolonization.* Stanford, CA: Stanford University Press.
Taylor, Diana. 2012. "Save As." *emisférica* 9.1–2 (Summer). http://hemisphericinstitute.org/hemi/en/e-misferica-91/taylor

Contributors

Naomi Angel is a Mellon postdoctoral fellow at the Jackman Humanities Institute at the University of Toronto. She completed her PhD in the Department of Media, Culture, and Communication at New York University. Her research explores issues of visual culture, transitional justice, testimony and translation, and the labors of memory. More specifically, she focuses on the Canadian Truth and Reconciliation Commission and the process of reconciliation between indigenous and non-indigenous Canadians.

Rachel Daniell is a doctoral student in anthropology at The Graduate Center, City University of New York. Her work centers on the intersection of evidence, documentation, and representation with historical memory and state violence. She holds an MA in Liberal Studies-International Studies from The Graduate Center and was formerly the associate director of the Center for Human Rights and Peace Studies at Lehman College. Her current research examines practices of documentation around human rights violations committed by the United States in the "War on Terror."

Nicole Doerr has a PhD from the European University Institute and an MA in Political and Social Sciences from the Institute d'Etudes Politiques de Paris. After her Marie Curie Fellowship at UC Irvine and at Harvard University she started her new position as assistant professor in International Relations at Mount Holyoke College. Doerr's work addresses questions of democracy, memory, culture, and political translation in social movements in Europe, the U.S. and in South Africa, and questions of gender, intersectionality, political discourse and visual analysis. Doerr's academic writings have been published in *Mobilization, Globalizations, Feminist Review, Social Movement Studies, Journal of International Women's Studies, European Foreign Affairs Review, Partecipazione e Conflitto, Berliner Debatte Initial,* and *European Political Science Review.* Her recent co-authored work with Alice Mattoni and Simon Teune, "Advances in the Visual Analysis of Social Movements" just appeared in *RSMCC.*

Lindsey A. Freeman is an assistant professor of sociology at SUNY Buffalo State. Her work largely concerns collective memory, nostalgia, utopia, space/place, atomic history, and sometimes art. She is currently at work on a manuscript about the rise and decline of the Atomic Age, which centers on the former secret atomic city of Oak Ridge, Tennessee, *Longing for the Bomb: Atomic Nostalgia in a Post-Nuclear Landscape,* forthcoming from The University of North Carolina Press. She received her PhD in sociology and historical studies from The New School for Social Research.

Timothy J. McMillan is a three-time graduate (1980, 1981, 1988) of the University of North Carolina at Chapel Hill. His PhD in cultural anthropology focused on resistance to colonialism in highland Kenya. Currently Dr. McMillan teaches in the Department of African, African-American, and Diaspora Studies at UNC-Chapel Hill and conducts research related to memories of race and slavery in the commemorative landscape. He regularly conducts a "Black and Blue" walking tour of campus that will soon have a digital presence through UNC libraries.

Laliv Melamed is a PhD candidate in the Cinema Studies Department at New York University. Her research examines aspects of memory, politics and aesthetics in documentary, television and home movies. More specifically she focuses on familial and amateur commemoration of militarized death in Israel.

Joanna Beata Michlic is a social and cultural historian, and founder and Director of HBI (Hadassah-Brandeis Institute) Project on Families, Children, and the Holocaust at Brandeis University. In September 2013, she has also been appointed a lecturer in Contemporary History at the Faculty of the Department of Historical Studies at Bristol University, UK. Her major publications include *Neighbors Respond: The Controversy about Jedwabne* (2004; coedited with Antony Polonsky) and *Poland's Threatening Other: The Image of the Jew from 1880 to the Present* and *Bringing the Dark to Light: The Reception of the Holocaust in Postcommunist Europe,* coedited with John-Paul Himka (Lincoln, NUP, July 2013). She is also the editor of the forthcoming *Jewish Families in Europe, 1939–Present: History, Representation, and Memory,* (University Press of New England/ Brandeis University Press, 2014). Her two current research topics are the history of rescuers of Jews and East European Jewish childhood, 1945– 1950. She is a recipient of many academic awards and fellowships, most recently the Fulbright Senior Scholar Award, Haifa University.

Benjamin Nienass received his PhD from the Department of Politics at the New School for Social Research. He is currently a postdoctoral fellow at the *Collège d'études mondiales* in Paris. His research is concerned with the politics of memory in postnational contexts, specifically in the European Union.

Susan C. Pearce is assistant professor of sociology at East Carolina University. She earned her MA and PhD in sociology at the New School for Social Research. Her research is concerned with the political contexts of culture, with an emphasis on diversity and marginality in the United States and in countries experiencing democratic transformations. She is the co-author (with Elizabeth J. Clifford and Reena Tandon) of *Immigration and Women* (New York University Press, 2011). Her research on collective memory includes studies of the counter-amnesia of the New York African Burial Ground, memory of the Solidarity movement in Poland, and the twentieth anniversary commemorations of the 1989 revolutions in East-Central Europe. She also studies the experiences of intimate partner violence among immigrant women. She has been on the sociology faculties of Gettysburg College, West Virginia University, University of Gdańsk (Poland), and Central European University (Poland).

Amy Sodaro received her PhD in sociology from the New School for Social Research and is currently an assistant professor of sociology at the Borough of Manhattan Community College, City University of New York. Her research focuses on memory and memorialization of violence and atrocity. She has published articles on the U.S. Holocaust Memorial Museum, the Kigali Genocide Memorial Center in Rwanda, and the Jewish Museum Berlin, and she is coeditor of *Memory and the Future: Transnational Politics, Ethics and Culture* (Palgrave Macmillan, 2010).

Cecilia Sosa is an Argentinean sociologist and cultural journalist. She obtained her PhD in Drama from Queen Mary (University of London) and currently holds a postdoctoral position at the School of Arts and Digital Industries (University of East London). Her work on memory, affects, performance, and the transmission of trauma in postdictatorial Argentina has been published in articles, book chapters, media and festival catalogues. She is also the coeditor of a special issue on Cultural Memory for the *Journal of Latin American Cultural Studies* (July 2012). Her doctoral thesis was awarded as the most distinguished thesis of the year (2012) by the Association of Hispanists of Great Britain and Ireland and will be published by Tamesis Books in 2014.

Samuel Tobin is an assistant professor of communications media and game design at Fitchburg State University in Massachusetts who works on the intersection of play, media, and the quotidian. His forthcoming book is *Portable Play in Everyday Life: The Nintendo DS* (Palgrave Macmillan). He holds a doctorate in sociology from the New School for Social Research in New York.

Index

www.ingramcontent.com/pod-product-compliance
Lightning Source LLC
Chambersburg PA
CBHW071239050326
40690CB00011B/2184